THE
DISH

D1522361

*Stories spun from the only position player dumb
enough to squat beneath strangers who swing
big sticks inches from his head*

NEIL R. BELLER, JR.

ISBN: 9798787433104

In Memory of

Buddy Miller, my childhood friend who shared my love of baseball.

Dedication

To all those middle-aged men who watch professional baseball and still think they could be out on that field competing, beer belly and all.

Acknowledgements

Extreme thank you to coaches: Neil R. Beller, Sr., Herman C. Bell, III, Jim Miller, David Lott, Larry Butts, George Henderson, Mike DiCrispino and John Jancuska for all their guidance and motivation. Thank you to Dan Fielder for teaching me to hit to the opposite field, Kevin Wilkins for allowing me to cut his line drive throws, Chris Manouse for extending my post-prime catching career, and Jack Kelly for trusting me enough to play the infield. I also want to thank the many little women I coached who taught me that, yes, there is crying in baseball, and a special shout out to my family for ignoring the affair I had with my laptop. Appreciation to Amanda Milewski and Craig Schenning for their publishing knowledge.

Contents

I Heart Baseball

The game was almost over and I only had one ball hit to me. I routinely scooped it up and threw it to first before I turned and signaled "two outs" by holding up my index and pinkie fingers and waving them in a noticeable fashion. I always thought it a silly ritual, but understood the tradition. It came from the Pee Wee leagues when the three wayward kids in the outfield were in their own world counting clovers and chasing bees, so the infielders had to keep reminding them how many outs there were. That way, they knew how long they had to wait until the coach bought them a snowball. Traditions like that started very early in a baseballer's life, but some eventually faded away like yelling "Lefty" whenever a left-handed batter stepped up to the plate. I guess in high school, improved observation skills allowed outfielders to tell when a left-handed batter was up, but they still needed a reminder on how many outs there were. You know… snowballs.

Truth be told, the infield was foreign to me and I didn't like it. I kept looking over my shoulders and then to my left and right to note the locations of my teammates. I felt out of place standing and leaning over with my hands on my knees. My normal and favorite view of any baseball field was from behind home plate in a squatting fashion. I was a natural born catcher.

As a catcher, I had the honor of being the only player on the field to have all the other players stationed in front of me. Every movement by them or the opposing base runners was instantly noticed, keeping my interest at a heightened level. Catchers are surrounded by dirt, dust and chalk and during the course of an entire baseball game their feet might never actually touch grass. Their view of the world is from sock level, they are masters at sign language and they are also the only participating player on the field to play an entire baseball game in foul territory. I loved catching.

I experienced things that no other position player ever could. One interesting example was when a wooden bat fouled off a 90-mile per hour fastball, the friction of the wood and the leather of the ball created a burning smell. It only happened three times from the thousands of foul balls that zipped past my head, each time lasting a split second and resembling the start of a campfire. The first time it happened I was looking for flames and craving a s'more.

Instances like that can be the highlight of the game for a catcher, well until you take one to the balls. For the record, athletic cups don't prevent the immense pain of a direct hit to the dangly parts, they just spread it around to the rest of your body making sure the puke gland is notified. I'll touch more on that later.

As I am participating in a charity softball game however, taking one to the balls is not in my current thought pattern. I don't know three quarters of my teammates and when my friend, Jerry Kovack, asked me to play short I immediately said yes. He was blackmailing me about the whole incident with the thing at the place, but that wasn't my only motivation. Softball usually found me playing somewhere further from home plate like the outfield. Everyone knows there is a huge difference between softball and baseball, especially for catchers, and even more for catchers with 50-year-old knees. Third baseman, Brian Cueva, was playing like he was still 22 years-old, so my ego forced me to follow suit.

I had reached the point in my life where I wouldn't be able to transverse the stairs in the morning if I didn't have a railing to lean on. I stopped playing baseball competitively five years earlier, but the disconnect between the body, the brain and the heart left me yearning. Let me explain.

I grew up in Baltimore, Maryland where we experienced the extreme of each season. It could be three degrees in the winter and 103 in the summer. Local weathermen had to create new terms like "wind chill" and "heat index" to add or subtract even more degrees so not to worry viewers. That was to explain why car doors froze shut or small animals burst into flames. Although in any of those conditions, baseball was never far from my mind.

Once when I was a kid, I made 50 little snowmen, placed each on top of its own fence post and then spent all afternoon throwing snowballs to knock them down. I must have pitched two complete games that day and it was the dead of winter. Later in life, when we would experience a day of Indian summer, I would grab the glove and ball out of my trunk and play catch with a passing motorist, usually against their will. Baseball was in my blood, turning simple tasks like chopping wood into practicing my swing, or asking the doctor to use red thread when I needed stitches. I blame it all on my youth, Johnny Bench and my muscle memory.

I have played so many games of baseball my hand-eye coordination was off the charts. I would randomly catch things falling out of my medicine cabinet without even trying and I once snatched a Frisbee out of midair without spilling my beer, and I wasn't even playing Frisbee. As a catcher, I developed tremendous peripheral vision from constantly looking at first and third bases without moving my head. This was done so the base runners wouldn't know I was spying on them. Years later, this aided me greatly while babysitting, as I could keep an eye on the kids and watch the Orioles on TV at the same time. Unfortunately, there comes a time when the body stops keeping up with the brain and heart's desire to keep playing and that is when accidents happen.

As I leaned over watching the next pitch, the young batter ripped a ball in my general direction. It was clearly going to pass between Brian and myself and end up in left field, or so my brain thought. My body, however, thought differently and before I knew it, I took two steps to my right and went airborne. My right arm was completely outstretched and I was parallel to the ground when I froze in midair like Wile E. Coyote. I'm pretty sure that the words "Stupidicus Dumbassicus" were written in the air below me. What the hell was I doing? I don't remember turning. I don't remember jumping, but I will damn sure remember what it feels like when I finally crash back to Earth. I decided to prolong that misery as long as possible, and picked that moment to look back and ponder my entire baseball career. Put on your wristbands, your eye black, grab a hot dog and settle in.

Northside

Parents have been throwing items back and forth to their kids since the Stone Age when cavemen tossed their children a bone, literally. When hunger wasn't an issue, they did it for pleasure and after that, physical education class. According to Darwinian paleoanthropologists, wooden clubs were evident during the Cro-Magnon civilization, so of course that meant farm teams.

I was told I was barely sitting up when my father tossed me a ball for the first time. The next day he bought me a pair of cleats. They really tore up the carpet and made learning to walk a serious adventure. While I had several sets of baseball pajamas, a baseball bib and baseball sheets, osmosis made sure I would love the game and it worked to perfection.

I had never seen grass so green until I exited the tunnel leading to section 32 of Memorial Stadium. I was holding my father's hand at the time and I remember thinking that whoever painted the place never colored out of the lines. It was if chroma itself was on steroids. The seats were as blue as the sky and the brown dirt of the field looked like a carpet for the gods. I could not stop looking around at the spectacle and relived that memory with every game I attended afterward.

Workers on the field were perfectly manicuring the bases, which were snow white and the announcer's voice echoed throughout the cement columns until it magically touched my joy button. I think I smiled through the whole game. My dad was keeping score on a brand-new scorecard, which was the centerfold of the program he purchased from a downstairs vendor. I was startled by a man who yelled, "Cracker Jack" at the top of his lungs, before throwing a box of the special treat halfway across the section. A few innings later, I giggled as I participated in handing a stranger's money to the person next to me, before passing back a mustard covered hot dog. Everyone was so friendly, I lived for a moment, as if the world was full of pacifists, even the umpires.

The highlight of the game was when Frank Robinson singled. What made it extraordinary was the other team was playing four outfielders. The combined roar from the crowd sounded like a jet engine and gave me goose bumps. My senses were freaking out, and for some reason I wanted to smoke a cigar. The players had a glow about them and when they ran, it was a lesson in light speed. I never saw someone run so fast in my whole life as when Luis Aparicio legged out a double. The Orioles catcher had more letters on the back of his uniform than I could comprehend. They spelled E-T-C-H-E-B-A-R-R-E-N.

During the seventh-inning stretch, the grounds crew came out with giant mats on ropes. They walked backwards in a syncopated pattern and dragged the field clean leaving it looking as it had been untouched by humans. A beautiful woman with long blonde hair ran from base to base carrying a broom. She gently swept each base and before leaving third, smacked the opposing team's coach in the butt with the broom. The whole place erupted in laughter. It had been the happiest day of my life and when I left that day, I knew I wanted to be a major leaguer. Later that year, my Orioles won the greatest championship in the history of sports, The World Series.

We lived next door to Herman C. Bell, III and he happened to be the manager of Northside A.C., which was the dominating softball team in the area. Known simply as Northside, they played two games every Sunday and their start time coincided with the completion of Sunday school. Our dad would pick up my sister Karen and me from church, and take us home to change out of our Sunday best. He was already in his royal blue and white uniform with the number "1" on the back, and I couldn't wait to be in my baseball clothes.

I knew it was only a matter of months before I was a card-carrying member of Northside. I couldn't help but wonder which one of the current players I would replace. Maybe Woody Wilson, the young speedy outfielder with the cannon arm, or maybe the tall and thin Don Eccleston. I can still see him standing perfectly still at the plate with his face directed toward the pitcher, but his eyes locked skyward following the arc of the ball. I just knew it wouldn't be Junior Costin, the pitcher. He was the one who nicknamed my sister, Pic-a-nic. "Junie" was a staple on the mound, and I had not mastered the slow pitch yet, so there was still time for Mr. Herman to decide.

In the time it took our dad to turn the big blue Volkswagen bus around at the bottom of our dead-end street, Pic-a-nic and I would sprint into the house, change into our play clothes, and neatly put our good clothes away. (Okay, that last part was a total lie, as I have never put anything away in my life.) On the way out the front door, our mom would hand us an egg sandwich with ketchup wrapped in aluminum foil, and we would be at the end of the sidewalk as our father arrived. We ate the yummy sandwich during the five-minute ride to Northside's home field at Carney Elementary School. I still get excited thinking about those Sundays and my mother's egg sandwiches!

Several weeks before the season started, Northside would hold practices and I was allowed to participate. I chased foul balls, shagged flies and carried the bat bag to the field. I thought I was the man, but looking back I realize I was only doing things that the grown-ups didn't want to do and was therefore, an indentured servant. I didn't mind chasing foul balls, as that skill would come in handy later during my college career. (See Chapter 18, Don't be Afraid to Start a New Chapter, Shit!)

When the team practice was over, my practice would start. Late Sunday afternoons were my favorite time of the week, because my dad and Mr. Herman would share their baseball knowledge with me in the backyard. They would pick one skill and I would practice it for an hour while they drank beer, ate pit beef sandwiches and barked directions. I once spent so much time learning how to slide, I created bare spots all over the yard. It was so bad, Mr. Herman had to re-seed. I also permanently stained my jeans, my socks and my underwear. To this day, I have Perennial Ryegrass embedded in my right shin.

Looking back, they taught me things that would tire me out, but kept me busy. I even remember them heading in the house to grab another beer with promises of watching me out the window, so I kept running. The drill was how to round a base without creating a huge circle, like little kids do, and I mastered it. I had to because they put a huge trashcan five feet from the base, and if I rounded the bag too far, I would slam right in to it. The trick was to hit the bag and turn quickly, so I'd run on the inside of the trashcan. It was a good drill and I remember wondering if the Baltimore Orioles had trashcans in the baselines during their practices.

I found it amazing that they came up with such neat learning techniques, but later in life I understood it was the beer talking. I mean they had me throwing baseballs onto the roof of our Cape Cod and shagging them as they rolled off. It worked well because from where I was standing, I couldn't see the balls until they banged off the rainspout and popped into view. I'm certain my mother wasn't a fan of all the noise in the house, but she never complained.

I played a lot of ball by myself and spent hours just throwing the ball up in the air and catching it. I practiced the two-hand over-the-head infield catch, the low-basket outfield grab, and the behind-the-back no-look catch. The latter was in case any single women were watching.

"Step-ball" was another way to practice as nothing propels a rubber ball with more force and precision than a set of concrete steps. I learned how to pitch and field just by playing step-ball. Depending on where the ball hit the steps, long fly balls could be created, as well as grounders and line drives. I loved playing step-ball and even played in the pouring rain.

When a fastball ricocheted backward and smashed our glass storm door, my step-ball days were done. My life was almost over as well, because my father happened to be standing behind the door at the time. *Holy flying glass on dad's head Batman!* Counting my blessings and moving to the backyard, I started pitching to the wall of the house. The barn red shingles stopped about four feet from the ground while concrete continued to the earth, so I painted a one-foot-wide white circle on the wall of the house and the game continued. Note to young baseball players, don't paint white circles on the back of your house, especially with oil-based paint. Unfortunately, after I broke a few shingles, my days of pitching to the house ended, as well as my ability to sit down comfortably. (That was a reference to the ass whipping.)

Then, for my birthday I was given the greatest kid invention ever. Some lucky entrepreneur attached springs to a net and called it a *Pitch Back*. All I needed was a lawn and I could be entertained for an entire month barring bathroom breaks. The technology of the pitch back only worked if you threw the ball into the flexible net, then like magic, the net would catch it and throw it back. There was a fabric square in the center, which was the target, but depending on where you hit the net determined which direction the ball would go. It was just like step-ball without the glass door, which of course meant no sore ass. Genius!

I would squat like a catcher about 30-feet away and play catch with my invisible friend. I quickly learned to use many baseballs because the invisible friend wasn't programmed for retrieval. So, if I threw very hard and missed the net, I had to walk twice as far to find the ball. Silly entrepreneur.

I was certain Mr. Herman was watching me out his kitchen window and was penciling me in his lineup. Maybe my own father would be riding the pine and I wouldn't even be sorry. I couldn't wait until the next Sunday when hopefully I'd become a Northsider. Unfortunately, I ended up with the bat bag.

One Sunday in particular sticks out in my mind. Like the uncanny recall of Hall of Famer Jim Palmer, I can remember the temperature, the feel of the wooden bench on my thighs, the speed of the wind, the way the sun was reflecting off of my yellow t-shirt and the gentle sound of a distant whippoorwill. Well, maybe it was a yellow-bellied sapsucker. In any event, I was on the team bench of field No. 1 at Carney Elementary and Mr. Herman was teaching me how to keep score.

He was very patient as I riddled him with questions. I learned how to chart runs, hits and walks. I gained knowledge about what a fielder's choice was, how to register outs, the number assigned to each position and about 1,000 scorebook acronyms.

Acronyms are abundant in baseball, especially in the statistics department. POS, BB, SB, HR, AB, HBP, ERA, BA, OBP, BFD and the list goes on and on. My favorite acronym was RBI and I used the slang version--ribbies--all my life. It stood for runs batted in. It wasn't until the grammatically correct peeps infiltrated sports before it was changed from RBIs to RsBI with the latter sounding like a bad speech impediment. For the record, I have never officially acknowledged the change, I mean WTF?

The Tools of Ignorance

When I was eight years old, I watched cartoons every Saturday morning from 7 a.m. until my mother surgically removed me from the sofa. I usually consumed half a box of Kellogg's Frosted Flakes while I sat there, and if luck were on my side, I would find a 3D baseball card inside. Pete Rose was my favorite cereal flake find. For the record, I never rifled through the box searching, but on occasion opened the box from the bottom to curtail the wait.

The "Bugs Bunny Road Runner Hour" was by far my favorite cartoon with Ralph Wolf and Sam Sheepdog creating the most laughter, but any cartoon that featured baseball was a close second. I remember "Porky's Baseball Broadcast" where Porky Pig played the public address announcer stuttering out the regular clichés of blind umpires, a bat (the mammal) as the batboy and a turtle playing the position of catcher. Turtles already look like they were wearing catching gear. They just turned their hat around backward and their shell around forward, and they were ready to catch. With the exception of the mask, they were perfectly adorned with the "tools of ignorance."

The term "tools of ignorance" refers to the catcher's equipment and was coined by a real major league catcher named Muddy Ruel, who apparently was pretty ignorant. His career lasted 19 years, starting in 1915 and he played for six different teams. Muddy wasn't his given name, but after catching and sweating it was the perfect moniker.

Baseball historians have noted that people who willingly put on catching gear might be a little touched in the common-sense area of the cerebral cortex. Imagine being told to squat beneath someone who is swinging a 36-inch piece of hard wood over your head. At the same time, your teammate who is 60-feet and six inches away, was trying to throw a 100-mile-per-hour baseball past him. All that happens inches from your face. Brain damage? Yes indeed.

The first time I heard the term "tools of ignorance," was while I was playing summer baseball. My coach at the time was Mr. Jim Miller, who was the father of two of my best friends. I had been the first baseman for most of the preseason, but one day during batting practice Coach Miller told me to come in and put on the tools of ignorance. I searched the equipment bag for tools, but other than the catcher's gear, I found no hammers or screwdrivers. When he saw me struggling, he came over and directed my attention to the mask, chest protector and shin guards and said in an all-knowing voice, "I present the tools of ignorance, now put them on."

It took me 10 minutes to figure out how all the buckles, clips and straps worked. I had a bigger belly than most kids, so I had to loosen the chest protector a bit. It was huge, puffy and equipped with a big oval flap hanging down in the middle to protect the making of future generations. As I waddled up to the plate, I felt like I was wearing a fireman's turnout gear. When I squatted, the chest protector rose up and covered my nose causing the mask to slide up on my head. I instantly felt like a turtle. Ah, now I understood the Looney Tunes reference.

I hated every minute of catching and couldn't wait to take it all off. I had absolutely no peripheral vision, reeked of the combined sweat of all those before me, and the worn leather on the facemask scratched my cheeks and chin. I was miserable with a capital "M." Little did I know, that was day one and I would be wearing the tools of ignorance for the next 40 years.

Coach Miller decided I was the catcher and from that moment on my calves began to grow. It felt almost prison-like as my view of the world was now through metal bars. The learning experience was never-ending, as most of the pitchers couldn't hit the broad side of themselves, much less a catcher's mitt. Needless to say, I spent my first year as a catcher eating the dirt that was kicked up in my general direction and trying to determine my center point of gravity. My teammates referred to me as "Weeble" after the toy from Hasbro/ Romper Room that wobbled. The only difference was that I fell down a lot and Weebles only wobbled ... they didn't fall down. My usual direction for tilting over was backwards, but I made sure not to favor one direction. On one occasion I fell forward just as the ball arrived, so it cleared my body completely and hit the umpire. Oops!

Initially, the only benefit I saw to catching was while outfielders were sprinting to their positions and jogging back, I was casually walking 25 feet to the bench. I once calculated that in my lifetime, catching saved me from running an extra 837 miles. That's like running from Baltimore, Maryland to Tuscaloosa, Alabama. It's a good thing I didn't wear a Fitbit back then, because I might feel guilty.... not!

My mother couldn't understand why I came home from every practice with a big lump on the back of my head. I'm sure she thought some errant batter hit me during his swing. The truth was, even though I was wearing a series of metal bars over my face, when the ball was approaching my nose, I had a sudden uncontrollable reaction to turn my head. That was the natural reaction, right? Well only because I had time to react.

Since most pitchers were delivering their 39-mile-per-hour fastball five feet short of the plate, the balls would bounce up in regular fashion, causing me to turn my head. It was just what was done when something was approaching your face, you would turn your head. For those who think they wouldn't do that, try not to blink when you are standing next to someone hammering a nail. Can't be done. Think about how many times on T.V. you've seen fans sitting in the front row behind home plate jump out of the way of a foul ball, only to see it stopped by the screen. I always love their embarrassed laugh afterwards. It was so hard to stop a natural reaction.

To this day, I can still feel the ball smashing into the back of my skull. It only happened a couple dozen times before I let the mask do what it was designed to do. Nowadays, young catchers wear helmets under their masks, but we just wore our hat backwards and had no protection against a wooden bat. You can always tell the catcher in the team picture because his hat is filthy.

The shin guards were equally perplexing and obviously created by a deranged hockey goalie. The shell material was fashioned in vertical sections and held together with thick strips of old leather. These were intended to be pliable, but had the flexibility of a metal mixing bowl. Four or more straps with hooks at the open end were attached on metal oval rings. These were to be wrapped tightly around the lower legs and fastened to a small ring on the other side. The design prevented the guards from spinning around or sliding up and down when running might have occurred. The top one went straight across the lower thigh and the bottom went around the ankle. The ones in the middle needed to be altered in a pretty crisscross fashion to create an X on the back of the calf. Catchers with an X on the calf were much cooler than those without. I remember thinking it was a baseball fashion statement.

If the top straps of the guard were too loose, they would slide down and dig into the back of your knee. If they were too tight, they would slide down and dig into the back of your knee. The rule of thumb was that the back of your knees would be toast. If by some mental mistake you wore them so they connected on the inside of your legs, they would occasionally get caught on each other giving you one thick leg in the middle of your body, forcing you to hop over to the bench for assistance.

Since gravity is a condition on earth, which can't be avoided unless you are playing ball while standing on your head, all the perspiration will run down your body and puddle around your ankles, creating mud in your socks. I noticed some guys on the team didn't have to wash their uniform after the game or if ever. My mother used to bring a wash pail and a scrub brush right to the field and bang my uniform on a rock during the fourth inning. Let's face it, when I was catching, I was only a few DNA molecules away from actual soil. The tools of ignorance were a proper description.

Town and Country Datsun

The P.R.C. or Parkville Recreational Council governed all the leagues where I grew up in Baltimore County, Maryland. Local dads volunteered to be coaches and local businesses ponied up to be sponsors. All of the uniforms were exactly the same with *Parkville* written across the chest in a recently extinct writing form called cursive. To designate different teams, matching colored hats and stirrups were distributed and the back of the uniform was adorned with a big oval patch containing the sponsor's name.

To some, a team's success determined the perceived domination of the sponsor. Meaning, if *Rittenhouse Fuel* had a killer team and they lost the championship to *Woodcroft Exxon,* then for years, every time we got gas at *Woodcroft Exxon,* I nodded to their superiority. It also meant that friends were forever associated with the team they were on when they were nine. I still have friends I think of when I pass *Baskin Robbins,* where *Schulte & Tride* used to be and the parking lot where *Akhurst Lumber* lived. I'm sure others think of me whenever they see a *Town & Country Datsun.* Okay so they went out of business in 1970, but then again, so did I.

I couldn't wait to get that initial call from my new coach. He never talked to my parents, but asked to speak to the ball player in the house. My dad stood there in the kitchen and watched me on the phone while reliving his own childhood. If I were lucky, I might find out the name of my new team and some of my teammates. Afterwards, I would call several of my friends to find out who their coach was, and any information they might have learned about others. This same ritual played out all over Parkville.

Looking back, I'm surprised I survived at all, because I actually picked up the phone, dialed seven random numbers and talked to someone on the other end. How could that be? As word of mouth spread, whole teams began to take shape and upon learning our sponsor, preconceived expectations based on last year's outcome came to light. When I learned I was playing for *Ben Franklin's,* a local fabric store, I was very sad due to their last-place finish the previous year. However, we came in second that year, so Ben turned out to be pretty cool.

The first practice was awesome because we usually received our new hats. Baseball hats in the way back machine didn't have those adjustable straps in the back, so you had to try on several until you found the right one. This was long before the head lice infestation of 1973, so parents didn't mind the sharing of hats. Unlike today, when learning of an errant hat share, parents immediate drag their kids from school and completely shave them from head to toe.

I loved getting my new hat. I couldn't wait to fold the bill in the same manner my father did. He bent down the sides 90 degrees for sun deflection, as well as a small crease in the middle. The ending shape resembled a long house, which at the time was very cool. Presently, it is not cool and leaves a bad taste in my mouth along with the tilted off-center version some current major league relievers display. I loathe that look.

The uniform came later as well as the matching stirrups. Obtaining a favorite number was always exciting, but since they went from lowest to highest, in order of size, I usually ended up with three digits. At home in the privacy of my room, I would suit up for the first time in front of our mirror wall. A few years earlier, my brother and I switched bedrooms with our parents, and we ended up with an entire wall of one-foot mirror tiles. At least they weren't on the ceiling! I would walk back and forth like a runway model checking out my gait, and making sure my gig line was straight. The stirrups were the final accouterment to the baseball uniform, acting much like a fine string of pearls to any formal evening gown. The thick portion of the stirrup would stick out of the pants leg up to 10 inches, and then it tapered down to an inch wide strip before entering the shoe. When worn correctly, they would run under the foot, just in front of the heel, and up the sides of the leg joining the stripe that ran down the pants leg. When worn incorrectly, they resembled an old lady whose pantyhose have fallen out of her jumper.

Some guys used to cut the stirrup in the middle and sew in a piece of elastic. That would allow the thin part of the stirrup to rise beyond the calf, hiding the thick portion under the pants leg. It was definitely a fashion statement and led to many bleacher discussions about manhood. When it was discovered that Frank Robinson might have been the high-cut trendsetter, everybody started jacking up their stirrups. With a nice pair of white sanitaries underneath, it would accentuate one's calf muscles enabling more females to attend games. Unfortunately, most of these females were our mothers.

Mr. Miller taught me how to rock back and forth on my toes so I could lunge left or right to stop a wild pitch. He also taught me to throw the ball back to the pitcher without standing up. In fact, he used fear as a motivator. He told me to visualize home plate on fire. You heard me. I was to imagine actual flames were shooting out of the ground, so I wouldn't step on or over the plate. Most catchers my age, who were also just learning, would stand straight up and take two or three steps towards the pitcher's mound gathering momentum before throwing the ball. Talk about cranking up. Some kids would end up completely in front of the batter's box.

I only forgot one time and I have the stretch marks to prove it. It had been drizzling and home plate was getting wet. I jumped up to throw the ball and took a step right on home plate. When I planted, my foot slid right out in front of me and before I knew it, I was channeling Nadia Comaneci. I was in a complete split and I couldn't get out of it. Many ill-placed ice packs later, lesson learned.

Flying Coach

Mr. Miller was more than my first coach; he was the father of great friends. That meant that I also saw him in father mode. Based on the antics of my friends, I saw him in *severe* father mode. I also ate dinner at their house, held ghost tours in their basement and learned how to make someone wet their bed during sleepovers. That wasn't the case with the Lotts.

Mr. Lott was also the father of great friends but they lived on the other side of Carney, so I witnessed no one wetting the bed in their house. To date, he was to calmest coach I ever had, meaning I can't remember him ever yelling. Yelling is considered prerequisite No. 1 for most coaches, but he glossed right over that and opted for the more conversational Mr. Roger's approach. Come to think of it, he might have even worn a sweater.

Mr. Lott not only fielded a complete team he supplied the transportation. On many occasions, I stood at our mailbox and witnessed the Lott's blue station wagon turn the corner of my street. Upon opening the back door, I was greeted by half the team. Mr. Lott drove all over town picking up those who didn't have a ride to the game. Afterwards, he would do the same thing in reverse and drop everybody off. I can still see his sons Randy and Timmy peering out of the car in full uniform.

Our league selected all the players from scratch every year, so the teams were constantly changing. Of course, if your dad were a coach, you would be on his team, but all the others were pulled from a hat. Good luck and serendipity landed me on Mr. Lott's team several years, but not all in a row. I'm sure he needed Neil downtime. I met some great friends, which I never would have met outside of baseball, like Mark Guzzo, who in his day could have competed with Jim Palmer. I didn't mean as a pitcher, but as a Jockey underwear representative. I never saw him in his briefs, he just had that underwear model look, at least that's what all the girls said. He also reminded me of the lead singer of Styx, well, until I heard him sing.

Very early on when I was still learning the game, Mr. Lott put me in as a pitcher. I had never even thrown off the mound, but the previous pitcher was sitting at the corner of the bench crying, so I walked to the mound and looked down at the rubber. I had no idea at all where to stand, how to stand or what the rubber even meant. I used to watch others dig at it and kick around it, but I never knew why so I decided to fake it.

I had seen Wally Bunker and Dave McNally pitch, so how hard could it be? I stood in the very middle of the rubber with both feet together facing home plate. I looked at the catcher, who I couldn't even recognize through the facemask, and then at the runner on first base. Coach Lott was smiling and clapping his hands before turning to the crying player.

I pulled both arms to my chest, raised my left leg and pivoted like I had seen various major leaguers do many times. As I twisted sideways facing third base, I reared back to throw when the batter turned towards me and prepared to bunt. It really caught me by surprise and his jarring move stopped me in my tracks. I couldn't understand what he was doing because we had never been taught how to bunt. It happened to be the first and only time I'd ever see someone square to bunt from the front. It was a double learning experience for me, because when I stopped in mid-pitch, I committed a balk. A what? I thought the umpire was making up words and I remember laughing at the name: a balk. Needless to say, a few minutes later I was sitting at the other end of the bench crying.

Baseball is a great game because you never stop learning from it, and it never stops teaching. When we finally learned how to bunt and steal, we needed to know when to do it and why. I mean, the first batter of the game usually wouldn't bunt, but the second batter might. When we became proficient in practice, the coach would try to implement it into a game, and the way to do that was with a sign.

Sitting in a half circle behind first base one practice, we learned the team signs. When the coach swiped his hand across his shirt the batter was supposed to bunt. When he slid his hand down his leg the runners on base were supposed to steal. When he touched the bill of his hat that meant to take a pitch. Easy right? Wrong. What about the indicator? That meant that a sign was coming. What about the hand clap? That meant the play was on. So, I saw the indicator and I saw the sign but the coach didn't clap, does that mean I shouldn't bunt? Wait! I didn't see the wipe off, which was the special sign that cancels the play even after it was put on just in case the other team had figured out our signs and signaled each other with their own signs.

Keep in mind this was the last millennium, so illegal video cameras and body buzzers were still buried in the DNA thought process of future sign stealers. The only additional way to help a kid from the '60s was to physically yell from the third base coach's box, "BUNT!"

It was all so difficult for me, because I was busy worrying about all the rules of hitting I was told to remember. Keep your eye on the ball, keep your hands back, shift your weight, open your hips, throw your top hand, step towards the ball, follow through, and the most important rule of hitting…drop the bat.

I saw so many bats flying during my first few years of baseball I thought it was a separate competition. The majority of them never went into the field of play, but hit the backstop, the catcher, the umpire, the scorekeeper and even through the Styrofoam water cooler. One kid even swung the bat all the way around his body and smacked himself in the head. I'm sure if the Guinness folks had been present that kid would be forever memorialized in their book.

Coach Lott simplified signals in a perfect way and that was through letter association.

B = Belt = Bunt

S = Shirt = Steal

What a revolutionary idea! Anybody could remember that. He even threw in the indicator as pointing to his eye. Anyone who understands the world of homonyms knows that "I" and "eye" sound the same. Therefore, when he points to his eye that would mean "I" which starts the word indicator. Now if he could only wear a tie and point to it when he wanted us to "take" a pitch that would be all encompassing. Does the baseball learning ever stop? No. It only set the table for what was to come later.

In college, we had skin as an indicator, which meant face and hands. We also had verbal overrides with the letters that started words being the signals themselves. We also had multiple signs for each task and when all that failed it was body language such as foot placement, hands in back pockets or hat removal. If anything, baseball taught me to be hyper-observant of anyone standing in the third base coach's box. However, once at a crowded bank I saw a strange woman give me the sign to steal. Coincidence? I think not, but I didn't oblige.

As with anything, the more you practice, the more proficient you become. Whenever I played catch with my dad it always included a series of extreme pop-ups. I became very accomplished at catching anything that was at least 15 stories high. When he launched one in my yard, I had to maneuver around the swing set, trees, random toys, and sidewalks while spying the sky the whole time. It was part of my catcher's obstacle course. On the field, the only thing you could trip over was your own mask, the bat and of course your feet.

I was taught early on the proper order of catching a pop-up. The first thing to do was jump up in front of home plate and turn around. The ball usually had a backward spin and would eventually drift towards the field. How many times have you seen a catcher facing the field while chasing the pop-up towards the pitcher's mound only to dive at the last minute and face plant?

Removal of the mask was next step, but it was to remain in your right hand. Once the ball was spotted, its trajectory could be established so you knew which way to navigate. As soon as the stepping began, the mask was to be tossed in the complete opposite direction. This way the catcher would never have the opportunity to step on or trip over one of the tools of ignorance. There was nothing more embarrassing to a catcher than tripping over his own mask. Or, so I thought.

One incident in particular comes to mind. The game was at Parkville Senior High and the batter popped the pitch straight up. When I jumped up and turned around, I couldn't find the ball. It was a high sky and the mid-afternoon sun was hindering my view. When I finally found the ball, I could see it was behind the backstop to my left. It was very high and drifting towards the field, so I threw my mask to the right and started moving left. I was running full speed towards the fence, but I couldn't tell which side the ball would come down on. I was still running with both hands over my head when the ball skimmed down the fence and right into my glove. I caught the ball, but my momentum took me right into the fence at a strong gallop and I bounced straight backwards and onto my ass.

Directly on the other side of the fence a 50-gallon trash can was mounted on a cement square. My girth pushed the chain link so far that I smashed into the trashcan knocking it from its mount. It wobbled around for a bit counterclockwise, before walking 10 feet and completely falling over with a loud bang. The noise was pretty spectacular and was only drowned out by the laughter and applause in the stands that followed. Good thing I didn't trip over my mask or I might have been embarrassed.

The Team What?

Each team received the standard bag of equipment, which included, bats, balls, batting helmets, a scorebook, catching gear and a whole mess of inexperience. When I first started playing recreational baseball, bats were made of wood. When a fresh bat arrived, the coach would take white medical tape and start to slowly wrap it around the bat, gaining a half-inch with each rotation. When completed, after about 10 inches, it resembled something you might find in an Egyptian tomb. Minutes later, dirt from the field soiled the wrap, giving the batter a good seasoned grip.

There was no sound more wonderful than the crack of a wooden bat striking a pitched baseball. One could almost determine the outcome by the sound alone. Even on a sandlot, that sound represented power and could turn the head of anybody within earshot. When it happened at a stadium filled with 50,000 fans, it could trigger immediate joy or disabling sadness.

One of the first things I learned about hitting was how to hold the bat. I'm not talking about that amazingly painful feeling you'd get in your fingers from not holding the bat tight enough on a cold day. Many times, I hopped all the way to first base holding my fingers in my crotch waiting for the pain to subside. I am talking about the letters to heaven or the grain.

Stamped or burned into every bat was the seal of the manufacturer. When standing in the batter's box, the batter would constantly check the line to make sure the logo or letters were facing forward. I was informed that the logo was usually stamped on the weakest grain of the bat and if held improperly, the bat would split upon impacting the ball. I only broke one bat my entire life and the coach let me take it home. I drove a small nail in it and covered the whole thing with green electric tape and called it the hornet. It became a neighborhood favorite and many of my friends used it for years.

It was very frustrating when someone on your team broke your favorite bat because they were holding it wrong. It definitely took at least two weeks to forgive that blunder, however a complimentary snowball purchased by their dad immediately following the game wiped the slate clean. At least one time during each at bat it was customary to turn your bat over and bang the handle on home plate. If it were cracked the noise would sound splintered. While in the midst of banging it, the umpire and the catcher always chimed in with their thoughts of it being cracked or not. I usually asked their impressions to the sound. "What do you think?" It was a community thing.

One summer day, I was dropped off at the parking lot of Double Rock Park. As I walked down the big cement incline that crossed the stream before turning up towards the fields, I heard someone hammering. The constant pinging sound was echoing throughout the woods and rocky surroundings of the park, and I wondered if the snowball stand was being renovated. As I exited the woods and reached the fields, I expected to witness someone thumping on an old milk can, but what I saw was very perplexing.

Another team was taking batting practice and the clanging I heard didn't compute in my brain with the known sound associated with striking a baseball. How could that be? I stopped in my tracks and looked harder and saw a glint come from the bat. Oh my God they were using metal bats! I had to double take as I wondered what the hell was going on. I knew there was a paper shortage in school, but were trees really that sparse? And why ruin baseball, how stupid! What was going to happen next, metal toothpicks, ice cream sticks and tongue depressors? The horrible noise was pretty annoying actually, and as our practice continued, my eyes would turn every time I heard the pinging sound. By the end of practice, I had a major headache and it lasted 42 years.

What I had witnessed was a major change in baseball with the invention of the aluminum bat. These bats came with rubber handles instead of tape and were topped with a round black plastic cap. The ping of the metal replaced the crack of the bat and the only positive addition I saw was that no one could split one. It took a few games to get used to and find a favorite, but soon they became a part of every game I played for the next four decades.

The day on which I came to love the aluminum bat stands out in my mind but not for the reasons you'd think, even though I did go five for five. Near the end of the season our team was so far out in front of the standings we had first place locked up. As a treat, Coach Lott made the announcement that for the next game we could play any position we wanted. My body celebrated immediately because I was finally going to play a game in an upright position. I had been catching for so long, my view of the world was from the height perspective of E.T.

I was in the 8th grade at the time and the next game was going to be played at Pine Grove Junior High School, which I attended, so I knew the field well. I had squatted for the past eight years in position No. 2. I found it humorous that squatting and the No. 2 had several connotations, however, I was looking forward to standing in the afternoon sun from position No. 9, right field. It wasn't just the standing that excited me, but for the first time in what felt like forever, I was going to play a baseball game without wearing a cup. Woo-hoo!

To set a reference, most employees in the work place have an extra coffee cup on their desk where they store and protect their junk. The same thing happens on a baseball field, sans the desk and coffee. When catching, a cup is a very important necessity. It was not the most comfortable thing to wear and although it had enabled thousands of future babies to contribute to the tax code, it didn't always do the job intended.

Its initial design was somewhat cone-shaped. Picture the Apollo spacecraft that splashed down in the Indian Ocean. Now, slice it from top to bottom and lay it on its side with the flat side down. Punch some holes in it and that was what the cup looked like in the '60s and '70s. If it were oval, it would resemble a hockey mask. Can you imagine Jason's face from *Friday the 13th over your trouser stuff? Wait, what?*

To hold it in place, a wacky undergarment was invented. The jock strap looked as if someone ripped all the material out of a pair of tighty-whities leaving only the elastic around the waist and thighs. Attached to the very front was a cone shaped pocket for the cup to reside in with the top of the cone facing down. Snaps held the protector of the baby maker apparatus in place.

With all the technology and design, one would think that taking a direct hit would be successfully blocked by the cup, and in theory that was correct. However, occasionally the batter would foul tip a ball straight down into the dirt, which would then head straight up and into the catchers undercarriage. With no security to the dangly parts, they would sometimes relocate to the catcher's throat, causing a gurgling which can only be attributed to the sound Chewbacca made in Star Wars. As a matter of fact, every time I hear him, I reflex and quickly cross my legs. Nothing can prepare you for the experience except imaging the impact while listening to someone slapping fresh meat with a bare hand. To combat the undercarriage shot, manufacturers added a slight bend to the cup, so it would curve back and end somewhere near the taint. It didn't work.

Personally, I have been hit in the cup several times and have ascertained that while I have no permanent damage, the associated pain is quite enormous. Truth be told, it is astronomical. The initial blow was shocking because the pain was quickly distributed through every outlet of the central nervous system including the ends of each hair. Usually, these incidents took place in public with girls around, so it was not in your best interest to cry out, "Oh my balls, someone find my balls!"

The next 10 minutes involved wandering around home plate

thinking about the solar system while the umpire whispered questions like, "Do you see dead people?" These are the facts of the case and they are undisputed.

The only other time you'd grab your groin while in a baseball uniform was during a pregame ritual known as a cup check. This was when teammates would walk past you and punch your third leg to see if you were sporting a cup. Most of the time they wouldn't punch you, but fake a punch just to see you flinch and recoil. Good times.

So, it was the first inning and I was standing in right field. It felt good to run out there and warm up by throwing the ball to the other outfielders. Coach Lott's No. 2 son, Timmy, wanted to catch, and I turned over the tools of ignorance with gleeful abandon. There would be no dirt in my socks tonight I thought, as I imagined my mother's joy at not having to hire Mr. Clean to wash my uniform.

Everything was going to plan until the third inning. The team we were playing didn't possess the same laissez-faire attitude we mustered up for the game and they were trying to win. Who'd of thought? Their recent rally added five runs to their score and a play at the plate took Timmy Lott out of the game. I remember seeing him bend over to receive a ball from center field, when he was blindsided by a scoring runner. Coach Lott walked to the plate, looked down and then signaled for me to come in. Damn! As I jogged in, my first thought was "Shake it off, Timmy!" I had been run over many times when behind the dish and for an instant, I forgot how horrible it could be.

Upon further reflection, I had 30 pounds on Timmy and he didn't see the runner coming so he didn't have time to lean in and prepare for the approaching blunt force. I'm sure he was walking back to the bench trying to answer the imaginary phone, which was ringing in his head. I've heard that call several times and it was always a wrong number.

I dropped my Rick Monday official fielder's glove near my bag and retrieved my catcher's mitt. My dad gave it to me for my 12th birthday and I treasured it. As I sat on the bench to put on my shin guards, it dawned on me that I wasn't wearing my cup. In fact, I wasn't even wearing a jock. I sided up to Coach Lott and explained my dilemma. He shrugged it off and replied, "Why don't you just use the team cup?"

"The team what?" I had no idea there was a team cup. Sure enough, at the very bottom of the equipment bag, covered in dirt and years of DNA, lived a very ancient team cup. The whole game was on hold as they waited for me to get dressed. The coach told me to hurry up so he could deal with his son, who was currently speaking in tongues, so I didn't tell him about the missing jock. I merely placed the cup against my bare skin beneath my underwear and took my place behind home plate.

While in a squat, the tightness of my uniform pants kept the cup in place, but when I stood, it would start to go rogue. I have been questioned all my life as to the baseball player's constant attention to the groin area in the throes of competition. Some think that players like to tug at their package, as a form of nervousness, however cup adjustment is surely the answer. I quickly learned it could get much worse.

The next inning, I was up first up so I grabbed my new favorite bat, walked to the plate and dug in. I already had two hits and was feeling pretty good about my aluminum bat selection. When connecting with the ball in a solid fashion, bliss was extended all the way up your arms and down your spine triggering your legs to run. I was starting to like the pinging noise too. The pitcher threw a fastball and I struck it solidly. I was a pull hitter, so my natural spot was in the hole between third and short and that's where it went. I took off down the line and immediately the team cup slid out of my underwear. "Crap!"

I tried to stop it with my right hand, although it was almost impossible to sprint all out with one arm pinned to your leg, so I let go and started pumping my arms. The closer I neared first base the further the cup ran down my leg. As I crossed the bag safely and turned towards second, my cup was now guarding my right knee. "Oh, good lord!"

I quickly reached down my pants and maneuvered the cup back in junk mode, before turning and walking to the bag. In my embarrassment, I was sure everybody knew what was happening with the team cup, which is how embarrassment works. In reality, I was alone with my predicament. To make matters worse, my two-step lead was interrupted with the first pitch as it short hopped the catcher and ricocheted to the right. Instinct had me taking off immediately for second, and to my shock the cup didn't move. As I ran, I used some magical force within my body to make my thighs keep the instrument in place. As I neared the bag, I heard the other coach yell, "Throw him out'" so I knew the play would be close and I prepared to slide on the outfield side of the bag. Herman C. Bell III had taught me to slide as far away from the incoming throw as possible, and the backyard muscle memory kicked in.

To my chagrin, I misplayed my slide and rolled further over than anticipated, ending up on my belly as I slid into the bag. Immediately, my discomfort level skyrocketed. I hit the bag with great force, but not with my legs. I ended up in a slight spread eagle fashion and mashed the corner of the bag with the team cup. I had beaten the throw, so I called time out, slowly and gently pushed myself up and shuffled a few steps toward center field to dust myself off.

As I moved, I noticed I was unable to stand completely vertical. Something was prohibiting me and it originated in my midsection. Pretending to tuck in my shirt, I pulled the elastic '70s-style waistband out and glanced down into my nether region. My brain could not compute what my eyes witnessed requiring me to look a second time. I was sorry I had. When I struck the base, the team cup split open. To my horror, when the cup split open, my manly part came through before the cup closed again. All the men reading this just flinched with dread, and for that I apologize. My very first thought was that I had been castrated by second base. I wondered what the scorebook acronym was for castration. DIC-2?

The shock of it all, was taking longer than usual to comprehend as I stared into my pants for confirmation. The umpire told me to move along and take the bag. I didn't have the balls, no pun intended, to tell the umpire my fate, so I moved slowly to second base. Every step I took was a new adventure in pain, and my mind was swirling about the removal process. The pinching feeling was exasperating with every move, and I thought I was going to pass out when the batter swung at the first pitch and drove it into left center field. "Oh shit, I have to run!"

I took off towards third base without breathing. I felt like my package was in a vice and I tried to run as fast as I could without taking full steps. I was afraid of the agony I might experience with outstretched legs, so I ran like Tim Conway's old man impression doing the love muscle shuffle. The coach at third was waving me on and quite honestly, I planned on running right through third base regardless of his direction and head for home. My internal prayers were now audible as I asked the penis gods to grant me the ability to reach home without sliding and without the need to purchase an organ transport cooler.

The catcher started to make movements like the ball was coming and I quickly decided I was going to have to kill him and not in the hyperbole sense. I was a few feet away from murder when I saw him start to stand. He had no idea how close to death he came. Without breaking stride, I touched home, shuffled right past the catcher, out the opening in the fence, past some wayward fans, down a 30-foot hill and into the surrounding woods.

I dropped my pants to see my dilemma, and almost passed out. I have no words to describe the non-aesthetic tube steak extraction procedure I used to remove myself from the broken team cup, but if medical journals are interested, I used a rock, two sticks and half a bag of Bubble Chew.

I sat on a stump to gather the strength and chutzpah to head back up the hill to the bench and my curious teammates. The concocted yarn would have something to do with Mexican food and an urgent bathroom break, but I still needed to explain the broken pieces of the team cup in my hand. My thoughts were interrupted by a rustling noise to my right. Looking down, I saw a box turtle crawl out of a tiny bush.

He turned and looked up at me. Our eyes locked and I swear we entered some sort of Vulcan mind meld. I was overcome with the knowledge that I should only witness the baseball world from a crouch. I felt comfort with the idea of having lime and fine dirt sprayed in my face daily. The thought of never sprinting to a defensive position gave me serenity. I projected to later that evening when I reached my house, I'd be scouring my copy of *This Great Game* to glean all the advice for catchers. I acknowledged the seed had been planted deeply. I shuddered out of my trance and said goodbye to my little armored friend. When he turned and crawled away, I stood up knowing I'd be a catcher for the rest of my life and I threw the shattered pieces of the team cup into the woods.

Pitcher's Hand

I played baseball everywhere I went. It might not have been the game we'd all associate with, but in some recognizable form. If no one was around, I invented games to play by myself. I would lie on my back in the living room with my elbow at my side and my hand next to my shoulder. For hours, I would flip a rubber ball at the ceiling trying to get the ball as close to the ceiling as possible without actually hitting it. If I could accomplish that three times in a row, it would be considered a strike out. Once I found the proper amount of wrist thrust needed to just miss the ceiling, I could duplicate it over and over and pitch a complete game. Concentration on every single movement was the key. If I hit the ceiling it was a single, and runners would accumulate and score until I ended an inning. I should add that the reason I didn't bounce the ball off the ceiling wasn't initially to enhance my skill. It was my fear of it leaving a mark, which meant my father would leave his mark on my ass.

When I tired of pitching perfection, I changed the game to precision hitting. I moved my arm until it was outstretched over my head and I would throw the ball to just miss the ceiling before hitting a place on my body, which I previously designated as a hit. For example, if the ball just missed the ceiling and landed on my chest it was a single. If it landed on my stomach, I'd score it a double. The farther away the body part, the larger the hit. The fun was lying perfectly still not knowing where the pitch would land. The excitement was spectacular and scary as hell at the same time. I should have called the game *Unintentional Cup Check* because if the ball landed in the crotch area it was scored as a triple play--inning over!

The layout of the house helped me with my baseball boredom too. If I sat on the floor with my back against the closed front door, I had a whole set of interior stairs to play baseball with. I would try to climb the stairs one at a time by tossing the ball at the back of step one and have it bounce back. I would repeat that action with step two and three and so on, until I had climbed the whole set. This was a perfect game until my father came in the front door and smashed me into the wall. I had no clue at the time, but these little drills helped me significantly later in life. I mean how many of us have mastered office tournaments of precision trash ball or road sign quarterback?

In 1970, I was gifted a NERF ball and my indoor playing time tripled. Not only could I maintain my drive for pitching perfection, but I could bank a throw off of my little brother's head and not even get in trouble. Now if I soaked the NERF ball in water and threw it at my brother, that was a different story because a NERF ball could easily hold two gallons of water. Of course, I would never have done that. Ok, for the record, the sound of a soaked NERF ball hitting my brother was pretty hilarious.

Every backyard in my neighborhood was easily a baseball field and I'm pretty sure I played in all of them. Fences were an oddity unless someone had a dog, so sometimes we would use two or three yards at the same time. I complained once to my father about not having a real diamond to play on, and heard from his lips how when he was a kid, they played in an alley with broken glass as home plate and they all slid in headfirst. That story preceded the one about walking to school uphill in the snow with no shoes and the famous "we ate dirt for dinner and loved it" speech. I don't know how any of our parents' survived childhood.

Thankfully, across the street from my house, the Carney Community Association constructed a park. Missing Pine Park, used to be a plot of scary woods before the county cleared it out and planted grass and broken dreams. It was dotted with a few toys at the far end, like a swing set and a spin & puke and the rest was an open field. It was long and rectangular with a perfectly straight stream running along the right side, and a hedgerow separating the park from neighboring houses on the left. About 20 minutes after the grand opening of Missing Pine Park, we were playing baseball and since they erected a flagpole right smack in the middle, we used it as second base.

We used to play baseball with so many kids, I thought they were being bused in. If you drew a mile radius circle around the park, you would find on any given day, about 2,000 kids and that number tripled when cousins came to visit. Each team was made up of players of various skill levels and ages, so it was common to have 14 people playing in the field at the same time. They would be scattered all around and standing still like bumpers in a pinball machine. They had the same effect as a pinball bumper when they'd try to field the ball. The ball would bounce off of one kid and then another, until one of them stopped it and threw to the pitcher.

Due to the stream on the right, we never threw the ball to first base. We tried it originally, but the ball continuously went swimming in the crayfish- and minnow-laden stream. Since we usually only had one ball, we continued to play with it until it became heavier with every splash. By the end of the game, it felt like we were throwing around and hitting an eight-pound shot put. The next game we commenced using "pitcher's hand."

Pitcher's hand was used when you only had a few players or there was a stream behind first base. The object was for the fielder to throw the ball to the pitcher before the runner reached first base. A bang-bang play at first base was hard enough to decide the outcome, so imagine a bang-bang at first base and the pitcher's mound. If the play was close, all 28 players would rhubarb on the field until democracy kicked in. By democracy I mean the oldest player present made the call.

The same rules applied for pitcher's hand as first base, meaning the pitcher had to have his or her foot on the rubber when catching the ball, or the runner was safe. If you threw the ball to the pitcher who wasn't on the rubber, then not only was the runner safe, but the pitcher ended up in the stream. Hey, competition was tough in Missing Pine Park. By the way, when I said "rubber" I meant long stick or a mashed soda can.

As a matter of fact, all the bases were fashioned from some foreign object or potential litter. As long as I can remember, home plate was a piece of cardboard from a case of National Bohemian beer. First and third bases were just bare spots on the ground and second base was the flagpole. Sounds like the perfect baseball field to me.

You have never played proper sandlot baseball until you've slid into a flagpole. It was hilarious to watch people reach for it as they ran by. Some kids tried to step on the base of the pole as they sprinted past, and others ran headlong into it. The sound of a human head hitting a flagpole is pretty distinct and reminded me of the noise associated with banging a metal hammer on George Jetson's maid, Rosie. I don't ever remember a time when the game stopped because of a subdural hematoma, but I did witness lots of kids' shonbbeling. According to the urban dictionary, *shonbbel* is when you are crying so hard you end up covering everything in tears, snot and various other unnamed excrements. It was not a pretty sight.

Many times, before the baseball game actually started, we would warm up with a couple hours of rundown. Rundown was one of my all-time favorite things to do. For this game, only two bases were used, home and second. Everybody playing would stand on one of the two bases all at the same time, while two of the more experienced kids would act as the fielder guarding each base. They would throw the ball back and forth until someone decided to take off from one base, and try to make it to the other base. When the fielder quickly threw the ball, the runner would stop and try to get back, only to be hung up between the bases in an area we referred to as the kill zone. The goal was to try and tag that person out before they reached safely, by throwing the ball back and forth as the runner constantly changed direction. Traffic would increase as eventually another kid took off, adding to the chase. Sometimes so many kids took off running at the same time it resembled a jailbreak.

To enhance the runner's experience, we would occasionally throw the ball real high and the runners would try to time their steal before it was caught. My go-to move was the fake throw and tag. I caught many a kid with their front foot off the base and their back foot in mid-air. If a runner tried to dive into the base and was tagged out, he or she would either sit to the side until all the runners were out or they would take the place of the person who tagged them. We even had rules to speed up the game--you were out if you didn't take off after 10 throws.

Heaven forbid one of the fielders made a throwing error then everybody would take off in unison. Kids were running back and forth with so much laughter and frivolity that pretty soon there would be shonbbel all over the place. I can still visualize 19 kids of varying heights all standing next to second base with their outstretched arms touching the flagpole. The thought of it makes me smile.

Where Have You Gone Johnny Bench?

When I was in the 8th grade, I started a new hobby that I continue to this day. I started collecting autographs of famous athletes, with the majority being baseball players. In the way back machine, Google was called the public library and you had to leave your house and go there in person. I'm not kidding either! Once transportation was acquired to the nearest brick-and-mortar learning establishment, several hours were needed to look through periodicals, encyclopedias, magazines and an ancient acronym-based sorting system known as the card catalogue. This process was equivalent to searching for the perfect cornflake with a garden rake.

With the help of several pointed-glasses wearing ladies, who resided at the information desk, I eventually wrangled up the physical street address of every professional stadium, coliseum and sports venue in North America and it only took 15 and a half hours!

A few years earlier, my aunt Virginia gave me stationery for Christmas. I really loved it and considered it super special because she designed it. She was an art director for *Chesapeake Bay Magazine* and she placed an old sepia baseball scene across the top of the page with my name and address smartly sprawled across the bottom. It was very eye-catching and appealed to any athlete who loved the history of baseball.

With my cool stationery, I sat down and wrote a heartfelt letter to my hero, Johnny Bench. I informed him he was my idol, and I was practicing his style of catching, by keeping the throwing arm behind the back and catching with just the glove hand. It went against the grain of everything I had learned about keeping the throwing hand protected behind the glove. I mastered bringing my glove to my shoulder where my cocked arm was already perched to explode. I thanked him for teaching me how to gain power and quickness in my release. This was a few years before he starred in The Baseball Bunch, which I watched religiously every Saturday morning, so I knew he had some free time on his hands to answer me. I let him know I would be honored and thrilled if he could bestow me with his autograph.

For his convenience, I enclosed three blank index cards and a self-addressed stamped envelope. In the lower left-hand corner of the envelope, a sepia hand throwing a baseball gave the recipient a feeling of nostalgia. I was very proud of my letter and placed it in an envelope addressed to the Cincinnati Reds in care of Riverfront Stadium to the attention of Johnny Bench.

I was so excited, I personally hand delivered the letter to my mailman. For the record, he was impressed. I sent it on a Saturday so after two days for delivery and two days to send it back, I was assured I would have my autographs by Friday. Well, that was what I thought, but I also believed it was possible for an overweight toy maker to circumnavigate the globe in a single night.

After receiving nothing, a week later I sent out several more letters along with index cards and self-addressed stamped envelopes. I had an amazing enterprise going and it was costing me cash money. Postage stamps were a whole 13 cents, which meant 26 cents a letter plus index cards. I probably had five dollars invested in this venture, which in 1975 was about 29 cheeseburgers from McDonalds! That was quite the sacrifice for me.

On a hot July afternoon, my mother called me in from my daily meeting with the pitch back and handed me a letter. It was addressed to me by me, and the cancelled mail register was unreadable. I was holding in my hand the very first autograph. I was as giddy as my friend Tim, when his sister's friends came over in their tube tops.

I sat down on the front steps and opened the letter. It wasn't a letter at all but three signed index cards. I pulled them out and looked at them with reverence. They were handwritten with a black felt pen and personalized by one of the best pitchmen ever, Mr. Coffee.

I sat there in stunning fashion looking at the autographs sent to me by Joe DiMaggio. All three of them were different with my favorite being the third. He signed one of them "Joe DiMaggio," another "Best, Joe DiMaggio" and one "Best Wishes, Joe DiMaggio." I couldn't wait until my father arrived home from work so I could show him. He was super impressed and told me a few stories about Joltin' Joe. Until then, I had no idea he had been married to Marilyn Monroe, or that once a month he sent flowers to her grave. I just knew him as a gray-haired spokesman on television, but quickly learned of his epic baseball career. The fact that he took the time to write back was never lost on me. The only negative response I could muster was that I didn't drink coffee.

That summer was magical, as autographs kept trickling in, and they were all baseball Hall of Famers. Joe Sewell, Ernie Banks, Robin Roberts, Billy Herman, Judy Johnson, Jocko Conlan, Willie Mays, Duke Snider, Hank Aaron, Lou Boudreau, Stan Musial, Roy Campanella, George Kell, Luke Appling and Happy Al Chandler all came to me via my unsuspecting mailman. Harmon Killebrew didn't send back my index cards, but enclosed an autographed color picture instead. How awesome was that? I bought a photo album and started storing my collection properly. A follow up investigation led me to learn that these men were excellent baseball players. Thank God for the card catalogue!

I was so excited, I customized my letter and reached out to great athletes in other sports. I went back to the library and with some more painstaking and mind-numbing stone-age research, I discovered a book which listed athletes' home addresses. I learned the lack of privacy was lost on professional athletes, so I quickly looked up Dorothy Hamill. Unfortunately, she hadn't gone professional yet and was dating someone else. Bummer.

To my astonishment the other athletes responded as well. My hobby had turned into a complete heirloom. My collection of returned envelopes contained autographs from John Brodie, Rick Volk and Lynn Swan, who drew an actual swan using the "S" in his last name. I also received Gale Sayers, Joe Montana, Larry Bird, Wayne Gretzky, Johnny Unitas, Roger Staubach and Bob Griese. I even received an index card, which became an instant collector's item in 1994. It read, "To my friend, Neil. Best Wishes!" It was signed "O.J. Simpson." I propped it up on the television during the famous white Bronco chase.

Later that year, during the Thanksgiving break, I received one last envelope. I excitedly opened it up and was shocked at the contents. It was a response to the very first letter I sent to my idol, Johnny Bench. When I pulled out the first index card, I was somewhat let down. When I pulled out the second one, I was even more let down, and when I pulled the third one, Johnny fell off the top of my idol list. All three of the index cards had been stamped and not signed. They not only had been stamped, but they had been stamped with only one visit to the inkpad. You could see how the ink was less with each stamp.

Looking back now, I understand that he never even saw my letter. One of his handlers or maybe even someone at the stadium laid all three cards out on a table, pulled out a Johnny Bench rubber stamp, hit it in the inkpad and then bam, bam, bam. The big red machine was quite the baseball team in the mid '70s and I'm sure Johnny Bench received an enormous amount of mail. I should be happy that I received anything at all. Well, that's what my father told me as I was taking down my Johnny Bench poster. Tony Perez and Sparky Anderson were a part of that machine and they signed the cards, or did they? I guess I may never really know, unless I take them all to an authenticator and that is not happening. If I found out they were fake, I would feel like that woman who found out her Tiffany engagement ring cost six bucks and came from a cereal box. My heart bled for her.

Over the years, I received many autographs with this system. Some athletes even wrote me notes thanking me for what I mentioned in my letter. Roger Staubach thanked me for discussing his career. Clay Dalrymple replied that he was going to include my letter in his scrapbook, so his great-grandchildren could read it. I received a wonderful note from the wife of James "Cool Papa" Bell. She said that he had signed a card against his eye doctor's orders. She even included a copy of the doctor's note.

My summer project continues to this day, and I have received many wonderful autographs. My collection also includes some very interesting people who had nothing to do with sports. My favorite autograph acquisition took place in 1985. I was the deejay for an outdoor wedding, when this cute little old lady walked up and asked me to play her a song. Her voice was thick and raspy and she was quite the flirt. She strolled around to my side of the table to look at my records. I normally didn't allow this but for some reason I let her. While she shuffled through a box of 45s she blurted out, "If I was 60 years younger, I'd be all over you." My uncontrolled laughter didn't stop her monologue, as she told me she really liked my long curly hair and wanted to run her fingers through it. I tried my very best to let this uncomfortable experience roll off of me, and then she smacked me on the ass. The shock of it caused me to jump and although embarrassed, I was geeked out at the same time.

With continued bewilderment, I watched her walk away until she reached her table. She was sitting with a group of women, and apparently was regaling what just happened, because she was pointing at me and they were laughing. After a few minutes, one of the well-dressed women stood and walked over to me sporting a big smile. She was the old lady's granddaughter and came over to apologize. She was in her early 30s and very attractive, so I downplayed my embarrassment for a moment, but what she told me was a complete game changer.

That dainty old lady with the raspy voice who flirted with me, was crowned Miss America in 1921! Her name was Margaret Gorman Cahill and she held the distinction in American history, as the very first woman voted the title of Miss America. Of course, she was in her 80s, but at one point every male in the country lusted after her. If that doesn't do something for your ego, nothing will. I immediately was interested in talking with her, but was working, so I politely asked her granddaughter for her autograph. The only piece of paper I had was a business card, so she signed the back of it. I cherish the memory of being smacked on the ass by Miss America 1921, and I smile every time I look at her name on the back of a silly business card.

The whole autograph journey took a different route when I received a very interesting request from Johnny Mize. He didn't return my index cards, but wrote me a note instead. He stated that he would gladly give me his autograph, if I would make a donation to the Demorest, Georgia Boy Scouts of America. I thought it a very noble gesture for the Boy Scouts. He asked for a four-dollar contribution and although it was my Good Humor money, I sent it along. I was a Boy Scout at the time, and I imagined how cool it would have been with a Hall of Fame baseball player lobbying for our troop. A few weeks later, he sent me an autograph along with a thank you note for my contribution.

Almost overnight, every autograph I sent out came back with a similar request. Most of the requests were charity-related, however a few wanted the money themselves. Wow, I remember thinking, how brazen of these old dudes? I mean, a player from that era didn't make a fraction of the money players from my youth were making and the contracts were only getting bigger.

It must have burned their eyes whenever they read of the latest big-league contract and the buckets of money attached. Although, I felt bad and agreed with them, I didn't have the bankroll to entertain such an undertaking, so my outgoing letters greatly decreased before almost coming to a screeching halt.

In the mid-80s I became enamored, like the rest of baseball, with the Bash Brothers. Jose Canseco and Mark McGwire won back-to-back Rookie of the Year honors for the Oakland Athletics and had been the talk of baseball. Although not Hall of Famers, I wanted their autographs, so I lobbed out letters to each of them. In my mind, they would have been sitting next to each other in the clubhouse when they received them, so I made sure they were different, in case they read them out loud to each other. It could happen.

I never heard from Mr. McGwire, but Jose wrote me back after a few months. Keep in mind when these envelopes arrived, I had no idea who they were from, which made opening each one of them like Christmas morning. I was excited to see which present I had and unfortunately when I opened the one from Mr. Canseco, all I received was a pair of socks. Yes, that was an analogy.

Jose Canseco or his publicist, or maybe even his mother, sent me a preprinted form stating if I wanted Jose Canseco's autograph it was going to cost me 10 bucks a signature. Ten bucks! What the hell was going on here? I'm pretty sure that Jose was raking in the bucks and five years later would sign a $23.5 million deal, making him the richest player in the game. Did he really need to charge me 30 bucks for three autographs? My sun became darker that day, because soon everybody else followed suit and the asking price followed the inflation scale of a Starbuck's triple, venti, half sweet non-fat caramel macchiato. And to my detriment, I still didn't drink coffee.

Can of Corn

By the time I had reached high school, I had seen my father play in about 500 softball games. He still played on Northside with Herman C. Bell, III but he also played on his work team. E.J. Korvettes, was the name of a discount department store that was the precursor to the Wal-Marts and Costco's of today, and my father was a department manager there. The name was interesting and the theory of its creation spawned a great urban legend. Two World War II veterans, Eugene Ferkauf and Joe Zwillenberg created E.J. Korvettes. The initials represented their first names, Eugene and Joe, and Korvettes was the name given to the small Navy warships they served on.

If you asked anybody who grew up on the Eastern Seaboard of the United States who frequented these stores, they would say its name derived from **E**ight **J**ewish **Kor**ean War **Vet**erans. It sounds plausible and interesting as well, but totally illogical. That's like saying IKEA was named after some guy named **I**ngvar **K**amprad, his family farm **E**lmtaryd and the village of **A**quinnaryd. Wait, what?

The Korvette's softball team couldn't hold a candle to Northside talent-wise, but they far exceeded them in the wacky characters department. Sometimes you'd see a player do something that labeled them for the rest of their life and these guys all held that distinction. I remember seeing their center fielder run in and make a great catch, only to ruin the play by stopping and taunting the guy on third to tag. "Go ahead, go ahead, you'll never make it, I have a cannon."

The guy on third called his bluff and took off for home causing the mouthy fielder to cock his arm and launch the ball over the backstop, and into the parking lot denting his own car. I remember my father dropping his head chuckling in disbelief before saying, "asshole."

If anything, the Korvette's boys were entertaining and not always in a Bad News Bears sort of way. In their minds, they thought they were better than reality displayed, so they just acted like they were. Try to imagine a whole softball team full of Eddie the Eagles, sans the skis and you had the softball team of E. J. Korvettes. Today, they would all be wearing eye black, flip-up Velcro wristbands with shift schedules and sporting bat bags engraved with their names across the front.

The best things about these games were the after-parties. I would sit in some strange bar that happened to be near the field of play, and listen to their postgame accolades. At first, I thought they were describing a game they had seen on television or witnessed in person, but they were describing the game they just played. These crazy department store employees would use popular phrases of baseball-ease when they spoke, and none of them qualified.

During the game nobody had a base knock; they all hit *frozen ropes* or they *ripped a pea.* All of their plays were *bang-bang.* I learned that I didn't witness an outfielder giving up on a *Texas leaguer,* what I saw was a *dying quail.* When discussing the great defensive-play they made at the *hot corner,* it would be brushed off as a *can of corn.* Even though it was a *Baltimore chop* or a *worm burner* they always threw the ball *around the horn.* That one guy in the fourth inning shouldn't have been out at second base, because he had a *bad wheel,* and it was a *phantom tag* anyway. Finally, it should have been a *dinger,* but he only had *warning track power.* I heard so much useless baseball lingo from these guys, it became ingrained in my vocabulary, and I started to use it in my everyday life. Once at school, when the teacher asked me where the idea of Pickets Charge came from, I told her, *"out of left field."*

The one saving grace about the level of their performance was that I was a standout. During batting practice one day, I ended up in left field shagging one-hoppers. Okay, I was being nice they were actually five-hoppers. I was catching each one and firing them to second on a line. I think the second baseman even caught a couple. I'm not sure whose idea it was but before I knew it, I was in the lineup and batting seventh. They put me in left center, which was next to my father in left. It was the very first time I played with him and I was excitedly nervous.

Most softball teams have four outfielders stationed equally apart, but Korvette's used a short fielder. It must have been a discount department store thing, because it felt kind of cheap to me. It was my first experience with "the shift" and I was on the move the whole game. I would roam from short left to short center to short right. I even obtained a new nickname. I was hoping for something like "Slick" or "Rocket" but ended up with "Ralph."

You see, I was a junior as my father and I shared the same name. In fact, that is the actual definition of being a junior. I had been around the Northside players my whole life, so they referred to me as "Little Neil." When the Korvette's gang met me, I was about the same size if not larger than my dad, so the name "Little Neil" would have been more suited for my father. However, anyone who knew my father would never utter such a thing in his presence or behind his back either.

At first, when the ball was hit, the infielders started calling out the name "Neil." Since we both were named Neil, we both went for the ball and confusion ensued. I never superseded his range and always deferred to him to make the play, until one time he deferred to me and sadly the ball landed between us. Of course, it was my fault.

Between innings, it was discussed, and when I noted out loud, I wanted to "ralph" when the ball landed between my father and me, the name stuck. Someone also pointed out that I wore Ralph Lauren clothes as well, perfect. Years later, I relived that moment during "Back to The Future." Michael J. Fox went back in time and met his mother who called him Calvin because the name was written in his underwear. For the record, I did not wear Ralph Lauren underwear.

From that moment on, the rest of the team took great pride in yelling "Ralph" when there was a chance I might be involved in the play. When I was nowhere near the ball, shouts of "Not you Ralph" would echo around the field followed by old man giggles. Hilarious, not.

I thoroughly enjoyed playing softball with Korvette's, and not for the laughter, the headshakes and the embarrassment at their caliber of play. It was for the simple fact I was playing ball with my dad. He had taught me the game my entire life, and this was a great way to show him what I learned. He was a proud man, but let me know his satisfaction. The only thing I wish I had done was sit with him, have a beer and discuss the game. He passed away when I was 18.

Days With No Knights

I grew up eating massive amounts of processed sugar, but what kid didn't? When I was younger, it didn't matter because after I drank a gallon of Kool-Aid, and ate a box of Captain Crunch I would go outside and run 37 miles. Our neighborhood was our playground, and we used every square inch of it. The neighborhood corner store, Len Dees, sold every candy bar on the planet and I tried them all. My mouth always had a giant wad of bubble gum in it, and the daily trip to the snowball stand assured me of an ice-cold cup of flavored syrup. You could say Will Farrell got his idea of Elf food from my childhood in Carney, Maryland.

As I aged, I slowly gained weight and by the 10th grade, I was getting unhealthy for a ball player. Okay, I was unhealthy as a human and the other teenagers let me know all about it. So what, if I bought all my pants at the Husky department of Montgomery Ward. So what, if when I went camping, bears hid their food. So what, if I was born on May 5, 6 and 7. Believe me, I have heard every fat joke ever invented.

In my day, most professional baseball players were tall and thin and the idea of a Big Papi body type, was far from a scout's mind. However, if your last name was Ruth and you were from Baltimore, then anything goes, including hot dogs at a record pace. Coaches these days would be very supportive and accept my body type, but back then they would tell me to mix in a salad and run my ass off, literally!

With all that as bottled motivation, I really bore down and forced myself to change. In four months, I lost 53.5 pounds (that's 214 sticks of butter). The reason I know this was because one week I only lost ½ a pound and was extremely disappointed. My health coach said at the time, "Just think that was two sticks of butter!" When I thought about it in small measurements like that, it made it easier to stay the weight loss course and I owe it all to butter.

The main reason for my body change was so I could try out for the high school baseball team. Another reason of course was the girls, because it was, in fact, high school, and with multiple feeder schools there were plenty of them who didn't know I was a goofball yet. It was the mid '70s and tight clothes were all the rage. Enough said.

Unlike today's system, high school consisted of 10th, 11th and 12th grades while junior high school, handled seventh, eighth and ninth. For the record, there was no such thing as "middle school" until Jan Brady pointed out the middle child syndrome and lobbyists determined it needed to be recognized.

High school baseball had a varsity team and a junior varsity team. My inquiring mind led me to learn about my competition, and how sophomores hardly ever played varsity, so I prepared myself for JV. I had not only lowered my goal, but I was about to make a personal blunder that I regret to this day.

Pete Rock was two years older than I, and on his way to earning "Most Valuable Senior" accolades. He was an extraordinary drummer, and a member of the Rabble Rousers. These were very athletic males, who sided with the cheerleaders in firing up the crowd at basketball games. Pete used to walk out a few steps from the sidelines and do a complete flip in mid-air and land perfectly on his feet. I had never seen that before and it really made an impression. Unfortunately, he was also a standout catcher. I had seen him play a few games the previous year, and he was very good, although he performed no flips behind home plate.

A friend of mine, Pat Shanahan, with whom I shared many a beer, was a junior. I knew him from choir and we were members of an elite group of young men known as the "Dead Ends." We held that rank with distinction, although it was coined by the music teacher, Mrs. Johns, who told us during one of our daily class interruptions that we weren't going far in life, as we were a bunch of dead ends. He too was a catcher and just spent his sophomore year on JV. The demons in my head had me thinking I would not be able to start over either one of them, so on the day of tryouts, I joined the crew in the outfield in order to acquire my own baby blue uniform.

The mascot for Parkville Senior High was a knight. Our school colors were black and gold and that scheme was used in every sport's uniform with the exception of the baseball team. Their uniforms were baby blue with black and yellow lettering and trim, as well as black stirrups with yellow stripes. Throw in a pair of matching yellow sanitaries, and you had a very smart and unique-looking uniform.

When you traveled along Hiss Avenue from Joppa Road and passed the last house on the right, it opened up to the vastness of Parkville's baseball field. The very first time we were traveling on that road, and I saw the team off in the distance I couldn't wait to wear that uniform. I'm sure today's players look back on those uniforms the way most fans look at the bizarre colored stripes of the Houston Astros, but at the time they were the bomb.

I had never been to a try out before, as the recreational leagues took you no matter what your caliber. The JV coach was Mr. Norman Norris and the varsity coach was Mr. Larry Butts. A couple other coaches roamed around offering advice and instruction and soon small groups had formed all over the field. There was a contingency of us in left field shagging balls and throwing them to second, where infielders were practicing covering the bag. There were members of the varsity and JV teams, plus others like myself who were vying for a position on a team. I spied them with reverence knowing they accomplished something I hadn't yet.

The coach hitting the balls, called us all in for a little meeting and I sprinted as soon as he beckoned. Some others had taken to a jog until I ran past and soon everyone was racing. When we arrived, one of the varsity players looked at me and without saying it verbally, let me know he thought I was a kiss ass. I thought it was funny, because I had set the tone for the group and from that moment on, we sprinted everywhere.

There was a huge disparity in the level of talent, so the outfield coach started to explain how to field on the run while instituting a crow hop. One of the kids said, "I thought crow hops were only used by the infield" and the coach said, "Son, everybody on the field should use a crow hop including the catcher. If you don't crow hop, you don't play!" Hearing that made me look toward the plate where the catchers were practicing throws to second. As I watched some of them throw rainbows, I felt I should have been there rather than relearning what a crow hop was. I thought about how I only took one step, if that, when throwing the ball to second, but never crow-hopped behind the plate. When fielding a bunt, I crow-hopped every time, as that little hop helped generate power with my throw.

After about 10 minutes, we sprinted back to left field and generated a single-file line to start testing. We each took about 10 balls on the ground, to verify our glove wasn't just a useless showpiece, and lobbed them into the cut-off man standing in front of third. The coaches viewed us as we arched in to cut off the ball, and how we positioned our body to keep the ball in front of us. Secretly, I was making the cut list in my head, as I measured everyone's ability against mine.

The coach sent the cut-off man in front of second and soon we were directed to throw there. We each had three opportunities to run in, scoop up the ball and fire to second with those receivers alternating in and out. There were a lot of throws off-line and some guys totally avoided the cut-off man trying to reach second on the fly, however their throws were way too high and could possibly draw rain. I hit the cut-off man every time like I was throwing only to him. That was a big mistake, but I didn't know it at the time. The idea of course, was to try to reach second on the fly, but with your throw going through the cut-off man. If it takes more time for the cut-off man to catch your ball, before turning and throwing to second than it does on the fly, then you are surrendering second base to the runner. A quick cut-off man with a seamless transition will aide an outfielder with an assist, but you can't depend on that.

Batting practice ended the day, and we all had a chance to hit against pitchers trying to make the team. Although not ideal for batting practice, we all stood in, took 10 or so swings before running the last one out. Obviously, the last swing was the most important, because the fielders would play it like it was a live game and try to get you out. The last thing you wanted to do was foul a ball off or miss it completely, because then you had to sprint to first while cussing the pitcher under your breath. Well, it couldn't be our fault so it had to be a bad pitch.

The baseball field was the lowest of the fields and lived at the bottom of a 30-foot incline right below the soccer or lacrosse field. The hill itself was a great place to sit and watch a baseball game, because it resembled the angle used by bleacher seats in other parks and ran the entire length of the first base line all the way to Hiss Avenue. We all gathered and sat at the bottom part of the hill, as the coaches addressed us about the postings. These would take place early the following week, and list the names of the players who made each team.

I sat there pondering my performance when one of the coaches spoke. "Is there anybody else who can play catcher?" I perked up and friends who only knew me as a catcher, looked in my direction waiting for me to respond, but I didn't speak. At the time, I felt it would look like I didn't think I could make the team as an outfielder. I would have negated the last few hours, not to mention what it took to lose 214 sticks of butter. My thinking was to make the team first, and then tell them I could also catch. They were not looking for team players, they were looking for position players. Not knowing that, I remained silent.

Instantly, two players spoke up and were asked to stay while the rest of us were dismissed. Later, I learned the coaches had planned on moving Pat up to varsity to share the duties with Pete, leaving the JV catching spot wide open. When I checked the list later in the week, I was not on it. I had been cut from JV. While never showing his disappointment, my father told me to use this as pure motivation and chock it up to a learning experience. I chocked it up to stupidity.

A few months later, we were playing softball in gym class. I was playing third base and inexplicably put on a Brooks Robinson display of diving and catching everything that came near me. I even threw someone out from my knees. We used the girls' softball field, which was on the other side of Hiss Avenue near the track. The first baseline ran parallel with King's Ridge Road, which was about 30 yards away. Jeff Ficek, who had made the JV team, and I took great pleasure purposely drilling long foul balls down the first baseline, just to watch the right fielder try to catch one. He was kind of a jerk and this was the only accepted form of bullying we could think of. When we tired of that, we would bash home runs at will. I can still see Jeff laughing as the kid was falling all over himself.

After the game, the gym teacher caught up with me as we were heading back across the street to the school and he said "Hey Neil, why you didn't try out for the baseball team?" I shuddered at the question but looked at him and replied, "I did Coach Norris, but you cut me." I ran off with the rest of the class knowing for sure my outfield faux pas made no impression at all and was my biggest baseball mistake to date. However, I rest assured knowing there would be others.

Varsity Baby Blues

In my junior year at Parkville, I tried out for the team as a catcher and landed the starting position on varsity, finally obtaining my own baby blue uniform. I could have kicked my own ass for not trying out as a catcher the previous year. Actually, I did try but I couldn't reach it. So, on paper, I was cut from junior varsity and then played varsity the following two years. It doesn't make a lot of sense, but it was my own fault for disrespecting myself. I actually read about that possibility in a fortune cookie years earlier so you'd think I would have been on the lookout. It said, "You are almost there." Actually, that could have been referencing getting a "B" in geometry or losing my virginity, so I'm labeling that particular fortune cookie as conjecture.

The varsity coach was Larry Butts, and he was the first coach I ever wanted to win for. I am not saying that I wanted to lose before meeting him, which would just be ridiculous, because like Jimmy Connors used to say, "I hate to lose even more than I love to win." As a baseball player, the one combined goal of all the participants was to win the game, although some just played for the chicks. Up until that time, I wanted to win for myself, and concentrated on improving my personal statistics while becoming a better player, but Coach Butts changed my motivation.

He was strict without showing it and very regimented in his coaching. I learned so much from him about my role and the game itself, that I wanted to prove to him what I had learned, therefore, I wanted to win for him. Think about it, not every teacher is good at teaching, so when you find one who makes you excel, you want to show them off by being an excellent student. Now don't go quoting me as saying I was an excellent student, because every teacher I ever had would join together in a class-action lawsuit against me, because I was a certifiable Stephen King *nightmare of a student.*

Every day, we had schedules we followed to the minute to learn aspects of the game, which I thought I already knew. From 3:20 until 3:40 we practiced covering the bases. We would break into groups and literally practice covering the bag. Pitchers would take the mound, and the coach would hit the ball towards the hole between the mound and first. The pitchers would sprint to first base to take the throw from the first baseman. We did this over and over and over, and we did it every day. As the catcher, who some considered the field general, my role was to point at first base and yell "One!" Everybody would move on the play, so the right fielder ran towards the line to recover an overthrow, the second baseman might move towards first base or second depending on how many runners were on base, and while the pitcher covered the bag, I stood there, pointed and yelled, "One!"

One of the first things Coach Butts taught me was to count properly. I said that in jest, but meant it wholeheartedly. Think about how many games of baseball you've played in your lifetime. When the ball was hit to a fielder with runners on base, all the other players and coaches started yelling where to throw the ball. "Second! First base! Throw it to third!" On several occasions, I've seen infielders stutter step and do the Macarena in five different directions not sure where to throw the ball. Then, when they finally threw it to whatever base they decided, their pause and indecision allowed the runner to arrive safely.

Coach Butts determined I was the only player on the infield to yell where to throw the ball and I only yelled numbers. For the record, "Home" is not a number. One reason was, all four numbers only had one syllable, making them easy to repeat over and over, like "One! One! One! One!" If you heard me screaming that, chances are you would know to throw the ball to first base. If you threw the ball to third, well, you might be pulling splinters out of your ass sooner than later. The same went for the other bases with only one more word added, "Cut!" I was never allowed to yell "Cut Home!" because some people misunderstood that to be "Cut Hold!" If someone cut the ball and held it, that would make Coach Butts very mad, although he never showed it to us, so "Cut Four!" was the proper bellow. To be honest, I have heard on occasion that he was an avid weekend fisherman and took his pent-up aggression on the local small-mouth bass population.

Each drill was perfected the same way. We practiced cut-offs every day from 3:40 until 4:00. We were all at positions and Coach Butts hit the ball to a selected outfielder. He was king of the pop fly and could hit a fungo straight up in the air...I mean it, straight up! I know this because he would do it every day at least three times for my personal catching pop-up drill. The pitchers ran the bases to create an in-game situation and my heart bled for them. Not! Pitchers needed to have strong legs, so running was a prerequisite and our coach ran them to exhaustion. Poor bastards.

If the ball was hit to right side of the outfield, the first baseman would be the cut-off man, and the third baseman would be the cut-off man for everything hit to the left side. The cool thing was they both had to listen to my instructions and I loved yelling at them. The first baseman would position to the right of the mound, and my role was to line him up directly between the outfielder with the ball and myself. More one-word directions were yelled as I shouted things like, "Left two, left two, left one, Stop!" Use your imagination to visualize the first baseman taking steps left until told to stop. Then, before the ball reached him, I would yell more directions like "Cut three!" so he would immediately catch the ball and fire it to third. If the throw were strong enough and on-line, I wouldn't say anything at all and he would step out of the way while the ball came home or "four." If it needed more juice, I would yell, "Cut four!" and he would cut the ball before spinning and throwing home. We perfected the cut off and practiced it so much, I used one word demands at the dinner table, "Meat Neil!"

When that drill was completed, we practiced defensive bunt drills. Again, the pitchers despised it, because they had to run their asses off. I loved it, because I had the opportunity to throw as hard as I could to every base. My favorite drill was the run-down drill. Coach Butts had such a fool proofed run-down plan, we never failed in a game and I mean never. To this day, I see rundowns in professional games and I shake my head at their ineptness. Sometimes, the ball goes back and forth five and six times with the runner changing directions on the fly like a cat following a toy dangling from a stick. I was always at a loss they weren't following Coach Butt's formula. Small-mouthed bass beware.

If performed correctly, rundowns shouldn't be a rundown at all, but a simple chase with one and only one throw. Plus, you were to never ever, under the penalty of carrying all the wrestling mats to the attic, chase a runner to the next base. You always chased them back to the base they came from. It made sense because if they weren't tagged out, no ground was lost.

Later in life, I was on clubs where half the team was involved in a rundown, with fielders switching off after they threw the ball. The third baseman to the catcher to the shortstop to the pitcher to the left fielder to the first baseman, I mean it was a real scorecard tragedy and somewhere in the bleachers a volunteer mother was developing carpal tunnel syndrome trying to keep up. The official rule states that if an infielder impedes a runner by physical contact, the runner is awarded the next base due to obstruction. With so many fielders standing around after they threw the ball, it resembled a mosh pit. Coach Butts had a simple solution.

Let's say, for example, the pitcher picked the runner off of first base and he broke for second. The ball was immediately thrown to the second baseman, who was already sprinting towards the runner. Most of the time, the fielder just tagged the runner due to his inability to stop and turn on a dime. However, if the runner happened to be Deion Sanders, and could run faster than his shadow, and he turned back towards first, the second baseman would run him all the way back to the bag. It was very important not to fake it, by pretending to throw the ball and juke him out of his socks, because you could also be faking out the first baseman. The second baseman would be holding the ball at head level ready to throw until verbally signaled by the first baseman. Again, there was only one word, "Now!" It was all about timing, and we prepared until everyone could do it without thinking about it. You know, like meowing back at cats.

It was beautiful to see the ball snap out of the second baseman's hand and land in the first baseman's glove before tagging the sliding runner out. Once on a failed suicide squeeze, I chased the runner all the way back to third, tagged him out and then chased the runner coming to third all the way back to second tagging him out. It was my favorite double play of all time! It happened so fast and perfectly, that when it was over, I was wondering why I was all the way out at second base wearing the tools of perfection. See what I did there?

My God, we practiced this so often I can't remember a time in high school when anybody was safe in a rundown. It was different on our end because we had the likes of Mike O'Neil and Rick DiPeppe, who weren't only speedsters on the bases, but would literally jump over fielders trying to tag them out. Picture the Flying Wallendas in baby blue baseball uniforms. The whole adage of "practice like you play" was proven to be true by Coach Butts and his direction worked every time. Well, almost.

How many times have you heard a major league announcer claim, "I have never seen that before?" I wondered when every play, and every scenario, and every crazy thing that hadn't been witnessed before, will finally be seen. Fortunately, I was a part of not one but two of those unseen scenarios.

The first one was pretty unbelievable and even the umpire had to look it up. The field we were using had been really worn and someone had unsuccessfully tried to remove the pitcher's rubber. It was raised up more than normal and leaning back towards second base. A previous pitcher had dug out the front of the mound to garner a tremendous push off, so from home plate you could see almost the whole frontside of the rubber.

A batter on the other team hit a line drive up the middle that struck the front of the rubber and bounced all the way back to me, just like my pitch back used to do. I caught it while still in the crouch and threw to first. I hope you could picture that, because it was astounding to see. Eventually the umpire called him out, but the other team protested about me being in foul ground. That fact had nothing to do with it, because the rubber was considered a part of the ground. I'm pretty sure most of you have never seen that.

The other event was a wee bit more epic. It was a home game and I was up to bat. There was one out, and Shawn Shanahan was on third base. Shawn was our first baseman and I had known him since I was 10 years old when he plowed his football helmet into my stomach during a game of *bull in the ring.* I couldn't breathe for three hours. How can you forget the kid who did that?

With two strikes, I half swung at a bad pitch outside and the umpire called me out. However, the ball popped out of the catcher's mitt, which gave me another life. Our bench was on the first base side and the ball was on the ground about four feet towards first base. I was caught in a weird place, because that catcher ended up in front of me, so if I started running, he would just pick up the ball and tag me out. I decided to play it cool and pretended to walk up the line, like I was heading towards the bench, and then when I passed him, I would take off for first. Unfortunately, Coach Butts didn't launch his mind-reading mental telepathy ability to ascertain my thought process, and screamed, "RUN, RUN, RUN!"

I picked up my step to pass the catcher and took off towards first, however as the coach kept screaming, "RUN!" Shawn Shanahan thought he was referring to him, and he took off for home. The catcher had started after me but looked up and saw Shawn barreling down the line, sans a football helmet. He instantly forgot about me, grabbed the ball and dove for home just as Shawn slid in. The umpire spun around and called Shawn out. It was the craziest double play I had ever been a part of, or was it?

I was watching the whole play over my shoulder and as I crossed the bag, I realized that I wasn't really out. Even though the umpire called me out, the catcher dropped the ball. *Baseball rule 6.09 states:*

> *The batter becomes a runner when -- (a) He hits a fair ball; (b) The third strike called by the umpire is not caught, providing (1) first base is unoccupied, or (2) first base is occupied with two out.*

I made eye contact with a very frustrated Coach Butts, who had finally mastered mental telepathy, and I took off for second. The other team was running off the field thinking they had three outs, so I rounded second and headed towards third. The first baseman who was jogging past the mound, picked up the ball the catcher had rolled back, and started running towards third yelling the whole time for any one of the five players who were jogging in the area to play third. Nobody was listening, and I slid into third moments before he arrived with the ball.

By this time, all hell had broken loose. Players were screaming at each other, Coach Butts was discussing it with the umpire, and our team was busy jumping up and down while pointing all over the place. The other coach pulled his players off the field, and our team didn't take the field, so I alone stood on third base while the managerial discussion manifested. After 10 minutes, the umpire pointed at me and instructed me to go back to second. This caused the other manager to run out challenging the decision, and he channeled Earl Weaver to do it. He ranted and raved and kicked dirt and had a complete meltdown. I glanced at our surprised bench and bewildered fans several times, and as new fans arrived, I wondered what they thought of the scene.

It would have been different if I had banged a double, but I struck out and now I was standing alone at second base for what seemed like half a millennium. Five minutes later, the exhausted umpire pointed at me and sent me back to first base, causing our coach to come back out. This went on for another five minutes and in all my embarrassment, I actually sat down on first base. There was no instant replay, and I'm sure as firsthand witnesses described the incident, it was expanding exponentially.

When the discussions were over, the other team ambled back onto the field and I remained at first base. Vindication! However, the next batter swung at the first pitch, grounding out to the pitcher. It was a horrible ending to a horrible beginning. I could no longer say, but for all in attendance they could now say "I had never seen that before."

Southpaws

A year before the start of the Civil War, the *New York Herald* published a story about a bare-knuckle prizefighter named David Woods. He knocked out his opponent in the ninth round, and it was reported he "planted his south paw under his foe's chin, laying him out flat as a pancake." Although not a bare-knuckle prizefighter, my dad was a southpaw. He was the only left-hander in the family, which meant he saw life from the other side of the road. He was by trade a first baseman. I'm sure when he was a kid, they made him play first base because he was left-handed, just like they made me a catcher because I resembled a bowling ball.

I've always felt a left-handed pitcher had an advantage if only by their scarcity. Statistically, right-handers outnumber left-handers 10 to one, so out of 1,000 random people 100 might be left-handed. Most batters aren't used to seeing left-handed pitching; therefore, they are unfamiliar with the delivery and rotation of the ball making it difficult to hit.

Randy Lott was the first left-handed pitcher I caught for on a regular basis. We played rec ball together for years, and I was enamored with his candor on the mound. He was forceful in his pitch selection and would shake me off on a regular basis and usually for show. He was very good with the psychology of the game, and loved to get in the batter's head. For example, I would put down one finger meaning fastball and he would shake me off. I would put down two fingers meaning curve and he would shake me off. I would put down one finger again and he would accept with a head nod. It was the same pitch I asked for, but now the batter saw him shake off two pitches and might be thinking a change-up was coming. Most of the time, they had no clue and just had to react. It definitely made the game fun. However, sometimes his own head would explode when he was the one guessing in the batter's box.

I remember one time Randy, who was anticipating some heat, performed a perfect corkscrew in the batter's box when a change-up arrived. He then got up and shouted at the pitcher, "C'mon dammit, throw a fastball, will you?" The shocked pitcher didn't know how to react, which made it hilarious at the time, but I still laugh when I think about it.

Randy had the best pickoff move I had ever seen. He could definitely give Tippy Martinez a run for his money. Well, maybe not Tippy's money, because after all he was a major leaguer, so I'll say Randy's brother Timmy's money. Left-handed pitchers had the honor of staring right at first base, so a base stealer would need incredible insight and intuition on when to take off for second. It would be similar to doing something devious while your father is staring right at you, but doing it anyway. The majority of the time the end result would be certain death.

I love when a base runner was all hunched over staring at the pitcher, while he was standing perfectly still on the rubber staring right back. Like a crab, the runner took tiny little steps towards second, almost never lifting his foot off the soil, before digging in with his left foot. Everyone was waiting for the pitcher to deliver for what seems like an eternity, but they just keep staring each other down. When the pitcher finally lifted his leg to throw home, the runner exploded off the bag. Now, it was a race to see if the runner could get to the bag before the catcher threw the ball there. That scenario sounds exciting, doesn't it? Unfortunately, this was not the case with Randy on the hill.

I need to explain, so it is important to understand the official baseball rule.

Rule 8.05 states *If there is a runner, or runners, it is a balk when-(a) The pitcher, while touching his plate, makes any motion naturally associated with his pitch and fails to make such delivery; If a left-handed or right-handed pitcher swings his free foot past the back edge of the pitcher's rubber, he is required to pitch to the batter except to throw to second base on a pick off play.* The key sentence is: *swings his free foot past the back edge of the pitcher's rubber,* which was breaking the plane. Randy would look towards home and lift his right leg straight up, bent at the knee. He would never swing his foot over the back edge or even the rubber at all. To the runner, it looked like Randy was going home and he would take off towards second. However, Randy would just step towards first and throw the ball, almost without looking. He picked everybody off. Of course, the runner, his coach and the whole other team would scream "Balk!" and totally have a personal fit at the injustice they'd receive, after the runner was called out.

We always told the umpires before the game to pay special attention to Randy's move, and sometimes we even had to explain the rule to them. Once we did, they joined the pickoff party and became fans just like the rest of us. As a catcher, I always prided myself in throwing runners out, but never had the chance when Mr. Lott was on the bump.

Real life is not like the major leagues, where each organization literally scours the Earth to find the best left-handed pitchers in the world. Discovering a Warren Spahn, Sandy Koufax, Steve Carlton, Whitey Ford or Randy Johnson was an astounding accomplishment, but landing two of them on the same team would be a hard feat to overcome. Imagine if that were to happen on a high school team. It did.

My senior year at Parkville was amazing. It was 1979, and that spring baseball took hold of me, as it never had before. During the week, we practiced every day and played at least two games a week. On Saturdays, I would rise early to experience Mel Allen's *This Week in Baseball* or TWIB. He had such a way with words, I sometimes wished he could have just narrated my life as I went about my daily activities.

"There's Neil Beller zigzagging down the sidewalk to retrieve the mail while singing "My Sharona" by the Knack, how about that?" If you don't know of Mel Allen, that statement won't hold water until you Google him. By the way, if you didn't know "My Sharona" was the No. 1 song of 1979, then you probably don't know the origin of "Up your nose with a rubber hose" either, and that's just sad.

The Parkville Knights ended up in the state championship that year, only to lose to Winston Churchill High School, thanks to a leaping grab by their left fielder, Ron Mallow. We never would have even been there if it hadn't been for our two left-handed aces, Johnny Willet and Kevin Tomchic. Kevin was a year younger, but I had caught him for a few years in summer ball and loved his delivery. His fastball had natural movement and when he snapped off a curve, batters just stood in the batter's box and wet their pants with disbelief.

We got along swimmingly until one day during an outfield drill at Pine Grove Junior. I was hitting fly balls to the outfielders with a fungo bat, and Kevin was the cutoff man. Someone found a golf ball and threw it to me, and on the fly, I swung striking it solid. It snaked in towards Kevin like a scud missile and he jumped left and then right before it struck him solid in the chest, knocking him to the ground. He jumped up and sprinted towards me with fire in his eyes, and I seriously thought he was going to end me. I dropped the bat and walked towards him with both of my hands in front of me apologizing the whole time. When he lifted his shirt, the welt was already a foot in diameter. I know that had to hurt, but I didn't laugh, and that was after I marveled that I hit a golf ball on the fly with a fungo, I mean what are the odds? If only I could hit a baseball with such precision!

John was a senior and threw straight smoke. Even if you knew it was coming, you would still swing right through it. He threw hard all the time even in warm-ups. I had a solid bruise on my catching hand for two straight years, and it didn't go away until I stopped catching him. He had a great memory and would talk about the ones an umpire had missed, even after striking out the side.

I'll never forget one time John was warming up on the sideline and a foul ball rolled in his direction. Unlike the majors, where foul balls were souvenirs, we used the same three baseballs the whole game, so it was common to track them down and throw them back to the home plate umpire. The standard trajectory was a high pop-up, which would bounce once or twice in front of the umpire, so he could easily grab it on a hop. Bucking the norm, and upset at a call in the previous game, John picked up the ball and threw a line drive bullet right at the umpire. He jumped out of the way at the last minute, and Johnny just turned and laughed. Even now as I am writing about this memory, it made me giggle out loud.

The Day Baseball Died

I loved "American Pie." For the record, I am pretty much enamored with any kind of pie: pumpkin, cherry, shepherd's, even the 3.14 kind. However, I am not referring to the raunchy and hilarious 1999 movie, but to the 1971 song by Don McLean. He penned the death of rocker Buddy Holly as "the day the music died." The song contained nods to Elvis Presley, Janis Joplin, Bob Dylan and many historic events that took place in the late '50s and early '60s. I have debated with friends about the meaning of the content over many years and many beers, and still learn about the song. That was the beauty of interpretation.

1979 was a wonderful and tragic year for baseball. As a card-carrying member of the graduating class of 1979, I will be forever married to that year, and everything associated with it. Speaking of association, I give you the President's Day blizzard. For two days in February, cold white stuff fell from the sky at an alarming rate and when it was done, there was over 20 inches of snow on the ground. It was massive and overwhelming and the wind blew drifts of snow six feet high in places. Seriously, even Alaska was jealous and sent Maryland a proclamation on official stationery, which stated, "Cut it out!" Keep in mind this was before Doppler radar, and other wacky weather instruments like yardsticks, so nobody saw this coming. We were off school for a whole week, which I loved, but now as a parent, upon reflection, it must have been awful for my mom and dad.

The bad news for me continued and this time it was work-related. I was working at Toys R Us in Towson, Maryland. My role held massive appeal to fellow workers, as I was in charge of the game wall. It was my job to keep the wall jam-packed with every game imaginable and in alphabetical order. I needed to know important things like, does Chutes and Ladders come before Hungry Hungry Hippos and should I place Don't Spill the Beans under "D" or "B"? The struggle was real. Above the game wall, was an area referred to as overstock. Most humans could never reach that high, although on occasion they would attempt random vertical leaps trying to grab a box of Connect Four. Everything in overstock could be found on the game wall, and if you knew your ABCs, with or without singing, these games were easily found.

We were instructed by management to never leave a ladder in the aisle unattended, due to patrons wanting to use them. I thought this was a ridiculous rule because that's what ladders were for. Once the company lawyer set me straight, I complied and was diligent in my non-ladder-leaving ways. One night, I used one to get a box from overstock and walked 15 feet away to set it down, when I heard the sound of the ladder being moved. I spun around to see a man standing halfway up the ladder on one leg, while reaching perilously as far as he could for a game of Mouse Trap. I yelled, "Hey, get down from that ladder!" My shout alarmed the man and he almost fell, but caught his balance and climbed down. I walked up to him quickly to grab the ladder and realized I had just screamed at Baltimore Orioles shortstop, Mark Belanger. Shit! Now I'll never be a major leaguer, because surely, he would have me blacklisted from ever getting close to wearing the cherished black and orange, and all over a game of Mouse Trap.

When he climbed down, we both apologized to each other and he asked me for my autograph. Well, that's how it happened in my head, but in reality, he just took his Mouse Trap game and exited stage left with my professional baseball career.

On the local level, the Parkville Knights baseball team had a stellar year and competed for the state championship. Our lefthanders and drill retention, created a winning formula that was so prolific, Coach Larry

Butts won Baltimore County Coach of the Year honors. Our team was awesome and we had standouts at every position. As Hall of Famer Orioles manager Earl Weaver liked to say, "We had deep depth."

Two of my favorite teammates were second baseman Steve Regner and right fielder Jimmy Maguire. They were not only great ball players, they looked like great ball players and there was a difference. Jimmy had a tremendous and accurate arm and would use sound effects when he unleashed the ball. I loved sitting at home taking a throw from him. They were always on the proper line and reached me on the fly. A good throw would add to the adrenaline rush needed to catch the ball and turn into an oncoming train.

Steve had very quick hands and a flawless release. When the ball was hit in his general direction, I knew immediately it was an out. He would move sideways like his legs were meant to move that way. Upon observation, his movements didn't resemble a shuffle or a skip, just a fluid movement, causing some to believe he was an alien crossbreeding experiment from a planet whose inhabitants also loved baseball.

Collisions at the plate were my favorite thing and I usually came out the victor. On occasion, I would start to advance towards the runner rather than wait his arrival. This maneuver would always take them by surprise, while some just had the shit scared out of them. I'm sure they didn't lace up their spikes before the game thinking that they would be bull rushed by the catcher. Most of them would slow or try to alter course when I chose this action, but I always slammed into them.

In all my years of catching and all the plays at the plate, I only had my clock cleaned once. Unfortunately, it was a deep shampoo, five-star, Big Ben of a clock cleaning. Our pitcher tried to pick off a runner from third and unleashed an errant throw. Fortunately, the third baseman grabbed the ball in foul territory while running towards the left field bleachers.

Instead of stopping, planting and throwing a line drive to me, he decided to throw while he was running in the opposite direction. His ball resembled an over-the-shoulder alley-oop, almost like he was playing basketball. I immediately thought this wasn't going to end well. The ball had a huge arc and I stood there waiting its delivery, while this guy was steaming down the line like Hoss answering the Ponderosa dinner bell.

I kept looking at him and then the ball and then him and then the ball. I noticed he was breathing heavy, and the noise was getting louder. Finally, I had to jump up to catch the high arcing throw and that's when he hit me. Since I was off the ground, he took me out at the knees causing me to spin forward with great force. Lucky for me, I caught the ball and my forward inertia enabled me to tag him, as my arms slammed into his back. He continued under me and I came down on top of him still spinning while his forward momentum had me completing a 360. We both tumbled together, like we were performing some foreplay dance similar to those pictured in the "Kama Sutra," however, the tools of ignorance prevented penetration.

The runner was out, but so was I. I stood up quickly and showed the umpire the ball and made my way to the bench, hoping I could learn to breathe again. Unfortunately, my medulla oblongata seemed to stop working and my stupidity in proving I was a man by walking away from such an epic collision without having automated body function, was going to get the best of me. I kept trying to take a breath but my lungs left my body for a lunch date with the majority of my blood vessels, giving me exactly three seconds before I passed out. Three, two, one, black.

When I came to, I was lying on the ground in the middle of the bat pile reciting lines from "West Side Story." I tried to say, "How long was I out?" but it sounded like, "I just met a girl named Maria." I'm sure it meant something to somebody, but that person wasn't present. I was only unconscious for a minute and thankfully my lungs started working again, so I stood up to take off my equipment when the umpire uttered, "Hey Catch, there is only one out." I pretended I knew that and zigzagged back to the dish.

Our championship game took place at Dundalk Community College on a weekday. Girlfriends and parents were present, although sparingly for a championship game, but then it was a school night. It was the most important game of my life at the time, and I was on pins and needles. We were competing against Winston Churchill High School from Montgomery County, and upon extensive investigation, determined they were extremely good. Extensive can be equated to word-of-mouth hearsay from a classmate's cousin who knew the first baseman's sister, so it had to be true.

The game was pretty uneventful with the exception of one unbelievable and outstanding play. Late in the game, we were down by a few runs and managed to get bases loaded. Our big man, Kevin Leblanc, was up to bat with two outs, and as championship moments happen, crushed a ball to deep left field. The whole dugout collectively yelled and held their breath at the same time. I was actually bent over holding the top of my head, due to the immense pain I encountered when I jumped up and struck it on the roof of the concrete dugout.

I was wearing my baseball hat at the time and I drove that little button on the top deep into my fontanel. I can still feel the pain, as it rippled all the way down my spine before exiting through my left pinkie toe. Through my blurry vision, I looked down the left field line to watch the ball clear the fence. Today they would measure the trajectory, the climbing speed and the arc of the ball. All I could see was a grand slam and thinking it was a game winner. Well, almost.

Out of nowhere, their left fielder jumped up higher than the fence, and caught the ball before crash landing on the fence in a very painful-looking manner. He then crumbled to the ground. He lay motionless as teammates and the umpire ran out to his aid. All of a sudden, I saw the umpire make the animated "He's Out!" gesture. He caught the ball. He caught the damn ball. Right before the umpire arrived, he lifted his gloved arm holding the ball to the cheers and jeers of both teams. Son of a bitch!

His name was Ron Mallow and he made one of the greatest catches I had ever seen in person. There was no instant replay, and if you blinked you missed it, or in my case were suffering from a self-inflicted concussion. I'm positive over the years the catch became more spectacular than it actually was, but we lost the game and the championship, and to me the catch was the reason. I can still see him lying on the ground in an un-conscience state, the big ham. The newspaper credited the center fielder, Bobo Fitzpatrick for steering him in to the fence to catch the ball. To this day, I dislike anybody named Bobo and won't attend a child's birthday party if I know a clown will be in attendance. I have recently learned, however, that some guy from that same high school was responsible for creating "Game of Thrones," so they get a pass. . .except for Bobo.

During the game, Coach Butts took out the starter to give one of the nonstarters a chance to play in a championship game. I always respected him for doing that. The emotion was very high and as John Willet walked off the field, the applause he heard wasn't just for the game, but the entire season. Later that night, I reflected on that moment and wrote a poem for Coach Butts. While visiting him years later, I smiled when I saw it hanging on his office wall.

The Changing of the Guard

It's late in the war and the tension mounts your face,
Sweat lines your forehead as you watch the soldier's base.
Pressure is increasing, your fingertips are blue,
You've always dreaded what is happening to you.
Wishing it was over, you stand upon a hill,
Your shirtsleeve meets your forehead, sweat remains there still.
Acting in slow motion, a weapon in your hand
You double check your army, plan to take a stand.
You pinpoint your target, and check the soldier's lead,
The battery is programmed, your pores start to bleed.
Time to shoot your rifle, a kill you would admire,
Can't pull the trigger, commander ceases fire.

You hang your head as you conference on the field,
With the changing of the guard, sorrow is revealed.
A replacement now reigns, his gun begins to shoot,
You head towards the bunker as fellowmen salute.
Sitting in the dugout, it's all you can endure,
Extra innings of baseball, a long, drawn-out war.

In early August, I was on my way to work at English's Chicken & Steak House, when I heard some unnerving news. Our family car was a 1971 Chevrolet Impala, and the radio only received two stations. One was a litany of religious zealots who seemed to scream a lot, and the other was 98 Rock. Needless to say, I became a screaming religious zealot. Kidding.

I listened to 98 Rock every day of my life, and not just for the music, although rock music is still the soundtrack of my daily existence. Their news mouthpiece was a guy named Lopez, and he informed me on just about every important piece of news during my youth. I remember him reporting on Jim Jones and the tragic outcome in Guyana, the Three Mile Island nuclear disaster and even the Challenger explosion. He also filled me in on the birth of the first test tube baby, new Coke and of course the debut movie for a crazy bunch of rockers, "KISS Meets the Phantom of the Park." Seriously, look it up! However, on that particular day, he broke the news about Yankee catcher Thurman Munson's plane crash. It was August 2, 1979, the day baseball died.

Thurman Munson was a catcher for the New York Yankees. He also had a name that sounded a lot like Herman Munster, and for that reason alone he was cool. Thurman sported a mustache in the lines of the Mustache Gang of 1972. Remember when the Oakland A's all grew a mustache for $300? Well, Thurman's was not a fancy Rollie Fingers job, but more of a Mad Hungarian sort. In the words of Bob Uecker, it looked like a party favor blew up in his nose. His position on the field made me take notice and I admired his career. He was a pilot in the air and captain of the Yankees on the ground. The night of his funeral, the Yankees played my Orioles, and Bobby Mercer drove in all five runs for the Yankee win. It was still a very sad day all around.

That loss didn't hold the Orioles down and they went all the way to the World Series in 1979. Those who are not from Baltimore and who are not familiar with the term, "Orioles Magic," will never understand how exciting that year was. Third baseman, Doug DeCinces started it off on June 22 with a two-run home run in the bottom of the ninth to win the game. The very next night, Eddie Murray hit a walk-off three-run homer in the bottom of the 10th. It seemed every game that followed ended in a similar fashion and it was magical. The whole state of Maryland was in a baseball frenzy and even novices became fans.

A crazy cab driver from Dundalk, Maryland named "Wild" Bill Hagy took over the upper deck of section 34 and with his enthusiastic animated spelling of O-R-I-O-L-E-S, led Memorial Stadium nightly with the Baltimore alphabet. The "Roar from 34" could be heard for miles around and the new Orioles Magic theme song brought the home team on to the field nightly. Just hearing that song will take any O's fan back to great players like John Lowenstein, Al Bumbry, Ken Singleton and my favorite pinch hitter of all time, Terry Crowley.

Mike Flanagan had 23 wins and locked up the Cy Young, while Jim Palmer, Dennis Martinez, Scott McGregor and Tippy Martinez held down the fort. Throw in Tim Stoddard, Benny Ayala, Don Stanhouse, Gary Roenicke and Pat Kelly and the Orioles were never short of a crazy play or story to fill out the year. One of my favorites was when Pat Kelly told Earl Weaver that he wished he walked with the Lord and Weaver replied that he wanted him to walk with the bases loaded.

With 102 wins, the Orioles beat the Angels to represent the American League in the World Series. They went on to face the Pittsburgh Pirates for the second time in the decade, after losing to them in 1971. That series can be summed up in two words…Roberto Clemente.

While I will never forget the oddity of seeing the bright orange

Orioles uniforms and the bright yellow Pirates uniforms on the field at the same time, I wish I could forget the nausea I felt every time I heard Sister Sledge singing "We Are Family." That was the Pirates theme song, and to this day I throw up a little in my mouth when I hear it. As you figured out, my Orioles lost to the Pirates in seven games again, even after being up three games to one. It was very unmagical.

Although Willie Stargell was excellent and won the MVP for the series, his nickname "Pops" has reverberated through the Maryland grandparent community as a slang name NOT to be used for Baltimore grandfathers. 1979, ugh…the humanity of it all!

Sex and Meat Loaf

I have heard many times in my life that baseball is the perfect game. It's creation and design and layout are absolutely impeccable. Ninety feet between bases was an exceptional measurement, and has led to many close plays that wouldn't happen if the distance was a foot either way. The game would be boring and the term bang-bang wouldn't even exist.

When a famous ad campaign coined America's four favorite things in a jingle it was, "Baseball, Hot Dogs, Apple Pie and Chevrolet." If you remember that ditty you are singing it now. Notice, baseball was listed first. Like so many other meaningful associations in our lives, baseball has been correlated with most things good. Radio advertisers love saying things like, "We are located a long fly ball from Memorial Stadium," or "Choosing our insurance will be a home run!" They don't say it will be a "touchdown" or "nothing but the net," they say "Don't strike out with a competitor, our prices are in the ball park."

Baseball…some people say it is better than sex. Of course, those people are crazy, but they still say it. Actually, baseball is as perfect as sex, because they are both related. Just ask any high school boy or girl if they have ever been to second base. I can assure you; their first thought wasn't the square bag that is connected to the ground surrounded by dirt.

Writer Rosemary Brennan wrote an article for Glamour in which she settled the long-standing debate of what it means to circle the bases during sex. She listed getting to first base as *kissing or making out,* and second base was all about *copping a feel* which usually involved groping the soft bumpy parts of the body. Reaching third base meant getting your *hands in someone's pants* and a home run was *scoring* with actual sex. In all my years, I have never heard of someone boasting about how they *banked one off the crossbar* or *ended up in a bunker.* They banged a homer! Of course, other sports terms could apply so I'll let you use your imagination for, *drove my shuttlecock, took a low blow,* or even *dropped a birdie.* After all, it is *a game of inches.*

Baseball has become a measurement of how relationships progress. It has also helped connect two men, with very different nicknames, with sex. Are you following along? If so, you know I mean The Scooter and Meat Loaf.

In 1977, a talented man named Jim Steinman wrote an amazing song titled, "Paradise by the Dashboard Light." It was performed by a man named Meat Loaf, and appeared on the record album, "Bat Out of Hell." It instantly became a rock classic. The guitar work at the beginning almost resembles the charge trumpets play at most big-league ball parks. I, like many millions of others, were immediately intrigued and fell in love with the song and Meat Loaf.

I was in high school at the time, and the song resonated throughout the school and became an outline of progress in our dating lives. The story in the song is told by a boy who is parking with a girl, and as their hormones fly around the car like a swarm of sweat bees, his advancements are stopped by her questioning his undying love. When he answers with the notion of allowing him to sleep on it, we are treated with a play-by-play sex analogy that is truly genius.

Phil Rizzuto was a shortstop for the New York Yankees for 13 years, and during that time his team won seven World Championships. He held records for bunts and double plays, and in 1950 was voted the American League's Most Valuable Player. When his career ended, he migrated to the broadcast booth, where he spent 40 years as a television and radio announcer. One of his trademark phrases was, "Holy Cow!"

THE DISH

With their romantic actions illuminated by the light of the car dashboard, Phil Rizzuto follows their actions with a play-by-play radio call, as the boy is allowed to get to first base, second base, and third base before being abruptly halted at home. You can hear the two participants panting and groaning in the background, as he describes the progress and it was just radio perfection. I am certain that in the heat of passion, someone, somewhere in the world right this second, is hearing in his subconscious, "Holy Cow, I think he's going to make it!" I wonder if he was safe at home.

Side-Straddle Hops

Going to college wasn't in my game plan because, well, I didn't have a plan. To this day, when people ask me what I got on my SATs, I just laugh in their face because I simply can't relate. I never had to study for weeks on end, I never took a college prep test, and the only campus I ever visited was the Kiddie Campus for Juvenile Delinquents. When I was three, I did time for a hit-and-run, when I ran over the mailman with my stroller.

Thanks to Monty Python, I saw no need in filling my brain with useless information, because I already knew the air speed of an unladen swallow. I've always had a knack for trivia, which would help me if anyone ever inquired about the neighbor's kid's name on "The Dick Van Dyke Show." Freddie Helper, in case you were wondering. My brain was ready, however, the summer after I graduated high school, I was steadily getting my liver ready, as my beer intake was excelling flawlessly. The official term was, senior week, but we referred to it as Natty Boh beach

Growing up, my family had zero to very limited extraneous income, which meant getting a bucket of chicken was the highlight of the year. I honestly never thought about going to college, and before I was even out of high school, I secured a job on an assembly line at the Black and Decker plant in Hampstead, Maryland. I put a lot of thought into my new career and even nailed down the night shift for more money. This meant, not only would I never see my girlfriend, my friends or my sanity, but my bodily evacuation schedule would be screwed up for years, yay me!

My first week of work was horrible. I didn't mind the job, but I didn't know if I should sleep as soon as I arrived home, which was 8 a.m. or wait until 2 p.m. and sleep until 10. I compromised and slept from 8 a.m. until 10 p.m.; I'm all about a solution. Every night, I would sing at the top of my lungs and nobody ever heard me. That place was so loud you couldn't hear anything, but the loud banging of machinery. I ran a giant spot welder and taped to the front of it was my song list. I would start off slow with Harry Chapin's "Cats in the Cradle" and end up eight hours later with Simon & Garfunkel's "Bridge over Troubled Water." It was a hell of a concert, and on many occasions, people would walk by and stare in awe as I sang my ass off.

I also didn't know which meal to eat or when to eat it, and I hated to get in bed when it was 85 degrees outside. I forgot to mention, the summer of 1979 celebrated a gas shortage. Gas needed to be rationed, so the gas distribution people came up with a surefire way to disperse it equally. They invented the even-odd system, which meant that motorists could only get gas every other day. To verify this, on even-numbered days only people with an even number on the license plate could get gas. The same thing happened on odd days. Unfortunately, my odd-numbered license plate didn't jive with the even-numbered day when I ran out of gas. I was trapped 30 miles from home, with no gas and no way to get it. You might be asking yourself what happened. Well, do the words "farmer's tractor" and "rubber hose" paint any pictures?

All the fun of a full-time working life was immediately postponed, when my father summoned me downstairs for a phone call. In the way back machine, most homes had one telephone, and ours was wall-mounted next to the back door. When I approached the black phone hanging on the side of the mounted box, I mouthed to my father, "Who is it?" and he gave me his sarcastic version of, "I don't know, I'm not Kreskin," with his outward arms and shrugging shoulders. He was super curious though, so he stood within earshot of the whole conversation.

It turns out the man on the other end of the phone was George Henderson, the baseball coach at the Community College of Baltimore or CCB. He was totally wearing his recruiting hat and regaled me tall tales about the luxuries of coming to a college, where former Baltimore Orioles, like Mark Belanger (uh-oh) would be at our practices daily. A team which had the best talent on the East Coast, a team that was being built to win it all and he wanted me.

He actually offered me a scholarship to play baseball. What? He had contacted Coach Butts looking for some talent to round out his team, and had already secured Parkville teammates Jimmy Maguire and Steve Regner. I can still see my dad leaning on his arm against the wall, proudly smiling as he listened to me fill him in on the offer. He taught me the game, so this was a feather in his cap, not mine. I asked him what I should do and he immediately said it was my decision, however I knew that was just something to say.

I began the pros and cons drill. College? Nightshift? Baseball? Gas lines? Sleep? Constipation? The drill ended there, and I became a CCB Red Devil.

CCB was located on Liberty Heights Avenue right near Mondawmin Mall and the Baltimore Zoo. There was a lake nearby, which was referred to by teammates as Red Devil Lake, although no red devils lived there. I met with a counselor, who presented me with a predetermined schedule consisting of 12 whole credits of your basic nonsense. In all honesty, the academic curriculum resembled 13th grade.

Classes started before fall ball, so I had a few weeks to establish myself as a real-life college student before meeting the team. Since I was a commuter, half of my morning consisted of finding a parking space. I had recently purchased my first car for $600, which felt like a million in 1979. It was a tan Vega nicknamed Runt, which was great on gas, but drank oil like it was attending a bachelor party kegger. It had an aluminum block engine which expanded when it heated up, and the oil would blow right through it creating a thick, smoky exhaust trail. Conservationists loved me.

During the first week, I received five parking tickets and I only went to college four days. The most egregious ticket was for parking on Liberty Heights Avenue in a bus zone. I tried to get out of it by offering to drive some of the bus patrons to Lexington Market between classes, but the mass transit authority I was speaking to wasn't buying any of that.

I didn't know anybody at CCB, except Jim and Steve, but never saw them, so I kept to myself. The college had an awesome dental hygienist program, so there were lots of pretty girls to look at as I traversed the hallways, but I was wondering who the ball players were. The first one I met was by mistake, and I wasn't happy about the introduction. I was asked by my English teacher to stay after class one day along with another student who sat in the front of the class. I recognized him as the only other white guy in the class, and I sat in the back about seven rows behind him. He was mumbling as we waited and I noticed a row of fresh stitches on the side of his head.

The teacher assumed we knew each other and talked to us like we were a couple. Not a "couple" couple, but a couple of knuckleheads and accused us of cheating. I was dismayed at his candor, and asked him to explain. He told me I did great work and wondered why I always turned in everything late. I told him I have never been late with an assignment and was pretty adamant about it, and he believed me. Turning to the mumbling dude, he asked him why our papers were so similar. I was in complete shock and didn't understand what was going on when the other student finally fessed up.

Apparently, when I would pass my assignments up the row, this guy would take mine home, copy it and turn them both in late. What balls! Who would do such a thing? I asked him in the hall what his major malfunction was and he just smiled and said, "My name is Tim O'Malley and I am your first baseman." And so it went.

He told me the stitches on the side of his head were from a bar fight and that someone hit him with a bottle. I wasn't sure if I believed him, but I quickly learned what lunacy he was capable of. He talked me into following him to his house in Brooklyn, offering a wonderful home cooked meal via his mother. Who could turn down that offer?

I was following him in my oil-sucking car, when we ended up at a red light in front of historic Cardinal Gibbons High School. While we sat there, I noticed his car had a license plate that was labeled Maryland State Delegate. I learned later it belonged to his father. I had never seen the plate before and was admiring it when I noticed Tim's driver's door open. He got out of his car and started to stretch with his back to me. I thought it was odd that he was doing this in the middle of a very busy intersection, when all at once he dropped his gym shorts right to the ground.

He was standing there bare-assed at 5:00 in the evening during rush hour and I was losing it. Who was this guy? I knew he was doing this for my benefit, and the funny thing was most people in front of us couldn't see anything because he was shielded by his car door, however for me and the cars behind, it was a front-row seat to an unwanted all-male burlesque show.

Cars started turning left and driving right past him, but he still stood there stretching and then it happened. I saw him start to hurry back in his car and immediately a police car pulled up and jerked to a stop. These two cops jumped out so fast Tim didn't even have time to pull up his pants. I sat there through three lights while the two cops berated him. One moved to the back of the car and saw the plate before yelling, "Oh this is going to make the news!" The other one says, "What if I had my wife and kids in the car?" Tim just sat there dumbfounded and half naked.

When I was finally waved to pass, I noticed Tim sitting in his car with his feet on the ground trying to explain himself out of trouble. The whole time this was happening, his shorts were still on the ground. A life in politics was certainly in his future, but since I didn't know where he lived, I lost out on a wonderful dinner and just drove home.

THE DISH

In early October, a practice was scheduled and I was excited to finally meet the rest of the team. Unfortunately, rain cancelled the outdoor practice and it was moved inside to the gym. I arrived a few minutes after the call time, and realized by the camaraderie I witnessed, that I missed the introduction portion of the program. I shook hands and exchanged names with a few of the guys, but if immediately quizzed on their names I would have failed. All at once, we were called into formation in the middle of the gym.

George Henderson introduced himself and then coach Norm Gilden, and finally Pete Hamilton. I had heard of Norm as being a coach for Johnny's, which had won 37 straight Baltimore City titles and many of its players ended up in the majors. Al Kaline and Reggie Jackson played on the team, both of who became Hall of Famers. The full name was Johnny Leone's, and was managed by former Oriole scout, Walter Youse. The first prospect he discovered was Cal Ripken Sr., and he went on to spend many years finding talented young men to play baseball.

I was excited just to be within arm's reach of such nostalgia and baseball history, so I wanted to meet Coach Gilden. I walked over to introduce myself and the sound of loud clapping diverted my attention. Almost at once, others started clapping and moving into some kind of formation. The gym was exploding with excitement, so I filed in like a zombie, and while clapping, found a place in line next to Steve Regner. One of the players moved to the front and was facing us, I assumed he was the team captain.

His name was Terry Little and he exuded coolness. He had a toothpick sticking out of the side of his mouth, like he had just finished eating a good steak. He was straight-faced as he eyeballed each player and he did all this without discontinuing his clapping. When he stopped, everybody stopped. He positioned himself like he was about to start something and sternly said, "Fifteen side-straddle hops, ready begin."

I quickly looked around the room in the most panicked way, because I had never heard of a side-straddle hop. Holy shit, these city

95

guys have a whole routine I know nothing about. I hadn't even met anybody and I was about to look like an ass standing there as they all did side-straddle hops. I glanced at Steve, who had a similar fear about him, when Terry started moving and counting out loud. "One, two, three, ONE!"

Jumping jacks! He was doing jumping jacks, but apparently in the city they are called side-straddle hops. I have to admit that did sound a lot cooler than jumping jacks. I immediately started jumping in unison with the others. Terry would repeat the "One, two, three" and then everybody would shout "Two!" This continued all the way to 15, followed by more exuberant clapping like we had just finished climbing Everest.

Unison was a great word to describe the CCB Red Devils, because we did everything together and if anybody was doing something different, they were called out for it. I don't mean in a civic or personal way I mean as a team. I remember one time we had finished our team warm-up and took a lap around the field. One of the pitchers was wearing his jacket and stood out as nobody else had one on. He ended up running five extra laps for not being a team member.

We even had a team meeting where we had to learn how to get dressed. Yes, I said that out loud. I mean, who doesn't know how to put on their uniform? Well, apparently everybody. We actually had three uniforms, one all white with black and red horizontal stripes, one all black and one all red. They were all interchangeable, meaning you could wear the red shirt with white pants or the white shirt with black pants. Once we developed a winning streak while wearing the all red, that pretty much was all we wore.

Sitting in the locker room, we were taught to lock our socks. I had never heard of that, but it was very neat and the only way I wore my uniform from that day on. We were instructed to put on our 50/50, our shirt, our sanitaries and finally our stirrups. Then we would turn our pants inside out and put them on bottom first. Now pay attention while I try to describe this.

Starting at the bottom of the inside-out pants, each leg would go in first. Trial and error determined the next part depending on your leg length, but for me I pulled them up to right below my knee. With them still inside out, I would take the top of my stirrups and fold them down over the pants leg to about mid-calf. Can you picture this? By grabbing the waistband and pulling up the pants, they would only go as high as was allowed by the folded-over socks. What this did, was lock your pants right into your stirrups. If during the game you had to slide, they would never roll up because they were locked and dirt could never penetrate the lock. When you took your pants off, you would pull them all the way down and then unfold the stirrup before continuing. You couldn't get them off any other way, unless you pulled them down very hard and pulled off the stirrups at the same time. This was quite difficult and can only be compared to pulling all the meat off of a drumstick. Ouch!

The stripe on the side of the pants had to match up with the stripe on the shirt and heaven forbid the buttons on the shirt didn't line up exactly with the zipper from the pants, forming a perfect gig line. We all looked identical all the way down to our matching Brooks Robinson spikes. I didn't know it at the time, but Coach Henderson and Brooks Robinson had a sporting goods business together. Imagine that!

I was impressed with Terry, as the whole time he was calling out exercises and counting, his toothpick never wavered or even moved. He directed us through other staples such as "pinwheels" which were just out stretched arm toe touches, and "impossibles," where we stood open-legged and reached back through our legs as far as we could. I was quite impressed with the vernacular.

The session went that way for an hour and ended with the dreaded core exercise. Keep in mind this was 1979, and years before "Buns of Steel" or Jane Fonda's contribution to the Danskin world, so nobody had cool stomach exercises.

Lying on our backs, with our hands under our butts, we would lift our legs off the ground six inches and do whatever Terry said.

"Up………..spread 'em ………..together………….down."
I immediately thought, "Oh my God that was hard. I was happy that was over because…"
"Up………..spread 'em ………..together………….down."
…wait you mean we weren't done? I don't know if I can do another…
"Up………..spread 'em ………..together………….down."
…one and I'm not kidding."
It was all I could do to lift my legs, much less spread them and then Terry got all medieval on us.
"Up………..spread 'em ………..together…………. spread 'em ………..together…………. spread 'em ………..together…………. spread 'em ………..together………….down."
The collective sound of groans following feet hitting the ground, echoed throughout the gym. I could NOT wait to drop my feet and when I finally did, I realized they were already down. I have no idea how long they were on the ground, but I could swear I was doing the exercise. I'm pretty sure I popped a blood vessel in my head and spotted at the same time. I knew one thing for sure, academically this year was going to be easy, but physically it was going to be a bitch.

The Hardest Test

All my life, I have enjoyed writing poetry. I was a huge fan of Dr. Seuss, as my first time speaking in front of the class was to recite "Green Eggs and Ham" from memory. In high school, I had several poems published in the literary magazine, and I usually wrote something heartfelt for the girls I dated because mean poems made them cry. I was excited to take a college poetry class to see if I could mature my craft, and write more abstract meaningful pieces or make my classmates cry.

My professor gave the class an easy assignment, instructing us to go home, look out the window and write a poem. I usually needed some inspiration to write and when I told her I couldn't do that she said, "Then you will fail."

That night I sat in front of my bedroom window all disgruntled, struggling to write a poem. I thought about the beauty of baseball and how it would make great material for a poem, I mean "Casey at the Bat" was a classic. I had so many topics to write about, the batter, the fielder, the bench rider and even a funny public address announcer, ie: Bob Uecker. Unfortunately, I developed baseball writer's block, and couldn't come up with anything and even when I turned to the Orioles, nothing rhymed with orange. It was almost midnight and I needed something for the next day, anything.

Glancing out the window towards the neighbor's lamppost, I noticed it was starting to flurry. I watched the flakes dance in the light for a few minutes and then wrote about it. Ten minutes later, I had written "Forgotten Flight." I fell asleep that night proud of my accomplishment. I really liked it and couldn't wait to read it in class the next day.

Forgotten Flight

They gracefully fly from the plentiful sky,
No two use the same route to float.
Programmed for flight and incredibly light,
They furnish the ground with a coat.

They talk to each other in quest of their mother,
So not to fall victim to the sun.
The white crystal ice of virginity splice
All together to make themselves one.

They giggle and laugh as they lie in a bath
That absorbs them, the Caucasian clean.
To strive for perfection the greatest invention
Finds final glory in a stream.

The sun shouts aloud from its imprisoning cloud
And laughs back at the forgotten flight.
Very proudly they die refusing to cry.
When they melt what happens to the white?

I was the only white person in the class, but didn't think about that until after the professor asked the class what they thought. I was eviscerated! Some of my classmates didn't like the poem at all, some didn't understand it, but some others labeled it racist. I remember one guy banged his fist on the table while saying, "I think what he is saying is what is white is right!" I was stunned and became defensive explaining it was just a snowstorm out my window. The professor thanked me for reading, and instructed me to look deeper inside myself because, "The true writer lives in their heart, which determines how they see the world." I obviously never forgot that moment.

My father told me that if you have the mental fortitude, you can withstand any physical challenges you might not be ready for. However, it doesn't always work for emotional challenges, and definitely takes a back seat when challenged with tales from the heart. In October of 1979, my family was blindsided by my father's cancer diagnosis. He was only 45 years old and didn't have a grey hair on his head. He lost his brief battle with cancer in late March, and never had the chance to witness his son play baseball on a college diamond.

I remember sitting with him one night while he was in a hospital bed in our living room. He was listening with excited eyes as I told him about our most recent scrimmage game. He was smiling as I talked, and all at once a dormant reflex awakened from his past and he quickly raised his right hand to catch a ball. He pulled the imaginary ball from his invisible glove and threw it to nobody. He was reliving some long-forgotten moment from his youth, and for a second, I saw in his face, a child. When I asked him what he was doing he just smiled and said, "Playing catch." I will always remember how much joy baseball brought him, and thanked him for conveying in me a love for the game.

My poetry class also had a requirement to read at a recital for anyone who was willing to listen. For the assignment, we had to pick three poems to read, which represented our current state of mind. It was not a requirement that we authored them, and we could use any sort of prose or iambic pentameter we liked. I was nervous as I waited in the hall, and when it was my turn, I noticed the room was full of students and teachers who just happened to wander in during their hour break.

I had learned from Marsha's driving test on, "The Brady Bunch" that to combat nervousness one needed to picture everybody in the room wearing only their underwear. That sounds good in a sitcom, but the pretty dental hygienists in the front row would have had me all a frenzy, and more than likely approaching half a three quarters semi, so I opted for the older professor in the back.

I read my two favorite poems first, "The Changing of the Guard" and "Forgotten Flight" and then I explained to everyone that I had just lost my father. I conveyed to them how delicate life was and how ugly it could become, and then I read "Summer."

Summer

The sun was shining brightly,
And I could hardly wait
To ponder out my window
And gaze at my estate.

The wind was blowing briskly;
It made the flowers sway.
The garden was enchanting
On this inspiring day.

My eyes fell on a little bird
With a beautiful yellow bill.
I beckoned him to come light
Upon my window sill.

I smiled at him cheerfully
And gave him a crust of bread.
Then I quickly closed the window
And smashed his fucking head.

The room was filled with laughter, shock and sadness all at the same time. A perfect tribute to my father. It was the hardest test I had ever taken, and I didn't write another poem for 10 years.

Mr. Yuck

My suburban upbringing did little to prepare me for the diversity of the team. I made a lot of black friends' years earlier in life at YMCA's, Camp Koda, but knew those friendships were only as long as the camp. Baseball teams' gel in a whole different manner, and you spend more time with them than your own family. I was excited to get to know these guys and to this day still practice what they taught me.

The first thing I learned was that nicknames ruled at CCB. I learned that from Cheese Hawkins. I seriously don't even know his real name, I only ever called him Cheese as did everyone else. He was small and fast like Al Bumbry and he was always smiling. Another member of the team was Juice and there was Kingy, Mags, DJ and Dr. Strange Glove. Going around the room kind of resembled the introductions in the bar from "Good Fellas." I'll touch more on them later, as I had a nickname as well.

We were playing a scrimmage game at Salisbury State University on the Eastern Shore. They had a cool artificial turf infield, and to the left of home plate behind the backstop was the public address system announcer. He was given the lineup card and was introducing each player as they came to bat. I had never experienced that before and was very giddy about the prospect of hearing my name announced like a major league ball player. As I approached the batter's box he launched into his spiel. "Now batting number 22 the catcher...Ned Beller." Ned? My bench was rolling and they were all calling "Ned!" "C'mon Ned!"

"Get a hit Ned!" I can still hear Cheese laughing as he was yelling, "Ned." To this day, the 1980 CCB Red Devils know me as Ned.

I quickly fell in with these guys and any inhibitions I might have had regarding race just melted away. They pushed me towards physical goals I didn't know I could obtain. I was in the best shape of my life and was willing to do anything to make myself a legitimate ballplayer. I even tried Copenhagen.

We were sitting in the café eating lunch and playing cards, which happened so much I thought I was getting credits for it. Lunch was a daily occurrence but sometimes eating wasn't even involved. I noticed some of the guys were always dipping their fingers into these little round cylinders and putting something in their mouth. They were also spitting into plastic cups, which was gross and disgusting. They called it "dip" and insisted I try it.

They had Skoal and Copenhagen and I reluctantly opted for the latter because it sounded Canadian. I thought maybe it tasted like molasses or bacon. You can't go wrong with anything bacon-related, except maybe spitting it into a plastic cup. Just like the commercial used to say, I put a little pinch between my cheek and gums. It had a gritty sawdust texture and took a few minutes to get all the grains in place. Those of you who have eaten sawdust understand the ordeal of using your tongue as a shovel and rake. My friends were smiling and looking at me with apprehension like I was about to sprout spider arms or something.

At first it was no big deal. I spit in a cup like everybody else and the taste wasn't overwhelming. A few minutes into the experiment my speaking became slurred and I felt a little buzz coming on. My friends were laughing at me now and I totally remember Cheese right in my face looking like he was in a fisheye lens. The back of my head felt like someone hit me with a hammer and my mouth went numb causing me to spit down the front of my shirt like a newborn baby.

Within 30 seconds, I was regurgitating everything out and gargling in the nearest water fountain. Just like I thought, it was gross and disgusting. Years later, I've seen hundreds of ball players chewing tobacco and dipping during a ball game. Yuck! How could a catcher spit through his mask anyway? To this day, whenever I see someone buy a can of dip at a convenience store, I shudder a little.

It never mattered to the rest of the iron stomach Red Devils because most of them chewed, dipped and spit on a regular basis. These guys were tough. I remember one time we were warming up with a metal ball. It was like a tiny baseball-sized shot put and weighed about 3 pounds. The idea was to stand about 10 feet apart, and throw the heavy metal ball back and forth for a few minutes to warm up your arm, and then you could throw a baseball, which was significantly lighter, about 13 miles.

Playing catch is very communal, so when another guy showed up, he would just stand in line at one end and eventually someone would throw him the ball. However, we were playing catch with a cannon ball, which meant you had to catch it at your side and quickly move your glove backwards to lessen the weight, and also protect it from exploding like a rawhide firecracker. Knowing all this, I was surprised when Juice walked up and held up his glove. I threw him the ball and he tried to catch it right in front of his head. The weight of the ball propelled his glove right in to the center of his face, and he catapulted instantly to the ground. The impact sounded so painful I thought he lost all his teeth. I ran over to offer help and he just jumped up and said, "Jesus Ned, why didn't you tell me you had the metal ball?" Umm, I dunno.

Even our bus driver was a beast. He was the kindest little old man you ever met, and he was always smiling. What made him so special was the simple fact that he was somewhere between 75 and 150 years old and had no teeth. One day he drank some bad coffee and the face he made was hilarious. When I pointed out to the team that he had an uncanny resemblance to the poison prevention sticker of the time, the moniker stuck and he was known forever as, Mr. Yuck.

Sometimes he was just called Yuck, but he never questioned the origin of his nickname and continued to drive us everywhere. During an away game at Bowie State College, Mr. Yuck was sitting alone on a set of bleachers along the third base line. He used to roll his own cigarettes and was just finishing by licking one closed, when the batter pulled a wicked line drive right at him. The ball struck Mr. Yuck on the right side of his head so hard it caromed all the way into center field. The gasps could be heard for miles as everyone ran over hoping not to find a dead Mr. Yuck. However, Mr. Yuck's head just snapped right back in place and he continued to finish making and then lighting his cigarette.

I couldn't believe my eyes. I thought for sure he was in shock and that he would eventually just fall over, but Mr. Yuck just sat there acting like a mosquito had brushed by his face. That was one tough bus driver. I remember hearing someone say, "Don't be afraid to take one to the skull and keep smoking, shit!" That was when the catchphrase segment of CCB began.

Don't Be Afraid to Start a New Chapter, Shit!

Every now and then a catchphrase or just saying something silly becomes prominent, therefore defining the times. I mean who can forget, "I can't believe I ate the whole thing" or "Where's the beef?" These were utterances from television commercials, but when heard, takes one right back to the visualization associated with them. Ever since the Mr. Yuck incident, it became common practice to start almost every sentence with "Don't be afraid to" and end it with the exclamation, "Shit!" I have no idea why, it just happened and we ran with it and we ran with it for a long time.

If you were playing cards in the cafeteria at a table of four and someone walked up you might hear, "Don't be afraid to save me a seat, shit!" followed by, "Don't be afraid to show up on time, shit!" followed by, "Don't be afraid to pay attention to the game and take your turn, shit!" followed by, "Don't be afraid to kiss my ass, shit!"

This became the everyday language during my time at CCB and I was amazed that not everybody was talking that way. That year at Thanksgiving, I was regaling my family on the new way to begin and end each sentence. My mother was having a very hard time understanding the concept until she finally said, "Don't be afraid to eat turkey at Thanksgiving......" The long pause was deafening as my family waited patiently for her to finish. Out of nowhere, my 82-year-old grandmother said, "Shit! You have to end it with shit!" We all reacted accordingly and laughed for 20 minutes. My mother, however, took another two months before ending a sentence with the desired expletive although she had been doing it all my life.

The vernacular at CCB stayed with me a long time and on occasion even to this day you might hear me say, "Don't be afraid to cancel the baseball season due to a pandemic, shit!"

The raw talent at CCB was amazing and we won just about every game we played. The field was a horrible area, which backed up to woods, which ran down a long hill into an overgrown ravine. If someone fouled off a baseball behind the screen, you could pretty much kiss that ball goodbye. At one of our first practices, I saw a batter lose 12 balls in a row. I remember thinking someone had deep pockets, because baseballs were expensive. I made the mistake of mentioning this to Coach Henderson, who immediately sent me over the fence to wrangle up a baseball. I guess I was part baseball bloodhound, because I came back with about 25 balls. My performance backfired and that became my job. I can't tell you how many times I scaled that fence looking for baseballs, but it did keep me flexible.

When this would happen, I would be away from the game for some time and would miss spectacular and amazing plays our team would make. I did witness our first baseman, Tony Maggard, run in for a bunt only to see the pitcher grab it. He started back peddling towards the bag as quickly as he could, when the pitcher erratically tossed him the ball. He had no idea where the bag was, and as he caught the ball with his bare hand, his left heel found the bag and knocked him completely off his feet. A millisecond later the runner touched the bag and both of them went flying. The runner was out and I couldn't believe what I had just witnessed. Tony just got up laughing before whipping the ball around the horn. Things like that were a common occurrence.

Another time, Wayne King was playing center field when a long fly ball took him to the newly erected snow fence. He jumped up to catch the ball and the fence took out his legs. By some form of acrobatic sorcery, he caught the ball but was standing on the other side of the fence facing away from the field. He couldn't climb back over because the back of his pants and his belt were tangled in the fence.

There was never a dull moment and there was never a time when I didn't think we would win. We always won. After the game we would shake hands with the losers and jog to the right field foul line. The other team would watch in horror as we would do multiple 100-yard wind sprints towards Coach Gilden, who was deep in left center. We would beat down a team by 15 runs and then run our asses off after the game. I was in the best shape of my life.

I wasn't the starter, as Mark Eckerl held that distinction, but I played in many games. I could be found in the bullpen warming up a pitcher or brought in as a pinch hitter to bunt someone over. To my credit, I mastered the art of bunting for a hit. There was a big difference between that and giving yourself up as a sacrifice. I was thick and stocky and during pregame batting practice ripped line drives down third, so I was perfect to bring in to lay down an unexpected bunt. I'm pretty sure I had most of my hits that way and Coach Henderson told me that I was one of his favorite secret weapons. I think he liked my ability to find baseballs better.

We were playing Dundalk Community College at home and during the pregame team meeting I was in the bullpen with starting pitcher Ronny Caldwell. Ronny had a wicked curve and liked to work it with two speeds. When the game started, he ran onto the field and I walked back to the team bench. One of the first people I noticed was the first base coach for Dundalk. He was a huge man and reminded me of a funnel. I'll go one step further and relate his size and build to The Mangler, who appeared on the television cartoon, "The Flintstones." Fred was a jury foreman and read the verdict convicting The Mangler who swore out loud, "I'm going to get you Flintstone, if it's the last thing I ever do!" Well, long story short, The Mangler was coaching first base.

As the game went on, I spent lots of time in the woods chasing balls and lots of time cheering on my team. Ok, that was a bold-faced lie. We were not allowed to cheer on our team, we were coached to get in the head of the other team. We would say anything and at any time to get under the opponents' skin. We would chatter about them, their mothers, their sisters, their sexual habits with farm animals…anything was allowed and preferred. I remember driving all the way to Allegany Community College to play at their field and as Mr. Yuck was pulling the bus in the parking lot, guys were yelling out the windows at the other team. "Nice hair 27!" "Hey 16, I slept with your girlfriend." Keep in mind they didn't know who they were yelling at, so they used their uniform number as a reference. The other team was ready to fight before the first pitch.

As you can imagine with this type of instigation, rhubarbs and skirmishes would occasionally break out. When they subsided, all-out wars were launched. I had never played this type of ball before and rarely participated in the verbal side and was chastised for my nonparticipation. I don't remember my other Parkville teammates doing it either, but we all participated in the brawls. Before the season started, after our team physical, where a doctor literally walked right down a line of players grabbed our junk and told us each to turn our heads and cough, we had a team meeting. We were all still standing shoulder to shoulder, individually trying to get the medical assault we had just encountered out of our minds, when Coach Henderson walked in to address us.

He told us we would definitely be fighting this year and there were two types of people in a baseball fight, swingers and pullers. Swingers were the ones participating in the brawl, and pullers were launching themselves into the melee and pulling others out. We were instructed, under penalty of never playing a single inning, not to pull any of our own players out of a brawl, only members of the other team. His reasoning was that while you were holding a teammate by his arms after pulling him out of a brawl, he was available for someone to swing at his unprotected body.

The coach walked down the line and personally told each one of us which one we were. He started with the first person in the line, Tim O'Malley and said "Swinger." We all started laughing because Tim was a gamer and loved to stir things up with the other teams. Then he continued down the line, "Swinger, swinger, swinger, swinger, swinger, swinger, swinger, swinger." He went right down the row and labeled everyone a swinger. We had no pullers on the team. He reiterated that anyone pulling during a brawl would not play another inning for CCB. After the meeting, our third baseman, Jimmy Dipino or Dipper for short, had a gleam in his eye and told me, "This season was going to be crazy!" Don't be afraid to make an understatement, shit!"

So, it's about the third inning and I keep looking at the first base coach and how intimidating he seemed. He didn't even have a neck, his head just sat on top of his large shoulders. He was clapping his hands to cheer on his team and the sound actually hurt my ears. I commented to Steve that the guy reminded me of the Mangler from the "Flintstones" and Steve laughed. He said the guy does look like a murderer doesn't he and I agreed. He then dared me to yell something at him. Our bench was only about 25 feet away from first base and we were always yelling something so I took a deep breath and yelled, "Murderer!"

The guy turned in our direction and chuckled while continuing to clap his hands. I turned to Steve to laugh and he was gone. He was walking towards the other end of the bench in a swift fashion pretending he was looking for his glove or something. I called to him but he ignored me, so I stood up and started walking toward him. When he walked around the back of the bench and away from me, I knew something was up. Finally, another player walked over to me and said, "Jesus Neil, didn't you hear what the coach said?" "Um no, what the hell are you talking about?"

Apparently, in the pregame meeting, Coach Henderson told the team that if we were to get in a fight with these guys to stand clear of the first base coach. He had just been released on bail after killing someone in a bar fight. Oh reeeealy! Thanks guys, for letting me know.

Thanks for letting me sign my own death certificate. Don't be afraid to let me call the Mangler a murderer at the top of my lungs, shit! From that moment on, I changed my voice an octave deeper and kept it that way through the rest of the game. During the end-of-game cordial handshake, I thought for sure he would slug me, but he was very professional with his "Good game fellas" retort. He didn't know when I said, "Thank you," it was not for the game but for not ending me.

We were all standing in the coach's office for the postgame debriefing when Coach Henderson burst in. "Who in the hell yelled, 'Murderer!' in the middle of the game? Jesus Christ, didn't you assholes hear what I said?" All fingers were pointing in my direction and Coach Henderson walked over and planted himself inches from my face like Gunnery Sergeant Hartman in "Full Metal Jacket." Before he even said a word, I launched into a defensive tirade. "I didn't know because I was warming up Ronnie when you told the team, I bet he didn't know either did you Ronnie." Ronnie looked perplexed and uttered, "Know what?"

The coach backed up slightly and then his whole demeanor changed and he started laughing. "Beller, you have more balls than anybody on this team, you just need to get them polished!" The rest of the team started laughing as well, however the coach didn't like that. He then turned to the others and one by one began to verbally rip into each player pointing out their flaws and imperfections like Simon from "American Idol."

"Dipino! You think you are so good; you are a fucking butcher in the field! Luther! Your curve ball couldn't break a pane of glass! McCoy you couldn't hit a cut-off man if your life depended on it. O'Malley you have all your attention in your pants, try a little harder at the plate and hit the fucking ball!" Tim had actually gone two for three that day, so it was obvious the coach was reaching and felt the need to say something about everyone, whether it was factual or not. Coach Gilden just stood there with his arms crossed like he agreed with everything George was blasting out, and only field coach Pete Hamilton looked uncomfortable at the barrage. His son Pete Jr. was also on the team, and was not left out of the equal opportunity rant.

This went on all the time. We would win by 18 runs and still hear what we did wrong. It was an interesting way of coaching, but not one I would choose to use on anyone, unless of course I became a gunnery sergeant. In my mind I was saying, "Don't be afraid to be a dick, shit!" I'm not sure that would have gone over well if I had said that out loud.

The Winger

I have been on many different baseball teams and learned many different plays. I have personally witnessed well-orchestrated pickoffs, the hidden ball trick, bunts turned into slap hits and even the eephus pitch, but I was not prepared for the winger.

I honestly don't remember which coach introduced us to this play, but it changed how I look at Major League Baseball to this day. I need to set the stage. As a catcher, when there was a runner on first base, sometimes the batter became the second objective. I'm not saying that was correct, because the person at the plate was the point of interest, however, with that guy jumping around off of first base I just want him gone. If I think he might be going, I will order up a fastball when an off-speed pitch might be better. When the runner finally breaks and the pitch was on its way, my only concentration was on the runner. I couldn't tell you where the pitch even crossed the plate, I just caught it and immediately rifled it to second.

Most of the time I learned to throw to second from the crouch, so I wasted no time standing or stepping during my release. When in the zone, all I could see was the right-hand corner of second base and that was the line of fire. That was, of course, if the pitcher got out of the way.

In rec ball when we were little, pitchers weren't accustomed to leaving the mound during a steal so they would just duck. When that happened, catchers had a tendency to throw the ball high because they were afraid of striking them. I was taught very early to just throw the ball to the bag and the fielder would eventually get there. Sometimes they didn't, which would wake up the center fielder pretty quickly. By the time we reached high school, pitchers knew better and would exit the mound usually to their follow-through side. Well, not all of them. Pitchers are quirky by nature and most have some interesting deliveries. The first time I saw Kent Tekulve throw his sidearm pitch after almost dragging his knuckles on the ground, I was quite impressed and horrified at the same time. We had caught wind that the next team we were playing had a pitcher that struggled to get off the mound, so he would just duck. To combat that, the coaching staff at CCB introduced the winger. See if you can follow along because we practiced this ad nauseam.

Here was how it was designed to go down. If we had a runner on first, a special signal was relayed to the batter to swing and miss the ball on purpose. He was not only to miss the ball, but do it awkwardly while winging the bat towards the pitcher's knees. The pitcher, who was ducking down, would see the bat pinwheeling towards him and jump up in the air to get out of the way. The catcher, reacting as soon as he caught the ball, fired to second and drilled the pitcher in the chest. The batter, immediately puts on a show of remorse at letting the bat slip from his hands, by making embarrassed sounds and actions. End result? Runner on second, batter retrieving his bat from the shortstop, pitcher on the ground holding his chest, catcher kicking dirt for drilling his own pitcher, and the umpire walking in circles trying to figure out what the hell just happened.

We practiced this! During batting practice right before the last pitch, the coach would yell a position and the batter would hurl his bat in that direction and pretend it was a mistake. I have seen bats fly, all-around major-league parks, and have always wondered if it truly was an accident. Some players are really good at it, some are not. (Machado.)

One game comes to mind where we would have used the winger play, but opted for a more conventional approach to the other team. I remember that day specifically because it was my birthday and we were playing Montgomery Community College in Rockville. The pitcher on the other team was acting cocky from the get-go and was shooting off his mouth at regular intervals. Tim O'Malley had recently obtained the moniker Dr. Strange Glove, due to his inability to close his glove after the ball entered. He was playing first and the ball would bounce out of his glove like it struck a brick or something. Whenever it happened, he would get so angry he was totally unapproachable.

Earlier in the game, I hit a triple with the bases loaded and I was running very high on the accompanying birthday adrenaline. When you are having a good game sometimes you stop worrying about the little things. Ronnie was on the mound and was efficiently slicing through the other team yet the pitcher kept mouthing off. Tim struck out earlier and received an earful which led Tim to let the pitcher know, through a hand gesture, that we were No. 1. In the fifth inning, the pitcher walked and took the bag next to Tim. Words were exchanged for a few pitches before Tim gave him a suggestion about what his next meal should be. The guy jumped in Tim's face and before you could say, "Thrilla in Manila," Tim dropped him with a left hook.

I immediately stood up and started speed walking in that general direction when the guy jumped up, took a swing and missed and Tim dropped him again. Then things went all Keystone Cops. The guy got up and started running and Tim chased him all the way to center field. Center field! What happened next can only be equated to a western saloon square dance, after the caller told everyone to partner up. Everybody started fighting and I mean everybody. Two guys ran from the bleachers and tackled DJ, our outfielder, and started dragging him off the field. I was blindly tackled by two other guys, who took turns punching my face mask. The mayhem was outstanding! Coach Norm Gilden came flying off our bench swinging a 36-inch Easton. He never hit anyone, but used every expletive in the book as he fanned madly. As soon as one skirmish would settle down another would kick up dust, attracting everyone to rush over. Coaches were screaming, umpires were getting knocked down, girlfriends were yelling from the bleachers and Mr. Yuck was laughing his ass off.

THE DISH

When it finally ended 15 minutes later, both teams were disheveled and bloodied. My chest protector was ripped from my body and it wasn't even properly unsnapped. The two umpires had no idea what to do, so in spectacular fashion, just let the game resume. The next two innings were full of verbal digs mostly under one's breath, to let the coaches know we respected their decision not to allow us to commit actual manslaughter.

When the game ended there was no shaking of hands, and the obligatory offering of "good game" could only be heard on our bench. We showed off by running our usual wind sprints before heading to the locker room. As a team, we always showered, changed into street clothes and went out to dinner after a win, which usually meant Sizzler or Ponderosa. We definitely ate good at CCB.

I was changing at my locker when I heard some muffled yells and hints of an altercation. Some of the guys started hustling toward the showers, so I jumped up and followed suit. The locker room had a door that went into another room that was filled with showers. When I say showers, you might picture individual stalls, but they were actually evenly spaced poles throughout the whole room, with four shower heads on each pole. Visually, you would see four guys showering around each pole but that wasn't the scene I encountered.

On the other side of the room was another door which led to the other locker room. Both teams were showering in the same room and they were yelling at each other. I couldn't believe my eyes, as 40 naked men were bickering and pointing and laughing. My ears were alive at the hilarity as personal digs and jabs were flying with impunity. Nobody was going to continue a birthday suit physical alternation, so it was all verbal. The stinging ditties were abundant, "Don't be afraid to wipe the taste of your mother off my Johnson, shit!" but the one that made me laugh the most was, "I bet your girlfriend needs a roach clip to deal with that tiny dick!" Later, on the bus, I stood up and thanked everybody for the greatest Cinco de Mayo birthday party I had ever had.

Bad Seeds

The end of the season had us winning the 20th district tournament, and we were scheduled to play the winner of the 19th district in a one-game playoff. The winner would represent the Mid-Atlantic region and fly to Grand Junction, Colorado for the Junior College or JUCO World Series.

The team we played was Mercer Community College and they came all the way from New Jersey. Our ground crew, which consisted of one man with a pickup truck, worked on the field for days. He cemented in new benches, dumped new dirt on the baselines and mound, added new gravel on the walkways, he even had a couple Johnny on the Spots delivered. It looked like a real ball park! I can still see him precisely paving the walkway with crush and run, by gunning his pickup truck in reverse and hitting the brakes. Gravel shot out the back like a Civil War canister blast and covered a large area in which he later raked smooth. American ingenuity at its finest.

Throughout the year, favors were collected by our coaches to make sure we played every home game. I'm not saying they were blackmailing people; however, the outcomes were quite worthy if you'd let your mind wander. For example, once after an incredible rainstorm, a Sikorsky helicopter flew in and landed on the field. It sat there running for over an hour and literally blew the field dry. It was the most amazing thing I've ever seen on a pitcher's mound. I'm sure for some it was the precursor to "Red Dawn," but for us it was just a giant leaf blower.

Another time, gasoline was raked into the sopping infield dirt and set ablaze. For a few hours after, we would be raking and uncover an unburned pocket that leapt back to life. It was crazy, but it was baseball and needed to be played. That experience always reminded me of one of my favorite baseball quotes. Pete Rose said, "I would run through hell in a gasoline suit to play baseball." You have to love Charlie Hustle.

The championship game against Mercer was over as soon as it started. I honestly can't remember a single highlight but know we won hands down. I do remember we didn't run sprints after the game because we celebrated. We celebrated our team, our friendship and our diversity. We also drank a crapload of beer!

1980 was full of firsts for me. It was my first year of college, my first experience with African Americans as teammates and my first lesson on world events and how it affected me personally. There was a rather large contingency of Iranian students at CCB. In November of 1979, a group of Iranian college students stormed the American Embassy in Iran, and held Americans hostage, for 444 days. It was all over the news constantly and President Carter knew that as 39th president of the United States, he struggled to respond to formidable challenges, including a major energy crisis as well as high inflation and unemployment and although he placed greater emphasis on methods, procedures and instruments for making policy than on the content of policy itself, he failed in negotiating the return of the hostages until his last day in office. Oh, it was also a first for talking political bullshit as I have no idea what I just said. Did you buy any of that?

Unfortunately, at CCB there was an ongoing conflict with the large Iranian student population, as some of them were beaten up on a daily basis. Not by me or anyone I knew, unless of course they were moonlighting as players for Montgomery Community College.

Airplane travel wasn't as prevalent in 1980 as it is today, and I was very excited to fly. We all dressed in our Sunday best and were introduced on the plane over the PA by the pilot, who congratulated us for representing Maryland. I took a whole roll of film outside my window as I had never seen the country from above. The perfectly square and round patchwork of farms mesmerized me and I couldn't imagine laying all that out. I loved watching the single spec of an automobile crawl along an endless highway and wondered who the occupant was and where they were going. Ironically, I used to lay on my back in the yard and think the exact same thing while watching the contrails of jets in the sky.

The gold and green capaciousness of the country turned mountain brown and then white with snow as we approached the Rockies. It was all so beautiful from the air, and I knew somewhere down there in one of those fields, kids were playing baseball.

Grand Junction was on the other side of the Rockies, and not knowing what to expect when we landed, I prepared myself to disembark with the team in the midst of complete strangers. Boy was I wrong. When we walked off the airplane we were still out on the tarmac. As a group, we walked towards the terminal and arrived to the sound of applause and cheering. Standing behind a fence were about 100 people wearing CCB Red Devil baseball hats. What? Who were these people and how did they get our hats? It turns out they were the Redlands Rotary, a local group, and they were our sponsors. They informed us we were the very first team to arrive.

They were our transportation and chefs as they drove us around sight-seeing and then to a giant cookout with more steaks that I had ever seen and that includes Sizzler. They were the nicest people and became our cheerleaders when we played.

The next day there was a big baseball luncheon and all the teams were finally present. Looking around the room they all seemed ginormous to me. Most of these guys looked like the Bugs Bunny baseball cartoon, where these enormous men, absolutely identical in size and girth, walked on to the field of play totally blocking the sun in the process. With that in mind, I quietly referred to these players as Team Eclipse. We were slated to play such an eclipse the next day from Texas.

For the banquet entertainment, former Brooklyn Dodger and Boy of

Summer, Carl Erskine spoke. It was exciting to hear him talk about his two no-hitters and afterwards he came around and shook each of our hands. While shaking mine he looked me in the eyes and said, "Catcher, right?" I've always wondered how he knew.

Our seed had us playing at 5 p.m. the next day against McLennan Community College from Waco, Texas. I remember Coach Gilden saying that we had a bad seed. He thought it unlucky because the loser of our game would have to play at 8 a.m. the next morning. My first thought was, well let's not lose.

We hung around the motel and watched some of the other games on the local cable channel. Well, like most fun things in life, the hilarity was short-lived. Right before we were to leave the motel and head to the field for our first game, we were called to a team meeting. We all piled into one of the coaches' rooms to find Coach Henderson and Coach Gilden sitting upright at the head of a double bed. They had their outstretched legs in front of them and seemed very troubled and unhappy. I thought it was a ruse and prepared myself to hear the Knute Rockne speech of all time. You know, those words of encouragement from your leader about how you worked long and hard and were more than ready to slay the dragons that awaited us. Apparently, those words only appeared in the movies.

We all made a giant semicircle around our coach's double bed like they were going to perform a scene from "Barbarella." Without warning or a setup of any kind, Coach Henderson blurts out that two of our starters were caught getting high. He wanted the team to vote if we should let them play or not. What? It turns out that Cheese and Terry played the stupid card and smoked a joint in their room and got caught.

On day one of the first practice, the coach told us under no circumstances could anyone using drugs be allowed to start any baseball game. Now here we are in complete uniform standing over our horizontal coaches as they are putting the ball back in our court.

Did they really think that we vote to sit these guys? Of course not, that was why they gave the decision to us. Coach Henderson played the martyr card and blamed himself for not being a good coach. All of a sudden, he broke down and started crying because his sporting goods business with Brooks Robinson went bankrupt. Coach Gilden tried to console him but started crying too and announced his brother was in prison. WTF? I looked round the room in shock. I mean don't be afraid to fall the fuck apart in front of the whole team moments before the biggest game of our lives, shit! Even Dr. Strange Glove was tearing up. I was pissed and was about to say something when Coach Hamilton brought everybody back from the edge.

When the tears dried, it was decided that Cheese and Terry could play but they couldn't start the game. Nice save by technicality. I think they both were playing by the second inning, but it didn't matter because we lost 8-0. The loser's bracket had us playing at 8 a.m. the next morning, which just sucked.

Somehow, we managed to swing by the stadium for the night game and the place was hopping. It was awesome to see so many fans in attendance, as I was sure some of the closer teams had road trip fans. We weren't that lucky but discovered a group of young ladies who were hanging out behind the grandstand. After a short conversation with a few, I was amazed to find out they knew all about the top players. They knew pitcher's records, batting average stats and the name and location of every team in attendance. I remember thinking they were great fans of the game.

I was super impressed until I was informed, they were on the prowl for a meal ticket. I know that sounds horrible when spoken out loud, however, I physically witnessed a group of them talk to a player, ask him his average and then move on until they found another player with a higher one. I just thought they were being nice and caught up in the festival atmosphere, but one of them told us she was looking for a future millionaire. I immediately knew it would not be me.

Hijinks were running amuck and practical jokes were all the rage. I brought along a very popular old lady product to help with my humor. It was an automatic noise-activated electronic interrupter, but you might know it as The Clapper.

I snuck into a room and secretly hooked it up to the television. I turned the TV on and then clapped it off. Before leaving, I ratcheted the volume all the way up to 11 and snuck out of the room. Several hours later, when most of us were supposed to be sleeping, I put my plan into action. All of our rooms were on the second floor of a motel, so there was a walkway in front of every room. I asked Mark Eckerl to walk over to the window in front of the unsuspecting room, and clap as loud as he could. He thought just the clapping sound would scare the two guys inside, but when the television kicked on and started screaming, half the motel woke up. We dove back in our room and Mark ran like hell. The hilarious thing was seeing these guys trying to explain to Coach Henderson why their TV was so loud after curfew. Ah the hilarity.

The next morning, we played the Triton Trojans from River Grove, Illinois and lost 6-5. I grounded to third, in my only at bat, but I would never forget squatting behind the dish and seeing snow-capped mountains surrounding the park. We were the first team in and the first team out, which of course meant beer.

In 1980, it was illegal to sell Coors beer west of Colorado, so of course we filled the bathtub with it. There had to be 15 cases of beer in that tub, and the only thing I remember about that night was that I was smiling. This team and the way we bonded would set the tone for how to prepare one's body for college baseball. My liver too!

I don't even remember seeing the coaches after the game, so I assume their bathtubs were full of Coors as well. We all kicked back and unwound and I had some great conversations with these interesting but crazy ass guys. Reggie Smith, for some reason decided to talk to me about sliders. Not the pitch that eluded the skill set of most catchers as I could never throw one, but the little juicy hamburgers. He seemed to be obsessed with them.

Although I couldn't throw a slider, I had mastered the knuckleball, and on many occasions lobbed one down to second base between innings, just to see the reaction from the infielder. For the record, whenever I was mad at a pitcher who insisted on throwing and re-throwing curve balls only to never see them again, a perfectly thrown knuckleball back to the mound will instill lots of humility.

We left Grand Junction and I didn't see it again until Ally Sheedy picked up Matthew Broderick at the airport in "War Games." For the record, the airport looked better with her in it. We had an eight-hour layover in Denver and never left Stapleton. We were dressed in street clothes so the whole team was sporting our red baseball jackets, which had "Baltimore" written in script across the front. In 1980, the Colorado Rockies didn't exist, so baseball teams were seldom seen at Stapleton airport. When a lady walked up to Cheese and asked for his autograph he immediately signed. She went back to her family and showed them and then they all came over, as well as many others. They wanted to take pictures with us so we all posed and took many pictures and many of us signed autographs. When she walked away, she told us her sister lived in Washington, D.C. and loved us, so she couldn't wait to send her the pictures.

I thought it was nice that her sister followed CCB baseball until I learned Cheese had signed Al Bumbry. Some of the other guys had signed other current Orioles, but I wasn't in on the joke and signed Neil Beller. These innocent travelers thought we were the real Baltimore Orioles. I'm sure her sister loved the pictures!

The airport was considerably larger than Baltimore Washington International, and with lots of time to kill, I wandered off to be by myself for a while. I had only been in an airport once, and I liked to explore, so I walked every corridor. I remember seeing stores which sold items I never would have expected to see in an airport, like totem poles. I found a bank of vending machines and bought a Tab and a six-pack of cheese crackers. It was a mental game to drink diet soda while eating crackers loaded with carbs. I convinced myself they cancelled each other out, but I ended up just craving more carbs, which I'm sure was the manufacturer's intention.

I found a bank of chairs along the wall with tables inserted every 10 seats or so, like the kind found in a dentist's office. I took the first seat to the right of a table and placed my jacket on the chair next to me. There were some magazines on the table, so I picked one up and started paging through it. People were spaced out sporadically and since strangers in an airport like to remain strangers, many empty chairs separated everyone. A woman sat down on the other side of the table and placed her belongings to the left of her and settled in slightly facing the other way. A huge lamp separated our upper torso's visually, but I could easily see her legs. She was also drinking a soda, but hers was a regular high-octane Coke. I felt a little embarrassed at my drink of choice, but it had been made.

I opened the crackers, ate one and continued to leaf through the magazine when I noticed her arm reaching over and taking a cracker. I quickly looked up at her, but all I saw was lamp. I debated on whether I should say something, but she was still facing the other way, so I just smiled at her effrontery and let it go. A few minutes later, I took another cracker and then she did the same. I stopped in mid chew at the disbelief of what was happening. I leaned down this time only to see the back of her head. I looked around for Allen Funt of "Candid Camera," because I couldn't believe what was happening. I even looked around to see teammates for verification they had set it up, but in hindsight they were not that clever. I didn't say anything the first time, so now I was sort of tongue tied. I wasn't angry at her, but shocked at her actions. What kind of person does that? Obviously, one with huge gonads, who wasn't afraid to act brazenly.

I was just turning pages now and not even looking at the magazine when she took a third cracker and slid the rest of the packet towards me. She then stood, gathered her things and walked in the opposite direction. I sat there in a complete stupor as she walked away. I never even saw her face and had no idea how to share the story, I mean who would believe me? A few minutes later, Cheese walked up with a couple guys to tell me they had found an arcade. I popped the last cracker in my mouth, grabbed my Tab and stood to go with them. I leaned down for my jacket and sitting on the chair underneath, was my packet of cheese crackers. Holy Shit, I was the cracker thief! I always wondered what she was thinking. It just so happened, I had huge gonads and didn't even know it.

With my first year of college baseball under my belt, I had the whole world ahead of me and my desire to play major league baseball was one step closer. Unfortunately, sometimes people step in the wrong direction.

That summer I played on Coach Henderson's team. He still liked to see me bunt for a hit and would cackle every time I successfully reached base. After one game Coach Henderson called me over to talk as we walked to our cars. He bluntly passed on some pertinent and coldly delivered information. We had just reached the parking lot when he told me that since my father had died, he was sure I could get financial aid, so he was giving my scholarship to some fireball pitcher from Pennsylvania. The disdain I felt for him after he told me that was so palatable and although I never would have played college baseball without him, I never spoke to him again. It seemed my balls had been polished.

Lots of Pain, Lots of Gain

The rest of the summer just sucked on a monumental scale. My recently widowed mother and I argued constantly. In an ugly verbal altercation on a Sunday evening, she invited me to sleep elsewhere and showed me the door. I called my girlfriend, Carole, (pronounced Ca-**roll**-lee) to let her know I had just been kicked out of my house and was headed to Ocean City to hang out with my friend Larry Merrifield for the week. Larry was a lifeguard and was only about three minutes and 100 yards from 64 beach parties at any given minute, and that seemed like a good way to calm my jets for a while. She was upset at my homelife news, but more upset about the "cool my jets with Larry" plan and asked me to stop by her house first, so I threw some clothes in a bag and headed over. Her parents were the nicest people on the planet and talked me into spending the night, so I could gather my thoughts. I didn't leave for three weeks.

During this time, Carole gave me a gift which started a lifelong collection. It was a little plastic turtle wearing catching equipment. He was squatting and wore a backwards red hat and I just loved him. From that moment on, turtles of all shapes and sizes became the go-to gift for the person who had no idea which gift to get me if gifts were to be gotten. Ceramic, wood, glass and even anatomically correct turtles lined every shelf I owned and several shadow boxes. The original was by far my favorite and represented to me how to adapt when you are a man without a home. You just take your home with you.

My levelheaded older sister, Jan, suggested I might move in with my grandparents in Pasadena, Maryland. I went for a visit and told them my dilemma. I was unsure of their response, because the issues I had were with their daughter. We were sitting outside on their deck when, in the middle of the conversation, my grandfather got up and went inside the house. I stood up to leave, thinking I had upset him, when he came back and handed me a set of keys. He told me I could stay as long as I wanted. Grandparents, I know right!

I moved in immediately, landed a part-time job as a cook at Bob's Big Boy in Glen Burnie and planned to visit the coach at Anne Arundel Community College to see about transferring in and playing baseball. In the meantime, Carole planned a day trip to the York County fair. Hoping to chillax a bit and spend the whole day checking out the exhibits, we arrived early. By 9 a.m., I was looking sideways at all the runway games. It is common knowledge that no baseball player can walk past a speed gun or a carnival game which deals with throwing an object or swinging some sort of club without participating. It has nothing to do with winning prizes, and everything to do with showing off and measuring your skill.

The first game I came upon was the one where for a dollar you would get three chances to throw a ping-pong ball into a glass of water. Sounds simple, right? Well, the circumference of the glass was a microfiber larger than the ball, so the chances against winning were infinite. There were hundreds of water-filled glasses all rim to rim with some containing goldfish. In the very center of the exhibit, raised above the others, was a glass filled with red water. That looked to be the hardest so naturally I tried for that one. I tossed one ball underhand and watched it bang around a dozen times before falling to the side. I threw the second ball overhand, like I was playing beer pong, and it went right in the red water. Carole screamed.

People standing around cheered and the attendant spoke about how nobody ever gets it in the red water, especially at 9 a.m.! Unbeknownst to me, a ball in the red water gets you a live animal. I don't mean live as in goldfish, which I could swallow and cough up later when I got home, but live as in a ferret, a bunny rabbit or a bird. Unfortunately, they weren't offering turtles and I had no idea what to do with a bird and since ferrets reminded me of Frank Burns, we opted for a tiny brown bunny. When it was handed it to us, it fit in the palm of my hand. It couldn't have been a week old. Now what do we do? We can't get on the Tilt-a Whirl because the bunny would implode. We can't roam around and eat cotton candy because candy was Easter-related and he'd be confused, so we headed to the animal pavilion.

It was your typical smelly building filled with cows, sheep, pigs and various other quadrupeds and lo and behold, rabbits. I reached in a cage and stole a handful of rabbit chow and put it in my pocket. The pellets were too big for our little guy and since we had no idea how to take care of him, we headed home. It was only 10:30. On the way, we toyed with names because we had to call him something other than jelly bean maker. We came up with Eddie Rabbit, Water Bunny, Killer Rodent, and Hop Tart but settled on a tamer moniker, Brer. Carole's mom said no to a bunny tenant, so Brer moved in with me. I built a travel cage so we could have joint custody, but his main hotel was anchored in my grandparent's backyard.

I cashed my first Big Boy's check after working four whole days in two weeks and after taxes I owed 14 bucks. How could that be? Not completely sure how the commerce withholding system worked, I turned my mind back to baseball as I could formulate a batting average and earned run average with my eyes closed. I had heard coach Skip Brown was now the Anne Arundel Community College athletic director. When I met with him, he was impressed with my CCB past and assured me a walk-on position as a catcher with the Pioneers. He had turned the team over to Mike Desimone, whose only negative coaching issue was his inability to cut anyone. He kept 10 pitchers and four catchers, four! There were 14 of us in the battery alone, so needless to say our team was quite large.

It was a good bunch of guys, but when it came to fitness, the

Pioneers were the complete opposite of the Red Devils. In all honesty, the only thing they had in common was beer. The team captain was George Brown and I can promise you he had never even heard of a side -straddle hop. Can you believe that? We used to stretch as a team, but conditioning was the responsibility of each player while at home, which of course meant extra naps.

1980 was just about the end of the disco era--insert your own "Thank God," after that last sentence--but for some reason the team jackets were these bright red shiny disco jobs with "AACC Baseball" blazoned on the back. I mean the first time I saw several players wearing them I thought they were The Spinners getting ready to launch into *"The Rubberband Man!"* George had matching red spikes, so he was certainly the lead singer. I laughed thinking the other George (Henderson) would throw up in his mouth at all the uncoordinated outfits.

The first teammate I met was right fielder Kevin Wilkins. He questioned me in the café about the CCB T-shirt I was wearing, telling me I made a big mistake transferring to AACC, which he said stood for "Any Asshole Can Come." We hit it off immediately and are great friends to this day. Other players included pitchers Rick Miller and Charlie Hester, center fielder Kevin Hild, shortstop Randy Hall, and third baseman Steve Kowalski. I was friends with everybody on the team, but these were the guys who sparked the most memories and subsequent police involvement.

Very early in the fall, George decided to have a team party and invited everyone over to his house to watch a movie on this cool device called a VCR or video cassette recorder. It might have been a Betamax or even a dehumidifier for all I knew, but it was big, top-loading and played a movie without commercials right on his television. I enjoyed meeting the team and the others in attendance. Kevin brought his girlfriend, Mary Fran, and she added to the learning experience in spectacular fashion. At one point, the conversation digressed from baseball to a Civil War picture hanging on the wall. She perked up with interest and said, "Oh yeah, who won that?" She wasn't kidding. Kevin pretended like he didn't hear her, it was his only defense. I immediately answered with "The West of course," which triggered a peculiar look of acknowledgement.

Later, Kevin and I flanked her on the couch as the movie started. I am going to go on record and say the following barrage of questioning could only be equivalent to your average episode of, "Perry Mason." We had no idea what the movie was about, which was part of the mystique of watching it. In the movie, someone walked in the room and Mary Fran in a rapid-fire sequence asked, "Who is that? Why is he there? What is he doing? Why did he pick that up? Why did he put it down? What's he doing now? Why did he open that? Why did he go in there?" I looked over her to Kevin who was paying more attention to the queso dip on the table than Mary Fran. My first thought was, oh my God, is she like this all the time? The more questions she asked, the more Kevin ate. What I was witnessing was a slow boil. Honestly, Mary Fran had an adorable nature but was completely ruining the movie for me and I assume others. Finally, with a broken chip full of dip in his grasp Kevin emerged, "Jesus Christ Mary Fran, we are watching the same goddamn movie that you are!" The room erupted in laughter including Mary Fran. Kevin had told me she was crazy smart; I only saw the crazy part. My memory tells me she was more entertaining than the movie.

The day we received our disco jackets it was cold and breezy. It had rained earlier and the field was a little messy. The coach was running us through *situations,* and was hitting balls to the outfield with a fungo. Situations mimicked actual game scenarios, while preparing us to instantly react to a batted ball. We practiced cut offs, repositioning and backup placement. Backups are important in case of an overthrow and give everyone on the field accountability. For the record and only because I could, I would always cut any throw coming from Kevin Wilkins. He had a great arm and was 98% on line but I yelled, "Cut!" anyway. It really drove him crazy and when he questioned my actions, I told him it was only because I wanted to refer to him as Kevin "Cut Home" Wilkins. He still cusses me out about it 42 years later.

I always loved the dance you would see when everybody on the field was moving to be a backup. There is a visceral reaction which happens when a ball is fouled off. For that split second, every engaged player on the field thinks the ball is coming right at them, so they flinch in the direction of the foul. Having experienced this, I know all of your energy was amped up and released in an instant and then has to slowly recharge as you go back to ready position. It was kind of like being the human version of the heart attack paddles we grew up watching on "Emergency." "Clear!"

How many times have you watched a pitcher give up a base hit and before he can even beat himself up about making such a lousy pitch, he has to run behind third or home to back up the throw? Most of the time they are cursing their ancestry as the run.

Like most drills we practiced, pitchers were used as the other team so they could also get in their running. I mentioned we had 10 pitchers so there was never a lack of runners. Charlie Hester was tall and muscular and resembled Clint Walker who played Samson Posey in "The Dirty Dozen." He loved working out and invited me to his home to lift weights while overlooking the local scenic estuary he lived on. The only curls I could do were of the cheese variety, while he toyed with bags of cement and anvils. He drove an old pickup truck and had a kind heart just like Posey. He was my pick to follow into an on-the-field brawl, but in hindsight might only participate in making peace or organizing a community garden. I don't remember him ever shaking me off from the mound, but if he did, I'm sure he apologized later. He was a fine specimen of a man.

On that particular day, Earl Hadaway had forgotten his sweats, so he was wearing jeans and his shiny, new, bright red, disco baseball jacket. The coach wasn't happy. I was standing next to him fielding balls, like a catcher does, when he lined a shot to center. Earl was on first base and took off at a good clip. He rounded second and headed for third when Kevin Hild came up with the ball and unleashed a bullet towards third.

Some people might throw the bullshit card on this, but I have this uncanny ability to spot the trajectory of a baseball and quickly determine if the fielder has a chance of catching up with it or not. I don't know if it is based on relativity, or speed versus air velocity, or atmospheric density with unladen swallows or whatever, I just know. Many times, I went from first to third on a close play because I just knew the ball was going to drop in front of the outfielder. Afterwards, I was "talked to" by the coach who labeled the move idiotic, but at the end of the day, I was safe at third.

Anyway, I was watching the arc of the throw and Earl running and I knew he was about to get hit. What I didn't know was how epic it would be. About 15 feet from third base, the ball hit Earl right in the back of the head. Earl went down in slow motion like he had been shot by a sniper in a Sam Peckinpah movie. His flailing arms shot out, his back arched, his legs abandoned him and he fell face forward right in a 10-foot mud puddle and slid all the way past third. I immediately started laughing and when Coach Desimone dropped his bat and fell to the ground in hysterics, I was done. The whole team was dying while Earl rolled around in the mud. The coach got up on one knee, looked up at me with tears in his eyes and said, "Dipshit" and fell back on the ground. Steve Kowalski was playing third and almost wet his pants laughing while shortstop Randy Hall did. Earl's head was fine and he spent the rest of the practice wet and cold in his muddy but new, bright red, disco jacket. From that moment on, he was known as Earl "Dipshit" Hadaway. For the record, Dipshit could throw amazingly hard and was the first pitcher to break the rawhide strings on my catcher's mitt.

Fall ball consisted of workouts, practices and a series of pickup games at the U.S. Naval Academy in Annapolis. We piled into two 16-passenger prison vans and trekked a few miles to the Navy practice field. The plebs were all clean-cut, motivated and inspired me with their baseball skills as well as their service. I was impressed with the whole scene until a bit of encouragement from their third base coach sent me reeling.

He clapped his hands together and simply said, "C'mon Bobo, find your pitch." I immediately called time-out and stood to look at the right-handed batter who stepped out of the box to take a few swings. "Are you Bobo Fitzpatrick from Winston Churchill High School?" His answer was a snarky yes, and he didn't even inquire why I was asking. I told him I was the catcher at Parkville and he laughed. I immediately wanted to strike him out for the rest of his life, but that thought quickly passed when he mentioned how good our team was and that on any other day our team would have easily won the game and the state championship. We became friends and talked every time we played each other.

Later that night, I was filling in some of my teammates about Bobo when they introduced me to the drinking game, Quarters. The game required the participants to sit around a coffee cup filled with beer. When it was your turn, you would try to bounce a quarter on the table in an attempt to get it in the cup. If you succeeded, the person of your choice had to drink the beer in the cup. Hopefully, they wouldn't swallow the quarter. To make the game even more interesting, you were not allowed to say the words, "drink," "drank," or "drunk," and pointing was outlawed unless you were using your elbow. Every few minutes you would here a burst of laughter followed by people pointing with their elbows and yelling, "Consume!"

I never missed the cup, never, and would always make the same person consume at least three times in a row. My secret was speed and sleight of hand. On my right ring finger, I always wore my high school ring. I would turn the ring around so the stone was facing my palm. I would make a movement like I was bouncing the quarter when I was actually banging my ring on the table and throwing the quarter right in the cup. It worked every time and I became a Quartermaster or a master of Quarters.

I hit the proverbial wall that evening and suffered greatly the next morning. Who am I kidding? It was at least until the afternoon before the room slowed down. I convinced myself staying prone was much more important than the two classes I was ditching, because baseball practice started at 3:00.

Walking to my car was a real treat as each step felt like I was Roger Moore perambulating crocodiles in "Live and Let Die." I arrived at the field feeling about 37% and wasn't sure I would even reach 50. Faking this hangover was going to need some serious help and I found that help in Kevin. He was currently lying on his back stretching his hamstring so I laid down in the outfield grass next to him. I quickly learned he wasn't stretching but stuck. He was suffering the same fate as me and even produced sound effects to enhance his misery. I helped him regain the use of his legs and together we shuffled to my car.

Realizing we had nothing resembling actual sustenance in our bodies, we decided to hit the closest and cheapest nourishment center. Like "Christine," the car literally drove itself to the nearest 7-11. Inside we found the one and only doctor-recommended hangover cure in the form of a microwave burrito.

Upon taking a bite, I perked up like Marty McFly from "Back to the Future" during The Enchantment Under the Sea Dance. It was amazing. Within minutes, Kevin and I were humming along with the radio and performing other human traits. By the time we reached the field, we were 100% and had one of the best practices of our lives. "Learning baseball was better with burritos," became our mantra and we saluted 7-11s everywhere we went.

Kevin and I both owned cool cars although they were far from mint condition. Kevin had a gray 1966 Pontiac GTO and I had a 1974 Gran Torino. For those of you named Huggy Bear, you might know that to be the car "Starsky & Hutch" rode around in. Theirs was red with a white stripe while mine was faded blue. My friends and I referred to it as the Neil Mobile and it became our chariot. I even put a baseball on the end of the gear shift so I could hold it while I drove. Holding a baseball was one of the best feelings in the world.

THE DISH

When fall ball ended, we had a few months off but had to maintain our workout regimen to be ready for the spring. I had a plan which involved running the neighborhood and working out at the local gym. Unfortunately, my grandfather didn't approve of my plan because it interfered with his role of food pusher. The ongoing joke in my family was my grandfather yelling to the kitchen from the front door, "Marge, the kids are here, put on a turkey." Every evening at 5:30 p.m. we gathered upstairs in the den to watch "M*A*S*H" and laugh. It was a great way to eat dinner and immediately afterwards I would lay on the floor with the aid of massive throw pillows while my grandfather headed downstairs to prepare his evening cocktail. On occasion, he leaned down as he passed and rapped me on the head saying, "And that was for nothing!" Doing things like that are required by grandfathers.

As habits go, it was a great ritual until one night, he plopped a homemade ice cream sundae in front of me. I say sundae but it was actually a weekend because it included a Friday night and Saturday as well! It was basically your anti-healthy nightmare in a bowl. Ice cream, chocolate syrup, nuts, sprinkles, whipped cream, even a cherry. Before I knew it, I had gained 20 pounds and quickly leaned towards 30. My weight gain coincided with my rabbit turning into very large, rotund pony. He kept getting bigger to the point that his neck disappeared and was replaced with six chins. I couldn't understand it until I learned after I fed Brer in the morning and went to college, my grandfather would shove heads of lettuce into his cage all day long. He bought it by the skid. What a difference a year makes. Death and taxes and ice cream.

Road Trip

Television has always been one of my favorite escapes. I had been the king of multi-tasking while watching television, and often used it as background noise for required college reading, essay writing, wood chopping or telephone talking. My girlfriend sucked me into the soap opera, "Dynasty," and we used to watch it together while on the phone. Okay, maybe I sucked her into it, but glamorous rich women with major trust issues and tight dresses had all the makings of a high-speed train wreck, and I needed to watch it crash weekly. I mean, Krystle Carrington!

I had the ability to pull a television or movie line out of my cerebellum at any given moment and have used them to enhance any situation. "I'm not hungry for dinner yet," "Okay, no soup for you!" There were so many good lines, why not use them again? To me, they were like an old song, and when I heard them, I started to sing along.

"I thought he was dead." "He got better." I can still hear my father hilariously laughing at that Hawkeye and Trapper exchange as the lost Luxemburg Lieutenant stumbled by. "M*A*S*H" was my favorite "go to" show, as well as "Dick Van Dyke" and "Seinfeld." I recited random lines so often I didn't even know I was doing it. "Not that there's anything wrong with that."

Like most people with a crazy sense of humor, one of my all-time favorite movies was, "Animal House." The Delta House was already on double secret probation when the Dean showed up and had their illegal bar physically removed from the property. Just when things were going bad, they all gathered out front and held a short conversation.

"This is ridiculous."

"What are we going to do?"

"Road trip!"

The Delta House members were at the end of their rope, but I loved their attitude and I needed some of it. The timing was impeccable, because I received a call from an old high school friend, Doug Wann, who was in the pre-planning stage of a road trip. It seemed Doug was missing our mutual friend, Mark Slater, who was living comfortably on the multi-language floor of Washington College in Chestertown, Maryland. His plan involved a contingency of other compadres, including Jerry Diem, Greg Hoffman and myself, to drive to Chestertown on Friday, sneak into Mark's college dorm and kidnap him. What could possibly go wrong? I was in.

Greg insisted on driving his light blue Volkswagen Beetle, with a set of bison horns mounted on the roof and an illuminated naked lady with wings running point on the hood. It was far from the nice car destroyed in "Animal House," and kind of already looked destroyed, so the four of us piled in and we headed off to college. Our first stop, besides the liquor store, was a department store called, Ames. We were already wearing black, for stealth purposes, but we needed nylons to hide our faces, some form of antennae for increased jocularity and of course hand-held toy weapons.

We were back in the car drinking when we finally tried out our firearms of choice. Mine shot little round red coin sized disks, Jerry's shot sparks, Doug purchased a cap gun and Greg's was a hollow clown gun, which when squeezed made a popping sound and projected a plastic ball about three and a half feet. We were deadly.

The ride over the Bay Bridge was uneventful, however, we were all sitting shoulder to shoulder jammed in a VW bug, so if we happened to go over the side, we would have made a seismic tsunami, before sinking like OJ Simpson's fan base.

While driving to the kidnapping, I asked Jerry if he knew anything about Washington College's baseball team. Jerry was a pretty good left-handed pitcher himself, and was on one of my summer teams. I was driving him to a game once when he had me detour to a local cemetery, because he heard a rumor there was a cougar running around. Much to my chagrin, he was not referring to a hot older woman, but an actual four-legged animal. We slowly drove around the whole cemetery in hopes of spying a jungle beast. We both swore we heard a roar of some kind, while in the midst of the silent graveyard, but saw nothing strange. However, police reports came out later, that grieving visitors saw a strange blue car with two fully dressed baseball players meandering in and out of each and every lane, while growling and yelling, "Here kitty, kitty."

While pitching one summer, Jerry took a line drive off the nether regions, but kept his composure long enough to run a few steps over to the ball and pick it up before falling down in a fetal position when the pain caught up with him. I hate that feeling and over a thousand times in my life, I've stumped my toe and quickly grabbed it before the pain kicked in. Pain is never instant with smashed toes, but when the baby maker gets pinged, well that's a different interior scream all together.

The sound of the ball hitting Jerry's junk was deafening. To avoid flashbacks, and embarrassing therapy sessions with healers of junk shots, he wisely decided not to play high school ball. I know he missed it, but I totally understood that line of thinking as I have experienced such sessions.

Washington College were definitely known as a lacrosse school, but their baseball program started back in 1870. I mean, it was possible veterans of the Civil War decided to go to college and ended up playing baseball in Chestertown. There are documented pictures of soldiers playing baseball in just about every war and if they had cameras during the American revolution, I'm sure they would have captured George Washington carrying his glove and a 36-inch Easton bat across the Delaware.

When we finally reached the college, only Doug had been there before but wasn't sure where to go. When he blurted out. "Turn," Greg took the first road he saw and whipped into it. Unfortunately, Doug hadn't finished his instructions and what Greg turned into wasn't a road, but a hedge-lined sidewalk. The bushes were literally scraping against both sides of the car as we violated the walking space, and I prayed hard we wouldn't meet a pedestrian and send him airborne. The naked lady out front illuminated the way as we shot out the other side unscathed. Greg was channeling Mario Andretti as he drove, and after descending a small set of steps, power slid into a parking space and announced, "we're parked!" Stunt drivers everywhere shined down upon us as we landed next to the building we were about to charge. We grabbed our guns, and pulled our nylons down over our faces so we totally looked like a band of trouble. Our costumes were perfect with the exception of Greg, who misunderstood the whole nylon thing and had purchased a set of panty hose, so he ran inside with a cotton crotch strip across his face.

Not sure where we were going, I just kept the pace and protected our rear, as we sprinted up three flights of stairs and plowed through the door and into the hallway of the foreign language floor. I heard an intense female scream ahead of me, as an unsuspecting student from Lebanon walked out of the co-ed showers and into a cotton crotch man running down the hall. As we sprinted, I noticed all the doors were open and the rooms looked immaculate, which was unusual for a college dorm.

Jerry and Doug found Mark in the common room. He was sitting on a couch talking to friends with his back to the door, so they threw a blanket over him from behind and they all tumbled to the floor. Greg missed everything because he had turned around to make sure Lebanon wasn't leaving the United Nations. By the time I showed up, they were dragging Mark by his legs across the tile floor while some girl screamed and started kicking Doug. We were only about a year removed from the Iranian crisis and some thought our little prank might have been labeled, "too soon." His friends were in shock except for one or two who were in on the event.

To my surprise, I heard the muffled voice of Mark call out Doug by name and then Jerry before asking who else was with them. Dumbfounded at the accusation, they uncovered a laughing Mark who seemed to know about the aforementioned kidnapping. Earlier in the evening, he had randomly called Doug whose mother told him, "Oh, he and some friends were driving down to visit with you." Talk about letting the cat out of the bag. He knew all along people were coming, he just didn't know the identity of all the players, what their intensions were and what mayhem they were capable of. His biggest mistake, other than trusting us, was his failure to inform the transfer student from Lebanon.

After the initial shock wore off, his well-dressed friends were very accepting of us. Bravely, he told us we couldn't stay because the whole floor was 45 minutes away from experiencing a wine and cheese party with all the Deans and Professors involved with foreign language. We just laughed, because we knew we weren't going anywhere. His friends split up to find us some presentable clothes to wear and rooms for us to stay. Apparently, donning all black while sporting toy guns, antennas and panty liners were not the acceptable attire for a wine and cheese party. Who knew?

Mark didn't bat an eye as he introduced us to all his professors and Deans as visiting dignitaries from other colleges. We blended in splendidly and I even found a professor who was proficient in conversations about baseball. He had no idea what "The Winger" was but we talked Orioles for quite a while and I remember him being enamored with the four 20 game winners of the 1970 season. He pulled out some astronomical equation about how that was impossible. I agreed, but then so were the odds of I conversing with a baseball loving math professor while drinking Red, White and Blue beer out of a wine glass. Double secret probation my ass.

I don't even remember sleeping that night, but I do remember walking through a graveyard at the crack of dawn to find breakfast. We weren't planning on eating dead bodies or looking for cougars, but omelets at some diner on the other side of the cemetery. We shared a serious conversation about walking on or around the graves, so we meandered an extra two miles to make sure we weren't injuring anyone. I always look at tombstones, as they are the calling card for the person lying below. Many times, I have seen odes to baseball, either in mentioning accolades or the actual shape of the marker. Harmon Killebrew had a giant embossing of his swing, Honus Wagner had a simple stone with two small engraved crossing bats, while Jackie Robinson left an inspiring quote. All three are perfect representations of their careers.

Later that night, in adequate "Animal House" style, we attended a Toga party at one of the fraternities. "Men at Work" were all the rage and their album, *Business as Usual*, played non-stop throughout the party. I had never been to a party wearing nothing but a sheet, so that was a first. The only garb I found, was on the bed in the room I was awarded, so I spent the night drinking and dancing in a pink and yellow floral designed queen fitted sheet. The elastic corners did a wonder keeping in all the dangly parts.

At one point in the evening, the music paused just long enough to see and hear a very intoxicated lad hurl his guts next to the couch he was wedged in. When the music started again, Doug Wann danced over and without missing a beat, sang everything the guy had eaten to the tune of, "Down Under." I was impressed with his observation and vocal presence.

All in all, Washington College will always remind me of John Belushi winning 20 games while drinking Red, White and Blue with an Australian accent and wearing panty liners from Lebanon. It was a much-needed road trip.

Why Did it Have to be Snakes?

As technology started to advance into the entertainment world, video games began to pop up in the commuter café. Giant boxes plugged into the wall had the ability to suck quarters right out of my pants. I fell in love with Asteroids and PAC-MAN and convinced myself I was developing excellent hand-eye coordination, which would assist me behind the plate.

I found the free time at Anne Arundel much more interesting than at CCB. Playing cards and spitting in a cup was replaced with throwing a half keg of beer in a car, and driving 15 minutes to the beach of Sandy Point State Park. That park, and its panoramic view of the Bay Bridge, was home to the Polar Bear Plunge, which was where attendees took a dip in the ice-cold bay at the end of January to raise money for the Special Olympics. It was a great organization and every year when I saw coverage of those brave individuals running into the icy bay, I am reminded of hot summer days and beer breaks.

I quickly made friends with some of the football players just so they wouldn't pick me up and throw me in the water when they were making their rounds. Helping them dig a hole in the sand to bury a keg of beer was all I needed to do to maintain my dry outlook and cool hair. One of these men was Mike McMahon, a truly interesting specimen who I would drive to and fro simply because he got in my car one day. He loved the Neil Mobile and was particularly enamored with the silver drive-in movie speakers I had hanging on the inside of the back doors.

They were given to me by my old friend, Greg Hoffman, when he moved to LA to become a stunt man, and the story about how they were acquired had many alterations with the least-believed being a legal yard sale purchase.

The electronics class I took in high school came in handy as these speakers had no off switch and constantly drained my battery. I drilled several small holes in my dashboard and put each of them on a toggle switch. I also did the same to the front speaker, the two I had on my front doors and the two living in the back dash over the trunk.

When people initially entered my car and I fired up my 8-track tape player, Journey, Boston or Pink Floyd's "The Wall" would start playing out of my lowly dash speaker to their dismay. Once I started driving, I threw the toggle switches one at a time until the Neil Mobile was a rolling rock concert. Someone commented with all the knobs and switches, my dash looked like the cockpit of a 727.

Rick Miller was one of my most cherished friends. Not only was he a pitcher with an intimidating curve ball, but he worked at Jumpers Hole Cinema. All I had to do was walk up to the door and in a few minutes, I was enjoying "Arthur," "Body Heat," "Stripes" or "Raiders of the Lost Ark" without spending a dime. I felt like one of the "Good Fellas"! Rick routinely offered up his doorman services, which saved me tons of money. Unfortunately, that money was eventually pumped into the Asteroids machine. Oh, it was a viscous cycle.

I used to call time-out and walk to the mound just to shoot the shit with Rick. I tried to get him to laugh, point out women in the stands who might or might not have been there to cheer him on, but mostly to find out what movies were playing. He always looked at me like I was crazy and I looked forward to it.

I think I saw "Raiders" at least five times and surprisingly enough Rick was working every time. I fell in love with the idea of Indiana Jones having two completely different lives, and totally related to him with his dislike of snakes. To this day when I see one, I repeat his famous retort.

Once, in a packed theater, one of our gang showed up after the movie started. I saw he and Rick trying to identify the back of our heads with some difficulty when suddenly Rick chirped in a non-theater bravado, "Neil!" Of course, the whole place turned around to see what the ruckus was as I sank lower in my seat. I raised my hand in embarrassment and Rick ushered him over. I remember him sitting down to Marion yelling, "I'm your goddamn partner!"

A few weeks later we were playing a home game with Mike McMahon and the usual crowd in attendance. He was carrying a large pillow case and, because it was Mike, it didn't seem that odd. Unbeknownst to me, he had a friend inside who was incapable of standing upright. Mike collected and raised snakes. Upon learning this, I quickly wondered if there was anything living in the Neil Mobile and if I was even going to look or just immediately burn it to the ground. Rick was on the mound and was for some reason causing me bodily harm with his 57-foot fastball.

The distance from the pitching rubber to home plate is 60 feet, 6 inches. All pitchers know this; hence they need to throw the ball at least that far and with enough speed and velocity to be elevated above the batter's knees. Rick wasn't currently on board with the math and accompanying trajectory, thus most of the pitches were ricocheting off the ground and into my body. I called time-out and walked to the mound to see what his deficiency was and what time "Porky's" started.

Just as I approached the mound and was prepared to say, "Rick why are you hurting me, I am your goddamn partner!" The other team came racing out of their dugout towards the mound. For a brief second, I channeled my CCB self and turned quickly prepared to do battle. However, they ran right past me and towards the field. Most of them were looking over their shoulders like they were being chased by a slow-walking guy in a hockey mask or a pissed-off prom date.

The distinct laughter from Mike McMahon told me otherwise. He thought it was a good idea to take the boa constrictor from its traveling cotton house and stick half of him through one of the vents at the back of the dugout. The force of the mass exodus can only be compared to the 1983 Black Friday sale of Cabbage Patch Dolls. Ask someone who participated and they will relay the horror of it all.

The umpire called a special time-out to remove the snake, and Mike took him on a field trip to the locker room so he could relax on the floor of the shower. Someone on our bench asked out loud if the other team had any bats in the dugout at all. I imagine if Mike had retrieved a flat-headed snake, he might have second-guessed his prank. Rick threw 64-foot strikes after that. My guess was he hated snakes too!

I heard later that Mike's snake had gone to slither heaven and the cause of death was athlete's foot poison. What does that tell you about the excretions of an average college baseball player? I hope the government has top men working on that. Top men.

Our season was less than stellar. We ended up with a winning record no thanks to my proficiency to hit home runs foul. I was a well-known pull hitter and sometimes would jump on a fastball so quickly, I would launch 425-foot foul balls. I can still see our third base dugout empty on the field to look to the extreme left, hoping the ball would draw fair. Not! Once I heard back-up catcher Jeff Irvine yell, "Holy shit, look at that thing go!" If only someone taught me to hit the ball to right field.

The Region 20 baseball tournament had us losing to Allegany in the first round with CCB winning it all and heading once again to Grand Junction for the JUCO World Series. Upon losing our game, we had to walk by CCB as we traded places on the field. I saw Dr. Strange Glove and greeted him with an extended hand and a smile. He just looked at me shockingly and said, "Ned, you got so fat!" Ah, camaraderie at its finest.

Yeah, Huh?

Summer ball usually consisted of college and high school players mixed in with wannabes and has-beens. Some were still learning and some were all learned out. One year a pitcher showed up named Dave who was 45 years old. When you are 19, a 45-year-old teammate was ancient. He was a good pitcher, but once when I attempted to throw out a runner at second, he caught the ball because he "didn't think I would get him." On most summer teams the coach was one of the player's fathers and almost everybody on the team was accountable as a player. Well, almost everybody. League games were twice a week with practices intermittent and specialty games outside our league occasionally took place when they fit in.

The first few practices were bestowed with the learning curve associated with meeting new players, discovering their talent or lack of, and figuring out who on the team would be your least favorite. Every team I ever played on had a prima donna whose biggest fan was himself. He was usually good, but his attitude created animosity and some teammates wanted to see him fail. One of my biggest hates in the whole world was wasted talent. Some players have a natural swing, an amazing arm or blazing speed, but don't realize what they have and don't use it to capacity. I always had the drive but lacked the raw talent so I had to work my ass off. I'm sure everyone can picture a player from their past who falls into one of these categories.

Each team usually had the player who hated to lose as well as the one who just didn't care. It is hard to keep everyone on the same page when they have a different desired outcome, but that was what made it fun. These teams reminded me of a Flip Wilson skit and many times while catching, I was laughing behind my face cage. My favorite teammate was the one who always looked and acted like they just woke up. Every now and then they would emerge from their coma and rip a triple or say something hilarious. Moments later, they would enter zombie land again and the practice would resume in an unpredictable fashion. I'm sure some of them are in politics now.

One night after such a practice, I was flipping through the channels and came across two of my favorite comedians, Jack Burns and Avery Schreiber. Burns and Schreiber made the rounds on variety shows, commercials and even had their own show. Jack Burns used to partner with George Carlin and was even Barney Fife's replacement in Mayberry.

One of their bits was where Burns was a passenger in Schreiber's taxi. He chats the whole time, pretty much driving Schreiber crazy. He constantly quizzes him to make sure he is listening and comprehending the useless information he is spewing. He does this using the slang word I would be punished for when I acted like I didn't hear my father, "Huh?" According to my dad, "huh" was never a proper answer and I had a sore ass to prove it.

Burns keeps repeating his questioning in a speedy fashion until the driver answers with a related follow-up.

For example, "It sure is cold outside, isn't it?"

"Yea."

"Huh?"

"Yea."

"Huh?"

"It's freezing, freezing outside."

I always thought their interaction hilarious and decided to use it on my team. It took me a while to teach it, because there can't be any pauses while you think of your witty answer, it has to be instantaneous.

The sequence could only be launched when you answered with "yea" and received the word "huh." When it caught on, it made the most mundane conversations that much more palatable.

"Did you drive here tonight?" "Yea." "Huh?" "Yea." "Huh?" "Brought my car."

"Are you hungry?" "Yea." "Huh?" "Yea." "Huh?" "Could eat a horse."

"That was a horrible call, didn't you think that was a ball?" "Yea." "Huh?" "Yea." "Huh?" "Low and outside, terrible call."

Sometimes it could be boring during slow parts of the game so anything to pass the time was applauded. It was also very easy to set someone up who was too enthusiastic to play or think on their feet.

"Are you just plain stupid?" "Yea." The conversation ended there with a head shake.

Most of these teams didn't recruit, so positions were flexible and had to be filled regardless of talent. It is hard to take sometimes when a true competitor is paired with an error-making novice and tempers have been known to flare. Our first baseman was such a player. His name was Rob Vereen and he was good, very good but he had a terrible attitude. I had heard stories about him, but chocked them up to just stories until I witnessed something with my own eyes.

Our third baseman was sick one night so the coach put a rookie in at third, his son. Throughout the game he booted some balls, misplayed a cutoff and didn't charge for a bunt. His dad talked to him a few times and nobody else chimed in because of who he was. Later in the game, with a runner on first, the ball was hit to third. It wasn't hit very hard so he hurried his throw and launched it over Rob's head. The field was wide and as Rob retrieved the ball, the first runner came all the way around and scored. It was very unfortunate and my thinking at the time was if Rob hurried there might be a play at the plate, but it didn't happen.

One run on an error wasn't enough for Rob. He jogged in with the ball like he was personally taking it to the pitcher, however, he didn't stop at the mound. He ran right over to the third baseman and punched him in the mouth. Don't be afraid to break etiquette and beat up a teammate in public, shit! I couldn't believe my eyes, but it wouldn't be the only time Rob surprised me. I'll bet money the umpires never had to break up that kind of fight before. I mean, no benches cleared and nobody was thrown out but damn! I prepared myself for a long season.

A few games later a new kid showed up, which sometimes happens in summer leagues as family vacations and parole hinders early participation. It seemed nobody knew him and he never made a practice, but here he was in full uniform taking infield at second base. He was small in stature but large in skill. In his first at bat, he punched a single between first and second and made it look easy. He stole second and third before scoring on a fielder's choice.

By the way, the FC is my favorite baseball action by name. When I hear the fielder had a choice, I am immediately reminded of the time it takes to order dinner from a menu or pick out a paint color. There was maybe half a nanosecond to decide where to throw the ball and no decision was worthy of a Fielder's Choice Award.

His second time at bat he slapped another ball between first and second. I hadn't done that my entire life and he did it twice in two at bats. His name was Dan Fielder and he was my Fielder of choice. I immediately sidled up next to him like George Kennedy did to Paul Newman in "Cool Hand Luke." Did I think he could eat 50 eggs? Um, no, so maybe that was a bad analogy.

Turned out Dan was more like Ferris Bueller. "He's very popular Ed. The sportos, the motorheads, geeks, sluts, bloods, waistoids, dweebies, dickheads--they all adore him. They think he's a righteous dude." Dan was a righteous dude and he mastered the art of hitting to the opposite field.

We hit it off immediately and before I knew it, we were at a local school field in the middle of a hot day with our gloves, two bats and a bucket of balls. We spent all day pitching to each other before walking the outfield and picking up the spoils. Of course, after I batted, we only had to walk deep left field and a little bit in center. For Dan we had to search everywhere. He explained his thinking on hitting the ball to the opposite field and unfortunately it required math.

Upon meeting his mother, I discovered he received the arithmetic knowledge maternally. She immediately recited my grandparents' phone number to me as she put it in memory when she first heard Dan mention it. She quickly ascertained the last four numbers 2958 were actually an equation in itself, as $29 \times 2 = 58$. I've known that number my whole life and never once made that distinction. I was totally impressed and asked her lottery advice. She said not to play.

Dan talked of angles, bat speed and time adjustment of my swing. I think back to my softball days. When I wanted to hit the ball to right field, I would turn my whole body towards right field and swing. That might work with a five-mile-an-hour arc but not when facing an 80-90-mile-an-hour fastball. We practiced his theory for a while and I started hitting the ball up the middle pretty regularly. Dan walked the bucket out to the hole between second and first and set it down. Then back on the mound he instructed me to swing normally but wait until I see the ball aligned with the bucket. I waited until the ball was at the bucket and swung. It seemed as if the pitch had already passed me but I struck it solidly and right at the bucket. WTH?

The elation I felt made my eyes swell with happiness, but they became angry. For the next half hour, I hit just about every outside pitch to the right side of the infield. The anger I felt was towards everybody in my baseball past. I wondered why no one took the time to teach me how to hit to the opposite field. I tried and tried my whole life and now here Ferris Fielder taught me in one afternoon. My guess was they didn't think I needed help. I was hitting home runs to left and drilling gappers with great proficiency. What I thought was broken, they thought was the norm. I grieved all the missed opportunity.

This was the very reason I can't fault Chris Davis for not being able to hit out of the shift. He was so busy bashing 500-foot home runs to right, no one taught him how to bunt and spray third base with his missiles. When you are a power hitter and in the heat of battle, you are looking for your pitch to explode on, not the one to slap on the ground. Now, I just have to practice and perfect my opposite field knowledge.

Teaching others to hit wasn't Dan's only talent. While spending the night at his house once, I learned we had something else in common, the love of old television shows and useless trivia. He loved to do characters from old shows and was super-strong in theme songs. In the pitch darkness of his room as I was drifting off, he started playing his mouth to a perfect rendition of "Sanford and Son." "Wha wha whaaa wha, wha wha whaa wha wha wha whaaa." My guess was that he was also a big Quincy Jones fan.

Dan's father was also on the baseball train and once drove us all the way to Erie, Pennsylvania for a tournament. He and Dan traded one-liners the whole way there. I had taught them the "Yeah, huh?" game and they were laughing like little kids watching Looney Tunes. Actually, they were laughing like me when I watched Looney Tunes.

We stayed at the Knights Inn. The interior design of each room was purple, red with gold medieval trim. The headboards were just planks nailed right to the wall. It was quite barf-worthy but right in our price zone. The night before the tournament, we had a team dinner and then split off in small groups before turning in. Around 2:30 a.m. there was a constant banging at my door and I opened it to find five or six very drunk and obnoxious teammates. I had been sound asleep and obviously in a better state of mind than these knuckleheads, who were ready to continue partying regardless of our 9 a.m. game. When reasoning didn't work and a beer was poured on my purple bedspread, I let the demons out and power blocked the pourer into the window AC unit. They had no problem going to sleep after that.

In the top of the first inning, Rob Vereen, who was looking quite the worse for wear, let it be known to a few of us that he was suppressing a monumental hangover. I felt sorry for him and since there was no microwave, nor burritos in our dugout, I advised him to get a drink of water from the fountain and take it easy. Moments later, he was on all fours throwing up in the floor drain at the corner of the dugout. I can still see his back arcing and convulsing when the coach said, "C'mon Rob, you're up!"

He stood up, wiped his mouth, grabbed his helmet and bat and strolled towards the plate. His motions were mannequin-like and as he stood in the batter's box staring down the pitcher, I perked up to see if he would puke on the umpire. Moments later, he hit the farthest bomb I had ever seen, barring the Major League home run contest. I swear it went over 500 feet and when it left the park over the center field stands, I lost sight of its' final destination, but I'm pretty sure it was Canada. I glanced around the dugout taking in reactions and only saw exasperation.

Rob dropped his bat and circled the bases in such a non-jovial manner you would have thought he was just given a death sentence for hurting the ball. I turned to Dan and said, "Do you believe that?"

"Yea."

"Huh?"

"Yea."

"Huh?"

"Seeing is believing, but damn!"

Rob high-fived some of us and half-smiled as he made his way through the dugout before getting back down on all fours to finish barfing. Truly, a natural ball player. I had no doubt at that moment he had the potential to be the next Mickey Mantle on his prison team.

Many summer games and practices later, Dan and I hit a 7-11 for hydration purposes. He likes to tell the story of how I filled up a Big Gulp and drank it down in one chug like Mean Joe Green did in a Coke commercial. I remember doing that but keeping my jersey. Like most endings of our antics, Dan's giggle became a follow quote. He enjoyed the silly part of life, but when it came to baseball, he was super-serious. Many times, during a game I would see him approach someone on our team and although I couldn't hear what he was saying, I could tell it was encouragement or advice on improvement. A player-coach for sure.

I walked around the corner of my gym one day and saw Dan sitting at the military press. He must have had 350 pounds on that monster and he was shifting his hands around to obtain a proper grip. Shocked at what I was seeing and knowing his second baseman stature, I had to quickly question his actions. "Are you going to lift all that?"

"Yeah."

"Huh?"

"Yeah."

"Huh?"

"Hydraulic elbows." I laughed for 10 straight minutes as that was the best Burns and Schreiber sequence, I ever participated in. For all I know Dan was sitting there for three hours waiting for me to come by so he could launch into our banter. Bottom line, baseball players are hilarious.

I had tried out for and landed the starting position for the Arundel Sun All-Stars. Our team was made up of players all around the county and we played one game against the Orioleland All Stars, who were major-league prospects from several of the surrounding states. There were about 2,000 fans in attendance, which was the most I played in front of at the time. I had a hit, an RBI and threw out a runner attempting to steal. During the game, I hit one of my patented 450-foot foul balls. That one was closer than most and I actually ran halfway to first before it was called foul. After the game, a man from the stands told me he expected to see me play in the big leagues someday. I can still hear his voice and although I am over 60, part of me thinks it will happen one day. That was what baseball does to you.

Thooooot!

With the addition of two fun-sucking summer classes, I had successfully obtained an Associate of Arts degree in American Studies. Now if only there were jobs in that arena I'd be set. Enter Jan with more advice. She suggested I transfer to the University of Maryland, Baltimore County or UMBC. Her husband, John Goedeke, just graduated from there and was inducted into their Sports Hall of Fame for his stellar basketball play and propensity to change lightbulbs without a ladder. I heard they had a decent baseball team too, so I decided to enroll and introduce myself to the coach.

I did zero research on our meeting, like learning tidbits of relevant UMBC information or how to pronounce his name. As a matter of fact, I didn't even know his name, I just heard his office was in the field house next to the indoor pool, so I walked up and knocked on the door. The plaque on the door read "Coach Jancuska" so when I knocked and he told me to enter I said, "Hi Coach Jan-coo-ska, my name is Neil Beller, I'm a catcher and I just transferred in." He was looking down at some paperwork and slowly looked up and said, "It's pronounced Jank-a-shay." Oops, so much for first impressions because I totally just crapped the bed. He also told me they already had a catcher who transferred in from AACC and went on about Jeff Irvine and his All-County status. Wait, what? I told him I was the starting catcher from AACC and Jeff was the backup. I'm not sure he believed me, but said I could come to fall ball as a walk-on to try to make the team. I thanked him and left his office with little confidence that I'd be playing college baseball again.

For the third time in three years, I was attending a different college to play baseball and had no idea who was on the team or when I would meet them. One week into the semester, I was standing outside my 500-student theater-style biology class after being asked to leave by one of my professors. We were learning about cell theory and the building blocks of life. The professor was running through the components of cells and their functions during copulation when he asked, "What happens to the genes?" My retort of, "They end up balled up on the floor of the car!" was not the proper answer apparently, so I was escorted from the class to applause and laughter.

As I walked out of the building, I heard a familiar voice from behind me, "Ned, is that you?" I turned around to see none other than Dr. Strange Glove. Don't be afraid to follow me to another college, shit! Tim O'Malley was the first teammate I met at CCB and then again at UMBC. After a short round of "What are you doing here?" and "No I won't lend you my homework," we talked about baseball and playing for the UMBC Retrievers.

The field at UMBC was pretty nice and backed up to the lacrosse installation. Basketball and lacrosse were the sports of reverence, so it was easy to see where the money was spent. I became familiar with home plate and took a few balls off the mound. It felt good to squat again.

I spent a lot of time in the off-season working my legs. Catchers need to have strong legs for a variety of reasons. Squatting, sprinting to back up first base, lunging left and right in defensive maneuvers and looking good in shorts were all viable reasons to work your legs. I knew I was in shape when I was purchasing pants for my thighs and not my waist. My calves were always locked and looked like I was perpetually wearing high heels.

I had a different workout regimen than most players which included sprinting backwards, crab walking and jumping rope in a squat. Yes, you read that right, I jumped rope in a squat. There were times at parties when everyone would be standing around talking, I would squat down and continue my conversation from knee level. It actually felt more comfortable down there than standing. I can't even tell you how many pairs of spikes I owned where the front set of cleats were worn all the way down to the soles from constantly being on my toes.

I also had three mitts--a single-fold mitt, a double-fold mitt and one larger mitt for uncertain pitchers who loved to throw in the dirt. My favorite was the double-fold mitt and I used it the most. Single folds are represented in most fielder gloves, but the double fold divided the mitt into three sections, which was perfect for framing the plate. By moving your glove along the edge of the strike zone, you can have a portion of your glove out of the strike zone making the zone a little larger. The umpire might not know exactly where the ball entered your glove so a ball will seem like a strike. Home plate is 17 inches wide, and if a portion of the ball crosses the corner, and your glove is even farther off the plate, the strike zone can seem 2 feet wide.

I was taught to frame the plate at an early age, but Coach Jancuska was a stickler for stealing strikes. If you watch film of a catcher in slow motion, you will notice when the batter swings, the catcher blinks his eyes. It only lasts a second and was almost impossible to avoid. Remember the hammering a nail example? The good thing was that umpires blinked too and sometimes longer. If a catcher can frame the plate and move his glove after catching the ball, the umpire can be fooled into thinking a strike had been thrown.

I was certain if I made the team, I would be using my large mitt, as the catching drills were a little scary. The batting cages lived in foul territory by right field. A pitching machine was set up and the coach called down all the players who might have the opportunity to spend some time behind the dish. I was the guinea pig for that drill, so I lifted the net and squatted behind the plate. We were required to leave our mitts outside and position ourselves in a squat with our arms behind us. Don't be afraid to catch a fastball without a glove, shit! He cranked up the machine to 90 miles an hour and directed it to hit in the dirt in front of the plate. The idea was to throw your body in front of the ball without letting it get by you. I can personally say with the honesty of knowing what a dentist's drill feels like, it hurt like a mother! I had bruises in places bruises shouldn't be forming. Even the tools didn't stop the ignorance as the pitching machine became our worst enemy.

The next day the machine was moved to the mound for batting practice where it became our best friend again. Halfway through the practice, the coach had to leave for an hour and the honor code kicked in. The honor code simply meant that we would behave ourselves and act like proper baseball players while the coach was within shouting distance. The team captain was senior Jeff Usilton, who was an amazing pitcher and unbelievable hitter. Fortunately for the rest of us, he had management issues and would rather have fun than be in charge. After BP, we decided to use the pitching machine as a tool for the catching pop-up drill. No one could hit the ball straight up, and throwing the ball as high as one could became old so we improvised.

We brought the machine behind home plate, dialed it to 60 miles an hour and pointed it straight up in the air. One of us would get in a squat facing the pitcher's mound with the machine behind us. Another catcher would run a ball through the spinning wheels making the familiar "thoooooot" sound as the ball left the machine. When the ball was in the air, "Now!" would be announced and the catcher would jump up, turn around and attempt to catch the ball. It must have looked like fun because others were lining up to give it a try. We laughed as awkward non-catchers tried in vain to chase one down. As soon as they stood and looked up, they were falling all over the place. It was much harder than it seemed and to make our case we cranked it up to 100 miles an hour. The "thoooooot" became a "thoot" and the ball became a speck in the sky. I am sure Baltimore/ Washington International Airport was seeing blips on radar. A couple of times the ball came down in centerfield causing the chaser to run all the way there while looking straight up only to miss the ball by a few feet. It was quite hilarious and entertaining until the coach came back early.

Running was a part of baseball, but it could also be a form of punishment. As we all huddled around home plate, we were singled out and divided up by speed into two teams. Meaning, if the coach thought two guys had similar speed, he placed one on each team. When the teams were picked, he informed us of his evil plan with a special treat for the losers. When he signaled, one player from each team sprinted down each foul line, touching the base and continuing on to the foul pole fence and back. The next guy couldn't go until their teammate touched home plate and then they took off doing the same horrible but necessary dash.

Here was where the coach was a genius and a psychopath at the same time. The losing team would be divided and made to run again. What? This misery would continue again and again until there were only two guys left and of course, an ambulance. Guess who was one of those two guys? Uh huh. Nobody wanted to lose and run again, so no one was holding anything back on the original race. The first time we ran, it was a 150% energy purge. When the fun was over, I was completely exhausted and never touched the pitching machine again.

Running and the horror associated with it didn't stop there. Please remember baseball was a game of starts and stops. Players walk everywhere, they jog and even casually stroll on and off the field. When someone hit the ball or was stealing, then the game turned into a fast-paced hectic sprint, but all in all baseball was a game of leisure. Long distance running was only for conditioning and was never used like it was in soccer, lacrosse or explosive diarrhea. The entire campus of UMBC, with the exception of the baseball and lacrosse fields, were inside a road loop. The road was actually called Hilltop Circle and its highest and lowest points are equivalent to Alaska and the Equator. At least it felt that way when running because it was 2.1 miles all the way around and some days, we had to run it twice. When finished, it kind of made you want to yell "Currahee!" Yes, that was a "Band of Brothers" reference.

On the last day of fall ball, I still wasn't sure if I had made the team. We were playing a scrimmage game against Johns Hopkins University at their field. The coach wouldn't hint either way and just told me to keep trying, but my teammates assured me I was a Retriever. I had an okay game but hadn't had a "wow" moment all fall. In my last at bat, I stepped into an inside fastball and drove it to left field. I took off running without looking at the ball and as I neared first base, the coach was looking towards left but waving me through. Most balls I pulled were usually called foul by now, so I thought maybe the left fielder had bobbled it as I headed towards second. I wanted to do everything right, and I glanced towards third to pick up the head coach before rounding second. He wasn't giving me any direction at all but had a smile on his face. As I approached third base, he held out his hand to shake mine and said, "You made the team." Apparently, I had hit a home run and didn't know it. An exuberant Tim O'Malley told me that the ball had not only left the field, it had cleared the road and the trees beyond, landing on the turf lacrosse field. It was the longest home run I had ever hit and now Coach Jan-coo-ska was stuck with me.

To celebrate our team, and to set a plan over the winter, we were informed that on the first day of spring training we would all be required to run a mile in under six minutes. If we failed, we would have to run again two days later and then again two days later. Spring training was months away, but I was already growing anxious. I had never broken a six- much less seven-minute mile. I wasn't even sure the Neil Mobile could do that. One thing I knew for certain, I was going to have a serious talk with my grandfather and his wholesale ice cream distributor.

The UMBC field house contained the basketball arena and was equipped with a small track which encircled it. The track was on the second level and its distance was a tenth of a mile. For those non-math majors, it meant we would have to run around 10 times in under six minutes. I decided to give it a go to see where I was time-wise and picked a day when the place wasn't crowded. On one of the walls there was a giant clock, with an equally large second hand, which constantly ticked away the seconds of my life. A simple calculation told me there were 360 seconds in 10 minutes, so if I ran each lap in 36 seconds or less, I would meet my mark.

I waited until the clock hit an even number and took off. I had never run around a track so small, and felt like I was in a perpetual left-hand turn. The first lap had me at 35 seconds and for a very brief second, I thought it would be a piece of cake. Unfortunately, the cake had a brick inside because my next lap was 39 seconds followed by 41 and 45. I was in a world of trouble and decided instead of running this mile, I would rather sort rattlesnakes by size and girth. It was that bad.

Formal Organizations

The winter of 1982 was cold and icy and made the side streets of Pasadena quite treacherous for running. In spite of working in a kitchen every weekend, I lost 15 pounds and remained diligent with my workout regime. It would have been very easy to snack on French fries at will, as I made them by the millions. I worked 5 p.m. to 5 a.m. Friday and Saturday evenings, so I cooked everything from pancakes to patty melts to turkey tetrazzini and all at the same time. I found cooking at Bob's Big Boy a satisfying challenge and each patron helped me to become more proficient.

For example, on the same ticket I might have a medium-well steak, a Western omelet with rye toast, a BLT and two sunny-side up eggs with extra-crispy hash browns. I learned to work backwards making the dish that took the longest first, and so on down the line until everything was ready at the same time. It was a constant learning experience as I literally was juggling ladles and knives while buttering bread and frying bacon. There were some cooks who would look at that ticket and immediately make the eggs and that just meant cold food for everyone. I didn't know it at the time, but it helped me organize my whole world, including baseball.

In baseball, everything is counted and tabulated and charted forever. As a player, you are compared to every person who ever played the game before you and after you. Organization was the key to keeping it that way, which was why players become coaches when their playing days are over. The game grabs a hold of the youth that lives deep in the fibers of your soul and never lets' go. Some people will do almost anything to keep playing, even when their bodies are telling them not to.

At AACC, we ran the steps of the football stadium as well as the field and I developed a nasty case of shin splints. They were the most painful injury I ever encountered because they never went away. I used to have the trainers rub down my shins with Atomic Bomb, which was like BENGAY 100 times over, before wrapping them in gauze. The burning sensation overpowered the pain, which I tried to cut with lots and lots of aspirin. Nothing worked.

A teammate had dislocated his ankle sliding into second and had to be carried off the field. Five days later he was back like nothing had happened. I immediately inquired to the miracle that fell upon him and he fed me the acronym, DMSO. Dimethyl sulfoxide was an industrial solvent used to rub down race horses and clean the chrome bumpers of various automobiles. It was also used as an anti-inflammatory, although the court is out on how that was ascertained. The selling point was that it reduced inflammation immediately, and since it was the swelling which caused the pain, why not? I heard a rumor that Jim Palmer used to soak his arm in it after pitching, and he was an amazing Hall of Fame player so how bad could it be? When I inquired about where I could obtain such a concoction, the conversation was reduced to a whisper. I was given an address, which was only a mile from my grandparent's house, but it wasn't a pharmacy nor a medical institution...it was a clock shop.

I pulled into the empty parking lot on a Thursday and made my way inside. I approached the totally stereotypical clock maker and asked him if he sold DMSO. He pulled back and slowly looked right and then left and in a hushed voice told me he'd be right back. He disappeared through a door in the back and I stood there thinking I was in the lobby of a speakeasy or some nefarious establishment that sold bazookas and other illegal products like unpasteurized milk.

THE DISH

He returned in the same sneaky manner and brought with him an old brown wooden box. He placed it on the counter like it contained nitroglycerin and carefully opened it. Inside were several blue bottles packed in cotton. My God, it was nitroglycerin! He pulled one out, blew off the dust and set it on the counter. Looking left and right again, he cautiously stated, "Dab it on with clean cotton balls and whatever you do, don't rub it in."

I slid the required cash across the counter and took my blue bottle of DMSO and left the clock shop for the first and last time. I made it to my room with fresh cotton balls acquired from my grandmother's pantry, locked the door and opened the bottle. I half-expected a genie to pop out but nothing magical happened. Not knowing what to expect, I wet the cotton ball and slowly dabbed it on my shins. The liquid was somewhat oily but instantly disappeared when it touched my skin. It was as if my pores went into suck mode and I could almost hear them slurping. I could feel it entering my veins, slowly moving about the blood highway of my body before reaching my mouth. All at once, I had a taste like I had just chewed a metal can used to house sauerkraut and soiled kitty litter.

I hid the bottle in my bookshelf and went about my normal routine not knowing if in 10 years I might be having a silver baby. The next day, I noticed the pain had decreased significantly. I had a one-on-one meeting with my counselor to create my spring schedule and then worked 12 hours at Bob's, but I felt great. I managed four hours of sleep before making my way to UMBC for a Saturday morning practice. After we stretched and loosened up, I took BP and warmed up several pitchers. Squatting gave me little discomfort which energized me and made me happy. We ended the practice by taking infield and outfield.

I had worked up a frothy sweat, so I peeled off my chest protector and left on my shin guards. Two other catchers and I were rotating in and out as the coach hit the ball saying, "Get one!' or "Get two!" All of a sudden, he stops hitting, turns to all three of us and in a loud voice asked, "Who is wearing DMSO?" I was shocked! Nobody answered as we were checking out each other to see who would fess up. Someone asked "DMS what?" He hit another ball and said, "Seriously, who is wearing it?" He walked over to us and in an instant chirped, "Beller!"

Apparently, a big side effect to using DMSO is the simple fact that it gives you death breath. Like "dead bird floating in the Inner Harbor" breath. It had been two days since I even used it and I brushed my teeth daily and gargled with Listerine mouthwash. My first thought was, "What did my counselor think?" We were in a small room together for almost an hour. Now, I have to buy her flowers and apologize for subjecting her to my dirty diaper impression. My second thought was that Coach Jancuska had visited my clock shop! He just shook his head like I had joined a cartel. Two stinky breath applications later, my shin splints were cured. A whole year of pain erased by a paranoid clock maker.

I was doing pretty good in all of my classes except one, Formal Organizations. I knew it was going to be the toughest hour and a half of my semester from the moment I walked in the room. I didn't know a soul but when I entered, I heard a familiar female voice say, "Neil, hey Neil sit here, sit next to me." That voice belonged to Kevin's girlfriend, Mary Fran. I was handcuffed, so with the pace of a three-legged turtle going uphill through a field of thumbtacks, I slowly walked over and sat next to Mary Fran. I prepared myself for a very long and painfully slow death.

Formal Organizations was a beast! It dealt with officially codified hierarchical arrangements of relationships between different jobs within the organizational units and relationships between departments within the organization. I had considered myself intelligent enough to understand anything if it were explained to me correctly, but I just couldn't understand any of that. To make matters worse and harm the way I revered my own intelligence, Mary Fran was acing the class. Are you freaking kidding me? It turns out Kevin was right she was smart as a whip. She even tried to help me understand, which humbled me to no end. I was at a serious dead-end when she suggested I meet with the professor after class, telling me he was really a great guy and her advisor.

Against my better judgement, I met him in his office, explaining my dilemma. He ate a cup of cereal as he listened, before telling me Mary Fran was one of the smartest students he ever taught. I asked him if he ever watched a movie with her and he just looked at me funny, so his answer could have gone either way. I was carrying my UMBC baseball hat and when he saw it, he asked me if I understood baseball. I laughed in a knowing manner and he perked up. I mean everybody understands baseball. Turns out this guy was a fan. He grew up with the Cardinals but followed the Orioles. We chatted baseball for a bit and then something amazing happened. He took the vernacular of Formal Organizations and changed it all to baseball. He explained that the legal advisors were the base coaches and the secretary was the scorekeeper and the staff was the bullpen. In an instant it just clicked and before I knew it, I was as smart as Mary Fran. I learned baseball was truly the foundation of everything including clock shops. If only I could invent some mouth spray that could mask the death breath DMSO caused, I'd make all the medical journals.

WUMD

As I anticipated, preparing for the six-minute mile was horrible. I worried about it all the time and it interfered with my sleep, work and drinking schedule. When the day finally hit my calendar, I was as ready as I'd ever be, so I walked to the starting line and waited to throw up. I am the type of runner who never talks or engages with any other runner. I simply can't. Every single breath I inhaled was needed to cross the line in an upright position and spending those breaths conversing with another runner was pointless. That was not the case for Bobby Bruchalski.

Bobby was our second baseman and in great shape, but didn't look like it. I could go on record and state that I never once saw him even sweat. During the mile he was talking with everybody. To rub it in, he spoke to us as he seamlessly passed by. He pretended he was running a marathon and reached out after every lap to grab a pretend bottle of water from an imaginary handler, drink it, and throw the imaginary bottle to the ground. My hate for him was not pretend. I was sucking wind so badly you'd have thought I was a chain-smoking, couch potato who ate daily bowls of buttered mashed potatoes while holding my breath underwater.

I was running in the middle of the pack and my eyes almost never veered from the giant clock. When I started the last lap, I had 45 seconds to go before the six-minute deadline. Mustering all the energy I had left, I reached out to God for assistance and pushed myself to the end. I crossed the line at 5:46 reaching my five-month goal. Even though the finish line was painted on the track, I tripped over it like it was 3 feet high and went down like a bag of hammers. The coach just smiled as I rolled by.

UMBC opened other sports outlets for me as well, and I landed a slot on WUMD radio. I joined the sports department and was assigned the duties of reporting national sports scores and various updates three times a day. Basketball standout Ricky Moreland was the sports director and together we held a weekly radio show. Ricky was as wholesome as Robert Young in "Father Knows Best" and was a tremendous basketball player, who went on to break almost every one of my brother-in-law's records. Weekly, I would call my sister to reveal another one of her husband's accomplishments had been surpassed. I'm sure they looked forward to my calls.

One of my other duties was as a color commentator alongside play-by-play announcer Rick Lagana for Retriever's basketball. We drove to colleges as far away as Kutztown University in Pennsylvania to make award-winning broadcasts. I took great pride in getting in at least one baseball mention during each show, usually referring to a Hall of Fame player, "That pass was horrible, I mean Brooks Robinson couldn't have caught that." Actually, Brooks Robinson could catch anything.

The word "digital" wasn't associated with radio yet, so we would pay to have our own phone line installed and make our analog broadcast on a long-distance phone call to the WUMD studio. If we had dependable staff members running the mixer, our programs were listened to by five, maybe eight, students. However, twice during the same broadcast, the guy at the sound board chatted with us during a commercial break and then hung up the phone. This meant we reported an entire basketball game for the creepy dude with the tool belt who was waiting to uninstall our analog phone line.

Working sports at the radio station was a blessing in disguise, as I met two people who would remain instrumental in my life for years and years and that was even after I took out credit cards in their names. One was the station manager, Shari Elliker and the other was Chris Strong. Chris and I actually met outside the radio station. We were taking a television production class which didn't start until 7 p.m. It was the second day of the semester and I had been going to classes since 9 a.m. I was feeling tired, hungry and slaphappy all at the same time. I was the first one to show up at the studio and found all the chairs in a circle, so I grabbed one with a view of the door and sat down.

As the other students began to stagger in, they all looked uninteresting and boring to me. You know that game you play when you are eyeing people up coming down the aisle of an airplane? That one looks crazy, that one looks stuck up, that one looks like a brainiac and that one was way too old to be in college. Other than describing the cast of "The Breakfast Club," that was my television production class until Chris walked in and sat on the other side of the circle. The class already had the makeup of a five-star emergency therapy session and he just looked like someone I would hang out with, so I decided to introduce myself. Since he was on the other side of the room, I did the only thing a mature college junior could do and fired a spitball at him. I immediately cracked up as the spitball stuck to his glasses. He pulled them off his shocked face, looked at me and mouthed, "What the hell is your problem?" When he finally started laughing, I knew we would be friends forever. Jump ahead 20 years and you'll see him holding my daughter during her baptism while becoming her godfather.

Chris and I immediately hit it off because we were both temporarily not liking our mothers. You'll have to read his book for that story. Shari and I bonded because she was the funniest woman I have ever met. Five minutes after we were introduced, I hired her to speak at my funeral. She knew absolutely nothing about baseball and never even saw a game, but judged every player by how good they looked in their uniform. For the record, she thought I displayed Hall of Fame pants.

In my junior year, I caught every inning of every game. What made that more of a feat for me, was I caught the last few games with a broken finger on my throwing hand. It didn't happen at a baseball

169

practice or game, but during a live basketball broadcast from Morgan State College. They didn't have a broadcast booth for us to use, so they perched a 6-foot folding table at the top of the bleachers. It looked rather sketchy as the front legs were propped up by phone books or some other nonsense to reach the next step down. When I inquired about the violation of OSHA regulations, I was assured by the home crew, other radio broadcasters used this same set up. Looking back, I see we participated in the first episode of "America's Funniest Home Videos."

We were in the third quarter dribbling on about dribbling when I felt the table start to move forward. While talking and holding the other team's roster in my left hand, I looked under the table to see one of the legs hanging in midair. Apparently, we had been slowly pushing the table forward and now it was in danger of going over.

I stood and leaned forward to grab the table and pull it back but my momentum, and the fact that my headphones were plugged into the mixer, took me and the table on a roller-coaster ride down an entire section. The noise was pretty spectacular and I think I might have broken several FCC regulations regarding expletives, as I was still on the air during my gymnastic routine. I stood up, with the help of the elderly gentleman I landed on, and glanced up the 30 rows at a bewildered Rick, who was still wearing his headphones and holding the plug in an outstretched hand. I shook off my embarrassment and while high-fiving some laughing patrons, felt my finger throbbing. Glancing down, its angle told me it was broken and I knew if I didn't get my high school ring off immediately it would have to be cut off later and I would never play quarters again. The swelling was immediate, so I pulled my ring off as gently as possible, which I don't remember because I almost blacked out. A trip to St. Agnes Hospital confirmed my suspicion, my finger was broken as well as my dignity and the promise I made to my girlfriend about being careful.

The next day we played a baseball game at Millersville University and I wasn't sure how to tell the coach two of the fingers on my throwing hand were taped together. When I finally did, he was pretty cool about it and just told me not to try to throw anyone out. That lasted one whole inning. In the bottom of the second, the first batter walked and took off on the next pitch. Without thinking, I just coiled and threw a pea to second. It was a natural reaction by now and I couldn't stop myself if I tried. I normally didn't hold a baseball with my ring finger, but it kind of rested on the side of it. With it taped to my pinkie it wouldn't bend so I had to grip the ball differently and it helped in my release as the runner was out by two steps. I had a great year behind the plate and threw out 17 of 21 runners (not that I was keeping track on a handwritten chart I made with a slide rule and my grandfather's graphing pencil that was taped to the corner of my bookshelf or anything).

I had a great day at the plate too. I launched a home run to deep left center that plugged in the side of the hill surrounding the field. It never moved after it landed. There were no fans out there and it took two innings before someone casually walked out there to retrieve it. I looked at it several times during the game and remember thinking it reminded me of a random golf ball one might see in an unreachable place. When the year ended, Coach Jancuska thanked me for walking into his office, saying I was a blessing in disguise. He also said I had harbor breath.

The German General

I became good friends with freshmen Vince Bucci and John Kaulius and played baseball with them for the better part of five years. Vince was a pitcher and John held down the hot corner. They were a few years younger so of course they looked up to me. Yeah, right, only if I was standing on a ladder. We laughed a lot and spent quality time together off the field. One afternoon, after I drove him home, John beat me in three straight games of Stratego at his kitchen table. I was super-impressed with his battlefield tactics, until I learned he had marked the back of my flag. He knew exactly where it was every time. I can still see him laughing, tricky bastard.

Once after working for 10 hours, I arrived at Vince's house in the middle of a Saturday night party. As I walked through the front door of his split-level, the party stopped like a sheriff had just entered the saloon. Everyone paused what they were doing and stared at me until Vince said, "Hey everybody this is Neil Beller, he is funny as shit!" Talk about being put on the spot. Now the first thing that exits my mouth needs to bring the house down so I quickly uttered, "That's what my therapist thinks."

Vince and I had an interesting relationship, because he was very headstrong with calling his pitches. He shook me off all the time. What he didn't realize was sometimes Coach Jancuska called pitches from the dugout. He set up a verbal system, which meant I not only had to pay attention to the game, the pitcher, and the runners, but I needed to listen for verbal cues. If he wanted a curveball, he would yell a sentence which started with the letter "C." "C'mon guys let's get an out," meant curveball. I had been calling games for years and years and he was the first and only coach who took that job from me. I have to admit he removed some accountability which made me feel less of a catcher, and I started catching without pitch thinking.

We had lots of verbal cues at UMBC and my favorites were for pickoffs. There was only one thing that pumped up a defensive catcher more than throwing out a runner and that was picking one off. When there were runners on first and third, catchers were on full alert because all kinds of things could happen. Double steals, delayed steals and running halfway to draw a throw, are just some of the tricky moves performed by base runners. To deal with such solid gold dancing, we had a series of verbal commands and we would announce them to the other team just to get in their heads. We even had three codes for each scenario in case we wanted to put the same play on again. As a catcher, I had three options for a first and third situation, so if I wanted to throw straight through to second base, I would walk out in front of home plate and announce to the field, "Two, two, two!"

That number had meaning to our team but caused the other team to look at each other for clarity. "Two" meant I was attempting to throw the runner out at second. If I yelled "One!" that meant the shortstop would cut the ball off and throw home to get the runner breaking from third. If I yelled "Three!" I would go through the motions of throwing the ball to second before shooting it to third hoping to catch the runner off guard. To add more confusion, when yelling I would touch my hand to my chest or rub my leg or both. These hand signals meant nothing at all, but made me feel devious.

I also did that for regular pitches. With a runner on second, they could see the signals I was giving the pitcher, so we would counter with a different sequence. Normally, I would give three signals and the pitcher would take the middle one. When that caught on, I would still give three signals, but give the pitcher an indicator about which signal to take. For example, if I touched the inside of my left thigh, it would be the first signal and the inside of my right thigh meant the third signal. When all that failed, I would place my mitt on my knee for a fastball, and next to me on the ground for a curve, all the while flashing a litany of finger signals which the pitcher ignored. Current day catchers have pretty colored fingernails for the pitcher to see and there was always texting.

The codes for picking runners off of first were "early" or "right," for second were "middle" or "center," and for third were "left" and "late." If I stood and talked to the pitcher as I threw the ball back saying, "C'mon Vince it's getting late," the third baseman could expect a throw from me following the next pitch. If I said, "Don't worry it's still early," I was throwing to first and "Let's go now, right down the middle!" meant second base. These plays worked to perfection and we were always picking off runners. I loved firing the ball to Kaulius because he played off the bag on purpose so the runner would get a bigger lead. He tagged out everybody and he did it with sound effects like Emeril Lagasse, "Bam!" These pickoff moves worked so well I used them on other teams for the next 20 years.

Once during an Orioles game with amazing seats, I could actually hear Cal Ripken talking to other payers as they put on plays. When the stadium became too noisy to talk, they would just open their mouth wide while hiding their gestures from the other team with their gloves. This determined who covered second base on the throw from the pitcher. I was very much in the know, but my girlfriend kept asking me why they were yawning.

We were playing a game at Widener University and had the opportunity beforehand to walk through their field house lobby. A tribute to Billy "White Shoes" Johnson caught my eye. He was one of the first NFL players to do an end zone dance. Nobody in baseball dances during a celebration. They just mob the hero player and jump up and down in place looking like a bunch of pogo sticks. A few innings later, I was wondering if Billy had ever pogo-sticked around home plate, when Vince called me to the mound. He had been shaking me off, but I kept giving him the same pitch. He wanted to throw more changeups but the coach wanted the heater. I told him I wasn't calling the game and he pleaded with me to ask the coach. We were just about arguing on the mound, so when the umpire came out, I walked away telling him to throw what I gave him.

The shaking off and mound visits continued until the coach wanted to know what the hell was going on. I walked a few steps toward the dugout and told him, "Vince wants to throw some more changeups." His reaction was less than understanding as he told me, in an Earl Weaver-type way, to get my ass behind the plate and tell Vince to shut up. Needless to say, I was pissed and the next time Vince shook me off I flipped him the bird. Aw, the love of battery mates.

My junior year we ended up with a 17-10 record. Only a handful of players moved on, so I knew our team would be powerful my senior year. That was going to be my last shot at getting signed so I traveled to a few major league try-out camps to show off my wares. One of the first things I noticed was that I was short. At 5' 10.5" I never thought I was vertically challenged but some of these other players were giants. I mean Wee Willie Keeler was only 5' 4", but he had the speed of a Greek god. I was anything but fast, and the only Greek god I resembled was the one who invented yogurt. At every camp I attended I scored better than most in the "pop to pop" time. That was the time between when the ball pops the catcher's mitt to the pop of the second baseman's glove. I consistently scored under two seconds, which was considered major league worthy. Now if I could only hit and hit with power, call every game perfectly and not flip off my pitchers I might have a chance for a major league career.

My baseball experiences continued to grow as I started another summer season. I was playing for the Andover Athletic Club and some of my favorite ghosts of baseball past joined along. Kevin Wilkins, Dan Fielder as well as Vince and John all joined in making sure my summer was filled with hilarity and international intrigue. The intrigue was delivered courtesy of the Korean All-Stars. They were a team of outstanding players who were touring America playing semi-pro teams all over the country. Somehow, we ended up on their schedule. Watching them take infield was quite impressive and reminded me of the Harlem Globetrotters when Meadowlark Lemon was passing under the basket. They were methodical and flawless and communicated with short bursts of verbal enthusiasm. It was clear from the get-go they didn't speak English because, well, they were Korean. They regenerated us and as someone mentioned on the bench, "It felt like the Olympics."

Hoping to show them the agony of defeat because we were representing the greater Glen Burnie region, we took the game seriously from the start. Vince was pitching and after getting the first two batters to ground out on fastballs, he decided to shake me off. Don't be afraid to ruin the flow, shit! I gave him the heater but he wanted to throw a curve. After going around a few times I gave up and let him throw his curve. He set his weight, lifted his leg and reared back to snap off his curveball. The only problem was it didn't snap and he drilled the right-handed batter on his elbow. It plucked the funny bone pretty solid and the batter jumped straight up in the air in pain and hopped all the way to first base holding his arm and uttering Korean expletives. One thing was pretty clear, pain was evident in any language, it was universal!

One of the unwritten rules of baseball was to never show pain. If you happened to be plucked by the pitcher, you were required to cease all your nerve endings from operating and your tear ducts from flowing. Most important was whatever you did, never rub it. That would give some credence to the pitcher's ability to be in charge. It didn't matter if blood was flowing from an open wound, we were taught at a very early age to suck it up and simply walk or jog to first base with a smile. It just so happened they didn't teach that lesson in Korea.

A few innings later, we were winning the game and it was visibly apparent they were not happy about it. They started tagging a little harder and running a little faster, but we just upped our game too until the "incident." I named it the "incident" because I am certain it created a black cloud over our two countries' international diplomacy. In remarkable fashion, and against most Vegas odds, history repeated itself. Vince shook me off before he drilled the same batter with the same pitch in the same elbow. As soon as he was plucked, I stood and walked towards the ball while shaking my head as the batter released a verbal assault towards the mound. Vince stood there unaffected and almost clueless as the batter continued his barrage until he picked up his bat and charged the mound. I immediately raced after him and could see Vince wide-eyed as he backpedaled. When the charger raised his bat above his head, Vince took off towards center field like a lion was chasing him. I started chuckling as I landed a giant bear hug on the pissed-off batter. I held him until his non-English speaking coach hustled out to intervene. He was yelling and pointing at Vince as well.

It happened so fast nobody on the field hardly moved. When I let him go, he was still uttering and emphasizing certain words, which obviously had "death to the pitcher" meaning, and walked over to first base. Dan went to the outfield to retrieve Vince and escort him back to the mound, as he was visibly shaken. I tossed the bat towards their standing team and made my way back towards home. The shocked umpire walked past me cackling and gestured towards the batter. I turned around to see him standing on first base which is the normal protocol after getting hit by a pitch, however, this wasn't normal.

The umpire was shaking his head while saying, "No, you are done," and pointing towards the bench. The batter had no understanding and kept pointing to his elbow and jabbering. His coach continued arguing as well but the umpire wouldn't budge and insisted the batter was out of the game for charging the mound with the bat. In an instant, we were smack in the middle of a Sid Caesar skit. The batter sprinted over to the umpire and in the most hilarious way was screaming in full Korean as he pointed to his elbow. What made it funny was he kept interjecting the English phrase of, "Two fucking times! Two fucking times!" I was immediately reminded of "The Show of Show's" skit "The German

General," where Sid Caesar was being dressed by Howard Morris like he was preparing for battle. They were uttering all kinds of German language until the very end. Google it, you will laugh.

I experienced the same flashback a few years later when I was editing for the World Wrestling Federation. When we had a completed show, we would play it back and record it again with a different announcer who spoke another language. Professional wrestling was huge in other countries so we made new shows in French, Spanish, German, even Arabic. We had no idea what they were saying, but occasionally a wrestler's name would be inserted like, "On dirait qu'il vient d'épingler Junk Yard Dog!"

So, this Korean player couldn't fathom that he was out of the game. Afterwards we laughed at the "incident" and for the rest of the year this could be heard from our dugout. "Was that dude just hit by the pitch?"

"Yeah."

"Huh?"

"Yeah."

"Huh?"

"Two fucking times!"

Osterizer

The "incident" wasn't the only time complete nonsense was yelled on a baseball diamond. My senior year at UMBC was super-exciting as I shared team captain honors with Dr. Strange Glove. Tim and I successfully took on the roles of good cop and bad cop, with me being the former. It was my last shot at getting noticed and possibly move on to the next stage of my baseball career and I didn't want to tarnish any chance I might have. Tim on the other hand was a realist and decided to just have fun. The team started the season with a southern road trip to play such schools as Norfolk State, Randolph-Macon and various others. It was exciting to jam everyone in Retriever vans and drive south for the spring. It was cold in Maryland so the thought of warmer spring weather had us all jacked up, too much actually.

We arrived at Norfolk State, ate some chili mac in their dining hall and the whole team retired to Gomer Pyle-style sleeping quarters. The entire room was filled with rows and rows of bunk beds and everybody picked their favorite. I think the place used to be a military establishment and I'm sure the cinder-block walls and concrete floor had seen their share of mischief. Coach Jancuska and Assistant Coach Jeff Usilton went off to sleep in a hotel and left Tim and me in charge. As soon as they left, the whole place turned into a giant slumber party. People running around like small children, baseballs were airborne, a pepper game was going on in the corner and John Kaulius was shooting bottle rockets off from one end of the room to the other. I'm not even kidding! One of them hit Dennis Ward right in the chest and set his blanket on fire. Pitcher's John Smith and Brian Butler were standing behind a support column like snipers taking cover between shots. I finally had to go from the good cop to the bad cop and started yelling. Tim immediately took a line from "Animal House" and coordinated a "road trip." A contingency of players followed suit and before you could say "Fat, drunk and stupid is no way to go through life, son," half the team departed.

Most of the freshmen stayed behind so we all hung out, sang "Kumbaya" and turned in before midnight. A few hours later, I was abruptly awakened as a loud and disruptive party train entered the concrete bunker. Tim and his band of very merry men were back and they were not alone. At one of the college parties they crashed, they found the Norfolk baseball team we were scheduled to play at 9 a.m., and brought them back to the bunkhouse. They were all smashed and I quickly learned talking any kind of sense into them was futile. Tim disappeared immediately leaving me with the extremely rowdy bunch only to return wearing nothing but a jockstrap.

When he walked out of the bathroom, our baseball counterparts lost it and were physically rolling on the floor in hysterics. The look on the faces of our freshmen was priceless and when Tim climbed on one of the 8-foot tables to perform a sing-along he ad-libbed, I had all but given up. I have to admit, seeing him march around wearing only a jockstrap was one of the funniest things I had seen in a long time and before I knew it, I was repeating his refrains with everyone else. The only thing that squelched the party were the blinking red and blue police lights outside the dorm windows. Don't be afraid to instantly clear out a room, shit!

Needless to say, the next morning Coach Jancuska was livid and Tim decided to get out of his interrogation by vigorously brushing his teeth for 15 solid minutes. After the coach stormed out, all Tim remembered about the beat down we received was that I kept saying, "I stayed inside with all the freshmen, coach." There was no way I was going to take full responsibility for the mass escape, the alcohol purchase and the hole burned in Dennis's blanket. It didn't matter as we were grounded for the rest of the trip.

To make matters worse, we ended up at Randolph-Macon on St. Patrick's Day, which would have been an excellent time to escape, but no one dared as our bridge had been burned. I could see the distress on the faces of team members as we ate chili mac in their dining hall. There were beautiful coeds everywhere and all my teammates could do was wave and smile. One group of women walked over to the table and invited us to a St. Patrick's Day party. I could swear I saw some guys tear up as the coach intervened and shooed them away. Life can be cruel, and I think about that every time I eat chili mac.

As the season progressed, we went on a winning tear and there was talk of qualifying for the NCAA tournament. That was my dream anyway, as it would top the JUCO World Series. I still had a glint of hope of being discovered and experiencing life in the minor leagues so I played out of my mind.

Each game was exciting, and Coach Jancuska made it that way because he was all about chatter. About 50 times a game he would engage the dugout from the third base coach's box by yelling, "C'mon let's get involved, let me hear some chatter!" For the next few minutes, you would hear teammates yelling, "Let's go!" "You've got this Bobby!" "Base hit Bobby!" and other similar stuff before slowly dying down. The coach would yell at us again and the enthusiasm would ramp up and then down the whole game. Between innings he would converse with me about "my guys," which was his way of reminding me I was their captain and needed to fire these guys up.

When I finally reached my threshold of exuberance, I realized it wasn't enough and called a dugout meeting. I explained in production class I learned how extras in a movie scene would say "peas and carrots" over and over and that it created the perfect background noise. I told the guys it didn't matter what we yelled, but we had to yell something and needed to pick a topic. They didn't understand so I decided to demonstrate and picked kitchen appliances. Their stunned looks took to laughter as I turned towards the batter's box and started clapping my hands as I yelled, in a very fast manner, a litany of nonsense. "Hey now blender baby, hit a toaster oven, dishwasher, dishwasher, c'mon coffee pot, Osterizer, Osterizer!" I really got into it and when the coach turned towards me and yelled, "Good chatter, good chatter," the rest of the team joined in. I doubt anybody in ear shot understood a thing they heard, but it fired up the coach and the batter ripped a double. To this day at Camden Yards, if I am in attendance, you will occasionally hear random appliances being yelled from the nether regions of the bleachers.

We ended our season 23-8 on a Friday and the coach assured us he was going to call everybody and their brother to get us in the tournament. The weekend felt like it was a year-long and I thought any minute the coach would call with the good news, but the phone never rang. I learned on Monday, we didn't receive a bid, the season was over. I left my fourth year of college baseball with the knowledge that I had done absolutely everything I could to further my major league dream. I played my very best, I occasionally hit the ball to right field, I threw out almost everybody, I even yelled Osterizer with extreme enthusiasm but my college baseball career ended on a sad note.

My depression lasted a few weeks until summer ball started. I had been pretty irritable and hoped hanging with old friends and playing baseball would cheer me up. We were scheduled to play a game in Crofton, Maryland which happened to be the hometown of Chris Strong. He thought it was a great idea to attend the game and packed a picnic basket and along with his father, decided to make it a long afternoon adventure. When the umpire showed up, I knew it was going to be a long game because we had history. Previously, we had disagreed on whether or not the black trim was a part of home plate, and if I was allowed to move before the pitcher threw during an intentional walk.

An intentional walk was something which was never practiced and I seriously never even thought about it happening until it did. I was 14 years old when the coach called my name and said, "Put him on." He was referring to the batter and wanted us to intentionally walk him. I had seen it done on television but never done it myself. I stood and held my throwing arm straight out to the side. The pitcher went through his motion and then launched the ball about 25 feet outside. I couldn't have caught that ball with a crab net. The runner on second came all the way around and scored as it was an intentional walk RBI disaster.

I learned most pitchers needed a target to throw to. To point to an imaginary spot in foul territory and then hope I and the ball both arrived there at the same time was not a proven method. To help the pitcher, and my sanity, I would stand, point, and then while he was in his motion, jump out a few steps so he could throw to me. It had worked for years until this umpire told me I couldn't move until the ball was thrown. He was right of course, but it really didn't matter or so I thought. In the course of my college career, three different pitchers threw the ball over my head or too far outside to catch, therefore, the runners moved up and eliminated the thought of a double play. In 2019, the major leagues changed the rule and now they do not have to pitch to the batter, he just immediately takes first base. I understand it speeds up the game, in theory, but it took away the chance of an errant throw. In any event, this umpire and I had danced before.

Chris and his dad hadn't shown up before the game started, so we had no interaction. We batted first and went three up, three down very unceremoniously, so I put on my mask and headed out to the field. I saw Chris and his dad walking down the hill and I was looking forward to meeting "Big Dan" after the game. Life had been shitty for a few weeks and I knew they would cheer me up. I squatted and gave the pitcher one finger which meant fastball. When he threw it, I didn't even move my mitt and the ball hit it squarely. I was about to throw the ball back when I heard the umpire yell, "Ball!" Ball? That pitch was right over the plate, what was he looking at?

Now, there was an unwritten rule that catchers can jaw with an umpire all game as long as they don't turn around and show them up.

On many occasions I have let them know what I thought about a call and even reminded them they now owe us one. There was a lot of give-and-take behind the plate. I have had umpires tell me they missed that one and would sometimes make it up later. It was hard to be an umpire but this was the first pitch of our game and it was perfect. I was disgusted so without turning around I decided to let him know my true feelings and uttered, "Ball? You're crazy!" He must have been waiting for my retort because immediately and with great fanfare he pulled off his mask, pointed off the field and yelled "You're gone!" He threw me out of the game after one pitch! I stood up turned around and ripped off my mask to unleash my verbal assault when over his shoulder I saw Big Dan with his extended arms holding an outstretched picnic blanket in midair. Here they had planned on spending the whole afternoon in the relaxed atmosphere of a baseball game and I had been ejected before they had even sat down. How embarrassing.

I felt like I had to make my displeasure even more memorable so I channeled Billy Martin and continued to argue. He not only threw me out of the game, he threw me off the field and then out of the parking lot. The parking lot! I apologized to my team about the same time Chris apologized to his father. They folded their blanket, picked up their picnic basket and invited me back to their house for a mood-swinging elixir. Big Dan was very understanding and not upset about our first encounter. He was a tremendous bartender and we became fast friends. He did ask me if I suffered from premature ejection. He thought that to be hilarious, so I almost had to shoot him in the face with a spitball. The fruit doesn't fall far from the Strong tree.

Later that night, while in the midst of a long shift at Bob's, I had some visitors. One of the waitresses came into the kitchen to tell me that a table of rowdy people had asked to see me. I walked out and found some very intoxicated teammates and their girlfriends ordering their 2 a.m. breakfast. Their vocal leader was Vince and they were still laughing about my early exit from the game. He went out of his way to tell me he was ordering pancakes and to "fix him up!" I wasn't sure what that meant, so I just assured him he was going to be taken care of and headed back to the kitchen.

Along the way, I wished I had my bottle of DMSO or some ex-lax to mix in the pancake batter. Those thoughts and the possible associated jail time had me take another route. I made the batter very thick and stacked up four huge pancakes. They were at least 3 inches high, so I removed the top pancake and carved a big hole in the remaining ones. As carefully as I could, I jammed all kinds of things in there like hamburgers, fries, onion rings, shredded cheese and some sliced tomatoes. I placed the remaining pancake on top and dropped a scoop of butter on the conglomeration. When the waitress removed the plate, it must have weighed 5 pounds and she almost dropped it. She looked at me in shock and laughed when I motioned for her to continue. A few minutes later I heard cheers and then Vince yelling, "Thanks Ned!"

The Anxious

Due to a major snafu, I lost 16 credits when I transferred in from AACC and had to do an extra semester. I had to have written permission from deans, chancellors and the guy who frequently handed me my parking tickets to take 27 credits my final semester, which was a bear. In order to accomplish such a course load, I needed to take internships, complete a ton of classes, sell my body for science, buy lunch for all my advisors and vacuum the cars of the administration staff. Since I was a commuter, I slept on the kitchen floor of a friend's apartment because their refrigerator made a great humming sound. This was the genesis to my constant need for white noise in order to sleep.

I survived a very long semester with a 3.25 grade point average and graduated in December with a BA in Television Production/Audio Media. I didn't walk the stage, but took an elevator to the 11th floor of the Admin. Building and received my diploma via a secretary who pulled it from a filing cabinet. Although my four-and-a-half-year college experience was super-anti-climactic, I was humming "Pomp and Circumstance" at the time, and then I drove home and slept for five straight weeks in front of my grandparent's refrigerator.

The extra semester didn't hinder me too much and was actually aided by the World Series run made by my Orioles against the Phillies. I, like thousands of others, was sitting in the stands a year earlier when the Orioles lost the last game of the season to Robin Yount and the Milwaukee Brewers. It was a heartbreaking end to the season and Earl

Weaver's last game as a manager until he came out of retirement a few years later.

For the series, his replacement, Joe Altobelli was victorious in five games. It was their third World Series in a row against a team from Pennsylvania and the third time was the charm. Eddie Murray and Cal Ripken Jr. were voted No. 1 and No. 2 in league MVPs with Jr. winning by a small margin. Great years were had by Ken Singleton, Mike Flanagan, Scott McGregor, Mike Boddicker, Storm Davis and Tippy Martinez, but it was a catcher, Rick Dempsey, who won the World Series MVP. He was definitely a favorite of mine and people compared me to him, not for his catching ability but for his sense of humor. Everyone remembers his rain delay antics, but I learned years later he was an amazing storyteller.

Since major league baseball wasn't in my future as a player, I continued to work, got married to Carole and together we purchased the house I grew up in, because being in debt was the grown-up thing to do. The day we moved into the house from our apartment was an interesting day. I don't like to pack or unpack, so I pulled all the drawers out of my dresser, still full of clothes, and set them on the brick wall out front. I went back inside for five minutes and returned to find two ladies rifling through my underwear drawer. They were driving by, saw the clothes and thought it was a yard sale, so I sold them six pairs of Hanes briefs and loaded up the car. In my fantasy world, moving into my childhood home meant teaching my children baseball in the same yard my father taught me. That proved to indeed be a fantasy and fell to the wayside with other fantasies such as fat-free food, marrying Dorothy Hamill and the service warranties associated with electronic devices.

Years of work-related softball games became the norm and I quickly learned my level of competition left me frustrated with novices. My job at a television production company connected me again with childhood baseball friend Tom Taylor. Although he was too mature to call "swipes" after a haircut, he understood we were playing with accountants, sales reps and various office personnel who have never played the game at our level and needed to be nurtured. I, on the other hand, was barking suggestions from the bench like they were veteran players. Baseball vernacular was lost as I yelled, "Hey Jason take the next pitch." The count was 3-0 and we had two runners on base with a power hitter on deck. To my chagrin, Jason swung at the next pitch and grounded to the pitcher. I immediately realized my mistake in thinking Jason knew what the word, "take" meant. He thought he was supposed to "take" a swing at the next pitch. To the laughter of both teams, I explained to him, "Taking a pitch was like taking a shit, you let it go." He immediately understood.

Work leagues saw sides of people that didn't exist in work life. While I was an electrician's helper and playing in a work league, I saw my brother-in-law flip out on an umpire and throw the game ball about 500 feet in frustration. His anger left him embarrassed, but left me wishing I had started him in the outfield, I mean what an arm! During a television production softball game, a fight broke out at home plate which had former interns, who now worked for the other team, kicking our downed cameraman like a scene from "Children of the Corn." There were enjoyable moments as well, like when we played the Babe Ruth Museum and everybody on the team wore the No. 3. These games were fun, but I missed and needed the competition.

Personal and professional changes happened at the same time as I took a job at WJZ television while in the midst of a divorce. The transition also moved me from softball back to baseball with a new league and a brand-new team. Chris Manouse was a few years behind me at Parkville and together we launched a new team whose home field was Overlea High School in Rosedale. Since we were very anxious to get started, we decided a perfect name for our team was The Overlea Anxious. We were sponsored by Della Roses, which was a bar/ restaurant on Belair road, where we frequently gathered anyway. I think one of our players, Nick Santoro, was a squatter in the basement. He was another baseball maniac, who immediately after a game at

Memorial Stadium, dressed up in the sweat saturated, Oriole bird outfit, to propose to his girlfriend, who was the Oriole ball girl at the time. Surprisingly, she said yes, and he was forced to find a proper residence.

The team was made up of local players, many of whom crossed paths with each other years earlier. The Lott brothers were present as well as some other familiar faces, however two of the staples were Ray Lawder and Carl Hucke. Ray was a premium hitter and a standout at third base while Carl was a power hitting outfielder. Remember how as a kid you would swing three or four bats at the same time in the on-deck circle? Carl would swing the whole bag. As a matter of fact, he didn't warm up with a bat at all, but swung a steel pole. I couldn't lift it with one arm, however he used it with such proficiency he had rust stains on his uniform where it rested on his shoulders.

Upon investigation, I learned he worked as a mason and carried around cinder blocks all day. My guess was that he ripped the pole off a passing semi or was awarded it from a superhero after an altercation. His shoulders were so large there was no way a pocketbook strap could ever live there. Not that he would ever carry a pocketbook, but had he been so inclined he would have done so without objection. Ray and Carl were also a vaudeville act, and would constantly entertain, sometimes in the middle of the game. I will never forget Ray getting on one knee in the third base coach's box before bellowing out "Too-Ra-Loo-Ra-Loo-Ral" at the top of his lungs. The other team didn't know what to think, neither did the umpires. I just sat on the bench and laughed myself silly as some fans actually joined in.

Manouse was always smiling and it was very easy to see that he enjoyed the game. The only time he didn't smile was when he was pitching. He completely changed character and went from a fun-loving guy to a demonic menace. He pulled his hat down to shade his eyes and glared in for my signals with extreme prejudice. He even made me uncomfortable and I was his catcher. We used to play a single game, Saturday evenings, followed by doubleheaders Sunday mornings. Uniforms weren't washed between games so Sunday mornings we were pretty disgusting. Unbathed and over saturated with alcohol, most of us weren't even functioning properly. The majority of the team was hung over, but as Ray liked to point out, some guys on the team were Neanderthals and hadn't yet mastered walking upright. He used to grab their hands to see if they obtained bloody knuckles from dragging them across the ground. Their manners were nonexistent as they would belch and fart unconditionally and with girlfriends sitting feet away in lawn chairs. We were not all fast friends which made me wonder if the 1927 Yankees, who are considered one of the greatest baseball teams ever assembled although they hated each other, had any bloody-knuckled farting Neanderthals in their dugout.

Early in the season, Chris made an announcement that we would be receiving a sponsor check from Della Rose's and that it might be a nice idea to patronize them after the game. The check was going to be a big one because it costs a lot to run a team. Uniforms, league fees, umpires, everything costs money. Baseballs were ten bucks a piece, so we needed monetary help and a bar was the perfect sponsor for us. Anyone in a group understands how unfair the dreaded "group check" can be. This baseball team was the poster child for skirting the check, which made it unfortunate for the first person to order because everything from that point on was in his name. This particular day, everyone's girlfriends showed up and after dinner and many, many rounds of drinks, the bill was over $1,200, so we just signed over the $1,000 check and coughed up another $200. I didn't say we were frugal or money-conscience by any means, just anxious.

One scary Sunday morning, I pulled on my dirty uniform and dragged myself to my car. I lived in a townhome with my sister Karen in Towson while we both worked at WJZ, and I wasn't looking forward to the 20-minute drive to Overlea for the game. When I got in my car, I noticed a white powder all over my dash. Upon further investigation it was everywhere as my steering wheel, seats and carpet were all covered with a white coating. Oh my God what did I do last night? In a panic, I started wiping it off but was just smearing it into cracks and crevices everywhere. If a cop were to pull me over, he would certainly question my cocaine use and lock me up. My thoughts were, I certainly didn't want to miss the game, but more importantly, do I need to contact an intervention counselor? I sat there befuddled trying to remember my actions the previous night. I've never done cocaine in my life so who was I driving around and why was white powder everywhere?

Glancing into the backseat for answers, I noticed an empty box of Dunkin' munchkins and remembered my late-night visit. Me devouring 25 white-powdered munchkins with the windows down came rushing back along with a stomachache, leaving me laughing at the residue in my car. I still might need an intervention. but for donuts instead of cocaine.

We had a stellar team, regardless of the bench smells, and played against Cecil Johnnies for the league championship. They were a powerhouse of a team and only lost two or three games all season. We had to win a double-header to pull off the feat, and prepared for a long day at their home field. They had intimidated the league for years, and had never lost a home double header in their history, which I understood to coincide with the year tube socks were invented. That's a long time.

Right before the game, the son and heir to be owner of Della Rose's walked up to our bench and in a Burgess Meredith voice screamed, "I want you to eat lightning and crap thunder!" Well, now we have to win. The jocularity quickly faded away, and we took the first game with ease as Randy Lott shut the door on them like they were an unwelcomed solicitor peddling used Q-tips. The last play of game one was a ball hit to Ray at third, which he uncharacteristically bobbled. He quickly picked it up and hurried a throw to second where it three-hopped right into an outstretched glove. It was a bang-bang play and too close for comfort but a win nonetheless.

The championship game started out quickly and we scored two runs in the first. Their coach had my number and before Joe Madden perfected the major league shift, he swung the second baseman around and had the third baseman hug the line. All series long, I was being robbed of doubles as the third baseman jumped in front of my line drives. Finally, I listened to Dan Fielder and smacked a base hit through the first base hole. The other coach catcalled me as I stood on first, which just made me want to win more than ever. Rob Ritter was pitching lights out, and that was after he drank a gallon of iced tea between games. Lefthander, Ray Dodson came in and finished the game, ending with a strike out. Our team swarmed the field and we celebrated like the running of the bulls in Pamplona, Spain.

That night at Della Rose's, Chris Manouse brought out the league trophy, which was so big it looked more like a piece of furniture than an award. We partied until the wee hours of the morning, participating in beer slides on the dirty floor, endless team shots and photo ops with all the girlfriends and wives. It felt good to win and that night nobody worried about the check.

Bang the Drum

Early in the fall, my girlfriend Kate and I took a trip to Cooperstown, New York to visit the National Baseball Hall of Fame. They change the displays often and it was such a thrill to go again. She grew up a sports fan and loved baseball, which was just one of the reasons she was a keeper. She could also recite all the collegiate football coaches' names at will, which I found to be sexually exciting. What man doesn't want their significant other to be a lover of sport.

A few months earlier we had flown to Chicago to join Kevin Wilkins and some other friends to watch the Orioles play their last game at Comiskey Park. I remember everything being painted with the same color of dark green, everything. The field was slightly elevated as the first few rows of seats seemed to be below field level. I was really hoping to see the Sox hit a home run so I could witness their exploding scoreboard in person. I kept panning the field hoping to catch a glimpse of a disco record flying through the air or hearing their organist play a forgotten tune or even Harry Caray singing "Take Me Out to the Ball Game," but that was a different team.

Under the stands, the eating establishments and bathrooms were small in size and had me thinking about the small stature of all the previous Americans who had visited. I mean it had opened in 1909, which meant many of baseball's best had walked these same corridors. The history of the game and the greats who played it was almost as exciting to me as playing the game myself. We are all judged by the same statistics, which meant on my best day I would almost be as good as the ghosts who walked the field. Unfortunately, some of those ghosts threw the World Series in 1919 right where I was standing.

Before we left Chicago, we took a picture outside of famous Wrigley Field as well. That one wasn't because of my love for the Chicago Cubs, or to commemorate Babe Ruth pointing out his shot, but for the hilarious scene Henry Gibson played as a disgruntled Illinois Nazi in "The Blues Brothers." We are on a mission from God.

We had a wonderful time in Cooperstown touring famous Doubleday Field, eating lunch at The Short Stop and shopping at all the baseball-themed stores in town. Cooperstown looked just like a Hallmark movie town and was very romantic.

I had been there one other time with my former father-in-law, Howard Flynn. That trip was not romantic, as we spent 10-12 hours a day reading every single plague on every single display. The whole place just reeked of history right down to the bricks of the building and I couldn't get enough. I started a collection of Hall of Fame cards, which I have updated every year since. The collection doesn't just have the greatest major leaguers ever, but umpires, executives and great stars from the Negro Leagues like James "Cool Papa" Bell.

The players' statistics are interesting, but I love the backstories, I mean, Honus Wagner was discovered throwing rocks clear across the Monongahela River. It was an interesting fact indeed, but I still want to know where the hell the name Honus came from. I have read just about every baseball book ever written and have limited shelf space to prove it. I actually have a baseball room in my house and I'm not kidding either as the doorknob to get in is an actual baseball. Baseball books line the shelves along with autographs, various baseball team hats and about 15,000 baseball cards in perfectly organized boxes. One of my college baseball bats is mounted on the wall being used as a hat rack. I used a band saw to slice it long ways down the middle and mounted pegs every six inches to display hats I have worn. Posters and pictures line the walls along with a drawing a friend from Bob's Big Boy, Mike

Hardesty, made for me. It depicts a catcher with many large protruding lumps coming out of his back as he addresses an extremely large pitcher on the pitcher's mound. The caption reads, "Take it easy on the fast balls big guy." I laugh every time I look at it.

One of the shelves is lined with VHS tapes of official MLB World Series highlights. They are original purchased copies therefore I don't need the expressed written permission of Major League Baseball to own them. There are also DVD masters of baseball events and movies. Baseball movies have always had a place in my heart and if I find one when perusing the channels, I will always stop and watch. I get excited, anxious or laugh or cry like the first time I saw them.

When Tom Selleck proves his worth in "Mr. Baseball" with the line, "Last season I led this club in doubles in the month of August," I still chuckle as it reminds me of actual dugout conversations I had with slumping players. When Annie yells, "Hit 'em where they ain't," from "Bull Durham," I hear every mother from every Parkville Rec game I ever played. I tear up when "Field of Dreams" character, Ray Kinsella asks his father's ghost, "Hey Dad, want to have a catch?" By the way, if your tear ducts don't open when you watch that scene, you fail to occupy a soul. Billy Beane stated a fact in "Moneyball" when he uttered, "It's hard not to be romantic about baseball." Brad Pitt nailed that performance and I felt the connection when he said, "I hate losing even more than I wan'na win."

Baltimore had a great baseball connection with "The Natural" as the director, Barry Levinson was born there. The movie is beautifully shot and the breathtaking golden hour scene with Roy Hobbs pitching to The Whammer in front of the parked train, was the prettiest movie scene I have ever witnessed. The setting sun backlit the scene as the two players competed against each other, creating lighting magic for the perfect duel. Baseball movies have everything from the innocence of "The Sandlot," and the comedy of "Major League' to the old school sentiment displayed in "Love of the Game." "Baseball is more than a game to me, it's a religion." -Bill Klem

On a cold Saturday when I was in junior high, I caught a baseball movie I hadn't seen before. Up to that point William Bendix in "The Babe Ruth Story," the original "Angels in the Outfield," and Gary Cooper as Lou Gehrig in "Pride of the Yankees," were the only baseball movies I had watched. "Bang the Drum Slowly" was about a New York Yankee catcher with a terminal illness and the relationship he had with his roommate pitcher. Robert De Niro played the catcher and Michael Moriarty played the pitcher. It was a bit hokey at times but totally gutted me and left me crying. As a catcher, I experienced this movie internally. I loved the pitcher-catcher relationship aspect of roommates and how they took care of each other. I wondered if it would be that way when I made the show. Sadly, I never found out.

While at the hall, I enjoyed researching the ghost players who walked from the Iowa cornfield and upon reliving their contribution to the game, I felt their visit was real. If only I could build such a field and play catch again with my father was an ongoing birthday cake wish I had every year.

My television and editing knowledge had me yearning for a significant change and where else but the mecca for my industry, Hollywood, California. One of my best friends growing up was Greg Hoffman and he was currently making a very nice living as a "key grip" on the left coast. His was one of those professions you saw in the credits right above "best boy" and wondered what the hell they did. He convinced me to move out there with visions of star hobnobbing and life-changing production work as well as perfect baseball weather. The latter sealed the deal, so I put in my notice at work, proposed to my girlfriend and together we prepared to move to lovely Southern California.

Two amazing and life-altering baseball-related events happened one month before we were to drive across the country with all our worldly possessions. The first was the end of an era as the Baltimore Orioles were going to play their last game at Memorial Stadium before moving to their new home, Oriole Park at Camden Yards. I already had a full-access press pass, which enabled me to go anywhere in Memorial

Stadium, including the field, but I wanted to take Kate and watch the game. Enter my all-time favorite Herr's representative, Bill Wilkins.

Bill was Kevin's older brother and he saved my life years earlier. I wrote saved my life, but I meant, he did not take it. Kevin had regaled me with hilarious stories of a raft ride down the Youghiogheny River he took every year with his brother and a bunch of friends. It sounded too good to be true and I wanted in. I pulled my standard Friday all-nighter at Bob's, went home to shower and waited for Kevin to arrive. He picked me up at 6:30 a.m. and we headed to the meeting place, which was Bill's apartment. Bill and his charming wife, LuAnn, lived in an apartment complex off of Route 100 and upon arrival Kevin parked in the lot behind the complex. A few parking spots away sat a huge delivery truck with "Herr's" blasted on the side. Bill was a delivery man for the snack company and well on his way to the management position he would obtain a few years later.

It was dawn when we arrived and as we neared the sliding rear entrance to Bill's apartment, Kevin turned to go back to his car for something hc forgot. He instructed me to continue on and go inside and even though I hadn't slept in 24 hours and had no idea where I was going, I listened. I opened the slider and reached in to move the curtain out of my way when the most obnoxious and loud sounding barrage of tumbling aluminum I ever heard, echoed through the early morning air. I stepped back to glance at Kevin, whose face resembled a child about to be punished, when someone angrily bellowed from inside, "What the hell is going on?" The curtain whipped open and there stood the biggest and angriest man I have ever seen at 6:52 in the morning. It was Bill.

"Who are you?" jumped out of his mouth and before I could answer an even bigger man, named Ed Jefferson, stepped into view from behind him, "Do you want me to end him, Bill?" For a brief moment I thought I had stuffed my last hamburger into a stack of pancakes when Kevin stepped in front of me, "He's with me, this is Neil!"

The two professional wrestlers stared me down before heading back in the apartment as Kevin told me not to worry while simultaneously asking me if I brought an extra pair of underwear. It turns out that Bill and Ed and several others inside had spent the entire night emptying and building a massive pyramid of beer cans in front of the curtain covering the sliding door. With one swipe I had knocked the whole thing over making them angry, waking Bill's wife and alerting the neighbors that Bill had lied when he told them, "You won't hear a peep from us." I sincerely hoped the theory of "first impressions matter" was in fact a bold-faced lie.

As it happened, Bill was one of the two nicest men I had ever met with Ed being the other one. These guys opened their homes and arms to me on many occasions and I have been enamored with their friendship and sincerity ever since. For the record, the Youghiogheny River trip was one of, if not the, most hilarious excursions I ever encountered. The actual raft ride was group-run and many of the other participants were families, on their vacations. Forty-eight hours of non-stop laughter with the craziest 35 strangers I had ever met, ruined those vacations. Acts of courage, feats of stupidity, and volumes of obscene actions are forever locked away in the vaults of the participants. Conveying them at this time would not be prudent, however, if you find me later in life with a cold beverage, I might be coerced to expound on such indecency and totally make your evening.

I mentioned Bill worked for Herr's and due to their heavy Orioles' sponsorship, he obtained four box seats to the Oriole's last home game at Memorial Stadium. There had been rumors around the sports department of the TV station that a "not to be missed" festivity was going to take place on the field after the game. With kindness in their hearts, Bill and LuAnn invited Kate and I to attend with them. I was beside myself with excitement. Kate's family had scheduled an engagement party later that evening, so I knew it was going to be a very memorable day. I advised her to not mention we were going to the game to her family in case we were running late.

The stadium was as electric as I had ever seen it. The game itself was uneventful as the Orioles lost 7-1 to the Detroit Tigers. Most fans were there for the post-game experience which started ramping up when Mike Flanagan came out of the bullpen to throw the last Orioles pitch ever at Memorial Stadium. As he walked to the mound, I started remembering every game I had ever seen there. The nostalgic feeling had tears in my eyes already.

Prior to the game, I walked down to the bottom of the section, showed the usher my press pass and walked on to the field. As you can imagine everything looked different from field level. I checked out some batting practice from behind the screen, had pictures taken with some of the players, sat in the dugout and even walked the runway back to the clubhouse. I was reliving my youth and dreams with every step. By the time I sat down in my seat to have a beer, my senses were already at a heightened capacity. Oh, and I have no idea how that catcher's helmet ended up in my procession.

When the ceremonies began, each event had the stadium cheering and clapping thinking there was nothing else in store. We couldn't have been more mistaken. With nobody on the field, Frank Robinson ran from the dugout to third base and waved to the crowd. He then jogged down the line and touched home plate for the very last time. I couldn't even imagine what was running through his head. He became an Oriole in the most lopsided trade in baseball history and ended his career in the Hall of Fame. A limo came out of the right field gate and drove on the field all the way to home plate. The grounds crew departed the ride, in full white with orange-trimmed tuxedos, and dug up home plate before driving away with it all the way to Camden Yards where Baltimore native, Jim McKay, hosted a brief ceremony on live video where it was installed in its now location.

For what seemed like an eternity nothing happened until music started playing from the movie "Field of Dreams." The stadium reverberated with the intense and nostalgic voice of James Earl Jones as he explained to Ray, "People will come, Ray." The words he spoke scrolled up the scoreboard until he finished with, "This field, this game: it's a part of our past, Ray. It reminds of us of all that once was good and it could be again. Oh... people will come Ray. People will most definitely come." The music crescendoed as Brooks Robinson ran right out of the past to his position at third base. You could see he was emotional as he kicked the dirt like he used to do while gazing towards the empty batter's box. I imagined he thought, "Just one more grounder." He absorbed the lasting cheers until Frank Robinson ran out to his position at right, then Jim Palmer, and Boog Powell. They all stood at their positions in period uniforms reliving their own youth on the field that witnessed them shine.

Like a never-ending-time machine, players ran from the dugout to the position they played and as each one touched the field, fathers in the crowd were pointing to them while leaning down and regaling their children about the heroes they didn't know. Tears were streaming down my face and Bill was as stoic as I had ever seen him. In the middle of it all, I thought about how my father took me to my first game there. I will hold that memory forever.

When it was over, 119 past Orioles were on the field. Some of them were presently playing for other teams but gained permission to attend and they were so glad they did. Kate and I stood there applauding for 45 straight minutes. All the players made a giant circle around the infield as a special 360-degree camera took their picture. Before the players exited, they threw baseballs into the stands and some of them even threw their hats. Finally, 51,000 people sang "Auld Lang Syne" together and the doors of Memorial Stadium closed forever.

It had been one of the most emotional days of my life and it wasn't over. On the way to the Bel Air home of my future in-laws for the engagement party, we wondered how to address the fact we were running extremely late. Time and all the appointments associated with it had been wiped from our minds. We didn't have the opportunity to offer an explanation as upon our entrance, Kate's sister Joan announced, "We saw you on TV at the last Orioles game!" Ruh Roh!

I tried to giggle it off until I learned that Kate's father, a huge Orioles fan himself, had his own company tickets to the game.

Unfortunately, his wife wouldn't let him go because of the party. He stared me down like it was my fault and to this day hasn't forgiven me. Bang the drum, slowly.

A few days later, the second event happened when someone burst into my post-production editing suite and excitedly asked me if I had heard. I sarcastically replied, "You mean that we are the only animals on the planet with chins?" After an interesting conversation about human anatomy, I learned Ken Burns, who treated the world to his amazing documentary about the Civil War, was about to do another one on the history of baseball. Are you kidding me? My goals in life immediately changed! I needed to be involved in some capacity, even if it meant fetching coffee, donuts or taste testing the different powdered chalks used to define baselines from all over the country. Gross I know, but as a catcher I have digested a lot of dirt so I was game.

The next morning, I went to the library and looked up any information I could find on Ken Burns including his need for editors, his tolerance for smart asses and his love of chocolate-chip cookies from a smart-ass baseball loving editor. His company was called Florentine Films and was located in Walpole, New Hampshire. I immediately sent him a letter outlining my skills as a television editor and more importantly my love and knowledge of baseball. I prepared myself mentally to relocate further north by purchasing a knit hat adorned with a Patriots logo.

I saw this as providential and felt it was meant to be. Although I told my girlfriend Walpole wouldn't be that bad, she was busy wondering about all the bathing suits she bought for the beaches of California. Research proved New Hampshire only had 18 miles of coastline and sunbathing was a lost form of leisure, which was replaced with making paper out of conifer trees. Her worry was for naught as I received a very courteous letter informing me my services wouldn't be needed in the land of "Live Free or Die." I was disappointed about the news, but even more sad I would miss the grand opening of Oriole Park at Camden Yards. California, here we come.

Medium Pitch

We ended up renting a spacious but expensive apartment in Valencia, California. Up to that point, my only knowledge of Valencia was from a commercial where Bing Crosby pointed out the window of a helicopter and said, "Look Nathanial, it's the orange grove." Sorry, but my mind is a steel trap filled with useless and obscure information.

The weather in Valencia was truly beautiful. The area was considered the high desert so as the day progressed, the heat of the sun generated a constant breeze. By dinner, it was really kicking, leaving grains of sand in all the window sills. Magically, as if a giant switch was thrown, everything stopped when the sun set. As nature goes it was pretty cool, as baseball goes the weather was frickin' awesome and I couldn't wait to play.

Through a connection with a freelance editor, I learned of a coed softball league which was centered in the valley. Living in the high desert made everything below us "The Valley" even though it went on for 30 miles. We signed up for the league and received a call from our coach about our first practice. When we arrived and met our team, we were excited about playing. Kate had played as a child and on several work leagues and upon playing catch with her I realized she was very softball-proficient. I knew this was going to be a recreational league and would be a huge step down from my "winner-take-all" baseball mentality, so I approached the league with a lackadaisical attitude.

I thought I had seen it all when it came to softball, but I was very surprised to learn I was mistaken. The league was referred to as medium-pitch, and came with its own set of rules. The first thing I learned, there were two first bases. They were connected together creating a rectangle and one of them resided in foul territory with the baseline running between them. It was explained to me that the outer base was to be used by the runner and the inner bag used by the first baseman, but only on the initial play at first. This configuration was designed for safety and I thought it was unnecessary but must have been implemented after some limb severing horrible collision took place, which left witnesses forever scarred.

Another oddity was from behind the dish. The catcher didn't squat like normal, instead he moved back in front of the screen. The umpire stood to the side facing the batter. Can you picture this deficiency? He laid down a specially designed mat, which was formed to fit against the back of the plate. It seriously looked like a car mat with a "V" cut out of it. He would watch to see if the arc of the ball crossed the batter. If the ball did and then hit the mat, it was an automatic strike. The catcher would retrieve the ball after several bounces and throw it back to the pitcher. I was impressed with the ball and strike-calling process and wondered why it was never put in place on the East Coast. I also thought it was odd that the catcher wasn't really a catcher at all, but a retriever. I could accept those new rules but had to clear my throat when the "four fouls and you were out" rule was announced. If one had two strikes on them and fouled off two pitches they'd be out. What the hell was this, kickball? However, during the course of the season this only happened two times, and it did speed up the game.

The big rule, and the one which set medium-pitch softball above slow-pitch in my tier of difficulty, was the addition of the windmill. The windmill was the motion used by all those talented female college softball pitchers, which enabled them to zip the ball past you at an enormous rate of speed triggering fear and progressed aging. I had seen these outstanding ladies play in person before, but never batted against one. To my astonishment, this league was riddled with them. When at bat, all men had to face a windmill whether they liked it or not, however women had a choice to face a slow-pitch arc instead. Every time a woman came to the plate, she would tell the umpire her choice and he would address the plate accordingly. Whenever I approached the plate, it was like preparing for the launch of a hip missile, so I was usually quietly reciting my will, just in case. For the record, some of these ladies could seriously bring it, and some men too!

This league found me playing center field and I was totally in my groove. I had flashbacks of warming up with Northside as I roamed back and forth catching balls at will. Our third baseman was the better half of a married couple and by accident we formulated a wonderful plan. One thing I forgot to mention was that stealing was allowed. You couldn't lead off the bag, and were required to stay on it until the ball passed the batter, but people were taking off all the time. Once an errant throw by the catcher came on through into center field and the runner took off towards third. I ran in, scooped up the ball and fired a shot to third base where she applied a slap tag to the sliding runner. He was out and turned to look at me in disbelief as he slowly walked to his bench.

During the break in the inning, we high-fived about it and then it happened again. Two catching-throwing errors and two outs at third. We decided to use it as a play and soon hoped people would steal just so we could throw them out at third. Even the pitcher would try to pick someone off at second and almost throw me the ball in the air. I can't remember one time it didn't work. Those are great memories. One not so great memory involved my right fielder, who just happened to be Kate. We were playing a pretty good team and someone sent a shot to right field and it was a real rainmaker. The ball was so high it seemed it had lost its arc and was coming straight down. As I was sprinting over to back her up, I could tell she was camped under the ball and was certainly going to catch it. She had her arms above her head, but for some reason at the last second, she moved her glove and the ball hit her square in the forehead. Her mouth was slightly open at the time and the noise that exited her body came from the bottom of her toes and was thick. It reminded me of an echoing rebound grunt made by a bear into a hollow drum. The ball bounced 15 feet straight up and had I not been concerned with her medical state, I could have caught it, forever living in the highlight reel for all those present. I picked up the ball and threw it towards the infield and turned to retrieve Kate as she walked in large circles.

The umpire sprinted ahead of both teams as he ran out to check on her condition. Other than a broken blood vessel in one of her beautiful blue eyes and a lump on her head she was fine. Embarrassment was abounding for sure and when the umpire was certain she was okay, he burst out laughing and he laughed very hard. I can chuckle now, but I was angry at the time. I couldn't understand why she moved her glove and since I knew she was going to live I was pissed I didn't catch the ball. A few years later Carlos Martinez of the Cleveland Indians had a home run after it bounced off Jose Canseco's head and over the fence. Kate was in good company.

The next week a very exciting day arrived for which I had been waiting impatiently. The Orioles were coming to Anaheim to play the Angels. I lived on Magic Mountain Parkway, about five miles away from Magic Mountain Amusement Park. For those of you who are Chevy Chase fans, Magic Mountain became Wally World for the National Lampoon movie, "Vacation," however in actuality there was no moose out front. I drove the 76 miles from Valencia to Anaheim, but because of California freeways and the idiots who drove them, it took about two and a half hours. I made a promise to myself that after living in California I would never, ever, complain about traffic again. It was like there was a permanent blue light special going on somewhere or they were giving away gold coins and not the chocolate kind, because the roads were always jammed. Unbeknownst to me at first, motorcycles were allowed to drive on the dotted lines between lanes. It was an invitation to mayhem and it showed up regularly. The only time I would ever consider sitting in intentional bumper-to-bumper traffic again would be for a double-double animal style at an In-N-Out Burger.

Once I reached the stadium, I found a place to park and started making my way towards the front gate. It was a day game and I didn't think I'd have a problem grabbing a ticket, so I made my way towards the ticket gate behind home plate. As I walked, I could see a few orange Orioles hats making their way, which made me happy. That was three decades before the Orioles Hawaiian shirt promotion, so there were none of them dotting the landscape like we see now on every away game of Orioles broadcasts. While living in California, I found it interesting when meeting someone from Maryland. A few months earlier, I walked over to a gentleman who was pumping gas because he was sporting a happy bird hat. I found out he was from Catonsville, Maryland. I would have passed him without notice in Maryland, but in another state, he became a person of interest. I still don't understand the significance or why the need to interact with home land strangers.

As I closed in on the line to buy tickets another man approached who was also wearing an Orioles hat. I smiled at him as he got closer and when he got in line behind me, I turned and started a conversation. We exchanged names and started small talking as we took a few steps when he asked what I did for a living. I told him I was a television editor and he calmly said, "Do you know Tom Taylor?" Now René Descartes, the inventor of analytical geometry, would have said the percentages of running into a man 3,000 miles away from home who knew anyone I knew would be astronomical. He was so wrong. I used to work at Spicer Productions with Tom Taylor and I played baseball with him when I was a kid. Holy crap, yes, I knew Tom Taylor! Turns out this guy, Cedric Snow, was his college roommate. Get the hell out of town! Instantly, we became fast friends as we celebrated our stories of Tom Taylor.

While laughing at the connection, a very kind lady in an Angel's hat turned around and asked us if we wanted her tickets. She went on to say she was a box seat season ticket holder, but was going to sit in another section with her friend so we could have her seats. She wouldn't accept our money either because in California they have anti-

THE DISH

scalping laws. I couldn't believe how sweet this woman was so I asked for her address and we actually corresponded about baseball for a few years. Her name was Helen Campbell and I will always be grateful for the gift she gave Cedric and I. We looked at each other bewildered and graciously took the tickets. Turns out, they were second row seats right behind home plate. During the National Anthem, several Baltimore fans from around the park who were dedicated to the cause yelled, "Oh!" at the desired time. It was indeed a superior and special day.

Three weeks later, Kate and I found ourselves sitting in Chavez Ravine with our next-door neighbors watching the Los Angeles Dodgers. Our friend, Sarah, worked for Safeco and they were sponsoring the game so her and her husband, Mike, invited us along. I had never seen so much Dodger blue in my whole life. The place was rocking, and as we sat in left-field I couldn't help but think that Frank and Brooks hit back-to-back home runs there during game one of the 1966 World Series. Nostalgia continued to capture my mind and heart as I visited these places of baseball worship.

My medium-pitch days were over when I found a baseball team looking for a catcher in Santa Monica. The coach was about 15 years older than me and let me call my own games. He also liked to catch a buzz in his car before each game, so he was always smiling. The Dynamos, as we were called, were made up of men of all ages from 23 to 60. It was an interesting league, full of interesting people. While chatting with an older catcher from the other team I learned he was an original member of the famous Chicago seven. These were not the Black Sox, as there were eight of them, these were the seven men who were charged with conspiracy for rioting during the 1968 Democratic National Convention. His name was Tom Hayden and he was a legend as an antiwar activist. He was also married to Jane Fonda for 17 years, so I assume he could Jazzercise. I was 31 at the time and he was 52 so I was impressed with his stamina, especially as a catcher.

I taught our team the verbal pick-off calls we used at UMBC and we picked off everybody. This league was totally invigorating for me as

I was a stand-out and led the team in all the offensive categories. I remember one game we played I could actually see the Pacific Ocean in the distance. I think of those memories every time I hear Billy Joel sing, "California Baseball" in "We Didn't Start the Fire."

That team was a lot of fun and after I moved back to Baltimore, they flew me back west twice for tournaments. The closest friend I had on the team was Drew Woerner. He was a real player with a great eye and led the team in walks. He also led the team in stolen bases which meant every time he saw ball four, the pitcher had just given up a double. I loved that about him and it was great to catch up every year.

During the first tournament, we had friends from California drive to Las Vegas to see us and they came to one of the games. During the game, I hit a double and was jumping off of second with a pretty good lead. The pitcher kept trying to look me back and stepped off a few times. One time the second baseman ran over to take a throw but there was none. However, he just stood between me and the bag so I ran into him knocking him to the ground. He didn't have the ball and I wasn't sure if it was coming and was just standing there so I took him out. He really took offense and started giving me an earful. I guess he thought I should have stopped, said excuse me and went around him, but I just told him he shouldn't block the bag and the umpire backed me up.

He walked to the pitcher's mound to have a personal discussion and I knew what was coming. I turned to the field umpire and told him to watch what was about to unfold. I didn't even move off of the bag as the pitcher toed the rubber, so it was very obvious when he stepped off and threw to the second baseman. He caught the ball and slap tagged me as hard as he could. I immediately looked at the umpire who had the Sergeant Schultz "I see nothing!" face, so I turned toward the player and went after him. Tim O'Malley would have been proud as I chased him into short center field. I just laughed at him as he ran, the little pussy. The umpires did nothing because it was a tournament and my visiting friends, who weren't baseball fans, asked me if it was normal to play football in the middle of a baseball game. Well, sometimes.

The second incident was in Phoenix, a year later, and this one let me know I was getting older. My eyes were already playing tricks on me because I had only slept about 30 minutes. I had a connecting flight through Denver, but unfortunately, I arrived there the same time as a blizzard and they shut down the airport. We circled for about an hour, before they let us land, and when we did it was the bumpiest ride, I had ever been a part of. At one point, I thought we were just going to take off again. I learned later, from the film crew that met us at the gate, we almost hit a snow plow. I can't imagine that would have been good.

After taxying for about 20 minutes, the plane just stopped and turned off right there on the runway. My final destination was Phoenix, and all I was wearing was a tee shirt and a pair of shorts. I looked out the window and watched the snow build up on the wing and thought I would never see the sun again and wished for warm weather.

Two hours later, we finally started moving. The problem was, they had no place to put us, because the gates were full and the pilot wasn't capable of double parking a 757. When we finally disembarked, and dealt with the TV crew, we learned all the transfers had been cancelled and we were stranded at the airport. I wandered for a bit, but refused to buy anything from an airport vending machine. Been there and done that.

About 4 a.m., I wrangled myself onto a plane heading for Tucson and rented a car to drive the 114 miles to Phoenix. I was exhausted, so I had to tap the adrenal glands and drive with the windows down just to stay awake. I was singing at the top of my lungs, but that didn't help either. I needed to stop by the airport first, because my luggage landed there. I had nothing, and if I couldn't find my toothbrush and baseball gear, I was going to have to play in shorts and with very bad breath.

When I finally found my belongings, they were in the midst of a suitcase pyramid. That was before 911, and all the subsequent regulations, so as people started to arrive, they climbed on the pile like children, and luggage was flying all over the place. It took about 15 minutes before finding both of my bags, and then I headed for the hotel.

After checking in, I took a shower and fell on the bed. My coma was interrupted 30 minutes later by my teammates, who said they were leaving for the field. They assumed I had been there all night, as my original arrival time was 10 p.m. I used all my remaining energy to brush my teeth.

It was an incredibly hot day and by 11 a.m. it was well over 100 degrees on the field. The only other time I had played in a baseball game that hot was for the Overlea Anxious. Our concrete dugout had to be 170 degrees that day, and I'm certain we were only an hour away before the bench would spontaneously combust. I lost over 12 pounds, and my catching gear was soaked through and through. John Horner, our accomplished third baseman, had told the team his father was going to bring us some food to eat between the games. It was a double header, and the first time in my life I wanted to bitch slap Ernie Banks for suggesting we play two!

I sat there thinking about the cold drinks and sandwiches we were going to receive, when I heard water pouring on the ground. I looked to my left to see outfielder extraordinaire, Kenny Yienger, sitting on the bench and leaning forward. Water was pouring off his nose like it was attached to a spigot. I thought he had dumped a bucket of cold water on his head for comfort, and these were the remnants, but it wasn't. It was his actual sweat glands coming together in unison on the top of his head, before streaming down his face and cascading off his nose, forming a puddle on the ground. I had never seen anything like it. A few minutes later, John's wonderful father walked around the corner carrying our lunch. It was a bucket of fried chicken. God bless him, but there was no way I was going to sit in an oven, and eat greasy, hot chicken. I didn't eat anything at all, and yes, that was a first.

My sweat glands were in hyperdrive and my eyes started playing tricks on me making the pitcher look like he was 50 yards away. You know how on very hot days when you look down a long road you can actually see the wavy lines of heat as they leave the asphalt? That was what the pitcher looked like to me. He was so blurry I couldn't make out his pitch until it was right in front of me. It was hard to tell if he was shaking me off or not, so I wasn't sure what pitch was coming. I found myself coiled and anxious as I looked for the ball, and then I had to snap at it when it came into view. It was more than a little scary. I had some reading glasses, but they didn't help either and that was after I taped them to my head. It wasn't like that when I was batting, only when I was squatting behind the plate. I knew my competitive playing days were coming to a head, so I started thinking about changing positions. All I knew was catching.

Fun Fact # 1456

In 1993, WJZ-TV flew me home to Baltimore for several weeks to work in their post-production suite. In the early '90s, post-production rooms consisted of gigantic 1-inch analog tape machines along with Grass Valley switchers, and editing controllers which cost over $1 million to construct. Unlike the thousand-dollar non-linear desktop editing systems used today, it took years of training to become proficient in such a room. The money private companies saved on training and equipment was now used to download self-help videos from the internet and purchase Otis Spunkmeyer cookie machines. Fair trade.

The woman I trained before departing for LA was taking an extended vacation, and the powers that be thought it would be easier and cheaper to fly me home than to train or hire someone who didn't know the system. That was the absolute perfect situation for me, because during my three-week stay in Baltimore, the All-Star game was going to take place at brand-new Oriole Park at Camden Yards. I did the only thing any capable man with a deathbed favor would do, I called and begged Bill Wilkins.

As luck would have it, he had possession of four center field tickets and one of them ended up in my pocket. Of course, I was required to cut his grass for the next 10 years and wash his dog every other Tuesday, but it was so worth it. Along with Bill, Kevin and hilarious fellow raft-rider and trouble-starter, Tom Howard, we had a date.

Baltimore was as jacked up as I have ever seen it, and that included the festivities surrounding the annual running of the infield urinals at the Preakness. Spotlights filled the sky, the Babe Ruth Birthplace Museum was all aglow, and giant video screens projected baseball icons on the grand warehouse. That would be any baseballer's wet dream.

A few days earlier, I had the pleasure of attending Fan Fest with Chris Strong. We went on Saturday morning, taking in all the exhibits before attending an afternoon game. It was the hottest and most uncomfortable day I had ever spent at any ballpark and resembled what I believed the humidity to be inside a pair of a person's yoga pants who suffered from hyperhidrosis. We were sitting in the upper deck, with the sun in our faces, wearing SPF 902 when Hall of Fame announcer Rex Barney proclaimed, "Temperature at game time...103 degrees!" Holy crap it was hot! It was so hot the devil himself avoided Baltimore that day.

Nobody moved or applauded and if someone had suggested generating the wave, they would have surely been unceremoniously removed from the outdoor facility by means of catapult. I saw no beer vendors, because they would have passed out navigating the steep stairs. Recognizing this, I bought one prior to the game but drank it before reaching my seat because it started to boil. I did notice, however, that ice cream, snowball and lemonade vendors were constantly selling out, because they were drinking and eating their own product. At one point, I thought I saw a hot dog vendor burst into flames, poor bastard.

When they announced the starting pitcher for the Orioles was Fernando Valenzuela, Chris turned to me and said, "He grew up near the equator, he'll probably throw a no-hitter." I wondered if he was wearing asbestos underwear. We lasted two innings before we relocated to the indoor air-conditioned bar and watched the rest of the game on TV with the overheated beer vendors.

The All-Star game was a complete sellout, but tickets were still being sold for standing-room-only fans. One such fan decided to introduce himself to our section, and stood at the rail with his back to the field shouting his proposition. "May I have your attention," he yelled while holding up something in his hand. Pointing to it he continued, "I am SRO or standing room only. However, I know as the alcoholic beverages begin to flow, many of you will have to get up and go to the bathroom. While you are gone, I will take your seat. When you return, I will gladly get up and move to another vacant seat. I might become your friend or even buy you a beer. If everyone is in agreement with my proposal please applaud." The section lit up with cheers of validation for Mr. SRO, and he quickly found a vacancy and sat down. This continued throughout the whole game and he made many, many friends that day. I am certain I saw him in at least 70 different seats. His tactics were very impressive.

Bill, Kevin and Tom were the perfect ingredients for baseball fun and that recipe was used many times in the future. We laughed and experienced a once-in-a-lifetime event at our own treasured ballpark. Baseball was better when it was a shared experience. The game itself was quite memorable at times with Pudge Rodriguez drilling a double which stuck in the left field fence, Randy Johnson's erratic fastball making John Kruk soil himself at the plate, Kirby Puckett driving in two to win the MVP and American League manager Cito Gaston getting booed for refusing to put in Oriole Mike Mussina to close it out. He deserved to be booed, I mean, really.

The day before, Ken Griffey Jr. hit the warehouse during the Home Run Derby contest, which was a first. I was forever grateful to Bill for including me, because I have never been to another All-Star game and more importantly, I never would have met Mr. SRO.

Recently, I opened a bottle of Snapple to find some baseball information printed on the inside of the top. It stated: Major League umpires wear black underwear in case they split their pants. It was Fun Fact #1456 and made perfect sense. I had been playing baseball for decades while inches from umpires, and never knew about their choice of undergarments. Tidbits like that were just some of the things to love about baseball. Unfortunately, that would be something I'd randomly bring up in conversation, so I'm surprised it never crossed my mind during pre-inning warm-ups.

Speaking of warm-ups, I have a small beef to get off my chest. This whole "pitch count" thing happening in the majors drives me batty. Somebody decided pitchers can only throw 100 pitches per game before they are removed. It is as if they throw 101 pitches, their arm would quickly start to disconnect from their shoulder, like a scene from "The Walking Dead." Between innings, pitchers throw at least six to eight fastballs to get loose, before the catcher throws to second, which ends the warm-up ritual. So, if a pitcher pitches six innings, he is somewhere north of 140 balls thrown. I have seen no science that proves pitcher's careers last longer or they become less-efficient by only throwing 100 pitches per game. Complete games are not even on the agenda anymore, which makes Jim Palmer's 211 complete games an outstanding anomaly, which will never be repeated. He alone was replaced with starters, relievers, middle relievers, set-up men, closers and sometimes random utility players, who just embarrass themselves and all their relatives. Okay, I'm done.

Sometimes total strangers around you at a professional game can make your experience that much more enjoyable. Once at Memorial Stadium, we were flanked by some loudmouth Yankee fans as we sat on the left field foul line just a few yards up from the third base dugout. They were pretty obnoxious the whole game and seemed to be getting on most people's nerves. During the seventh inning stretch, the grounds crew came out to drag the field and sweep the bases like they did every game. They were in staggered formation as they pulled chain-link pieces of material behind them and right before exiting the infield, they yanked hard in such a way, the whole mat flew up and was gathered under their arms, before they ran off the field. When the last guy jerked his mat, it flew up over his head and landed on him, sending him tumbling to the ground in a Laurel & Hardy sort of way. Instantly, one of the Yankee fans yelled, "Minimum wage!" and it was hilarious. Turns out these guys were only obnoxious because they were Yankee fans. Had they been Orioles fans, I would have been right there yucking it up with them.

That October, we moved back to Baltimore following the Rodney King riots and the destructive Northridge earthquake. Our California adventure came to a screeching halt and although I loved California baseball, fearing for our lives while driving to work or having the ceiling fall on the table while eating sushi wasn't part of the game plan. It was time for some sanity in our lives, so in one week, we drove across the country arriving on a Friday, found a place to live Saturday, moved in Sunday, started a new job on Monday and got married the following Saturday. If we would have banged out a kid in the meantime, we might have won a toaster. While flying to Hawaii for our honeymoon, we struggled to remember anything from the previous two weeks. So much for finding our sanity.

I was back on the Overlea Anxious and loving it, but all the games were now at Harford Community College, which was an hour from where we lived. I left work at 5 p.m., changed into my uniform as I drove Interstate 95 in rush hour, before I sprinted to the field arriving minutes before the game started at 6 p.m. Many times, I exchanged looks with gawking truck drivers who were wondering why the person in the car next to them was only wearing a jock. I prayed hard for no traffic incidents, as the "My mother told me to always wear clean underwear in case I were in an accident," defense wouldn't have worked.

Sometimes we had night games, which didn't start until 8 or 9, so I wasn't getting home until after midnight. It definitely made for a long day, but it was organized baseball and I was still viable. I played well into my late 30s, until the commute became an issue. One day, I looked around and noticed I was the oldest member of the team. Even the umpires were younger than me and when one of them whispered, "You know they have over-30 leagues," I figured it might be time to stop.

The last year I played for the Anxious, there were a lot of new faces on the team that hadn't started shaving yet. The younger players were all up in themselves and didn't take too kindly to suggestions or teaching. It seemed they knew everything there ever was to know about baseball and only cared about themselves. Some of the veterans weren't happy about it, and there were some verbal altercations during practice. It didn't affect me much, but I told Chris Manouse I wasn't going to let things slide and most likely would have something to say. He just smiled.

It didn't take long, as a matter of fact, it was in the first inning of the very first game of the season. We performed our normal pre-inning warm-ups and I fired the ball to second. For a catcher, that was always an important ritual, because it showed off your arm to the other team. Many times, I thought about throwing one in the dirt or in the outfield as a ruse, but my propensity to play well denied that from happening. I greeted the umpire and crouched down to start the game. The batter stepped in and I put down one finger for a fastball and the very young and very new pitcher shook me off. Are you kidding me? I gave it to him again and he shook me off a second time. Under my breath I mumbled, "Oh, for Christ's sake," but out loud I called, "Time out!" Those two words were magical because they could stop the game at any given moment. Unlike football, where you only had a certain amount of play stoppage, baseball wasn't limited to a time, so you could play forever.

I walked toward the mound to confront the pitcher. When I got there, he sarcastically said, "What?"

"Why are you shaking me off?"

"Because I want to throw a curveball."

"How old are you?"

"What?"

"How old are you?"

"19, why?"

"I have a corn on my foot that is 27. Just throw what I give you and maybe you'll see 20."

I plopped the ball in his glove and walked back to the plate. When I arrived the umpire said, "Kids, right?" He got it. I still loved the game and wanted to play as long as I could, but was starting to contemplate my involvement. To my surprise, my work life and play life were about to collide.

The company I worked for, along with the Crown Central Petroleum Corp., was tasked to create a commemorative video to celebrate the 40th anniversary of the Baltimore Orioles. Holy cow! I was so excited as I was the senior editor and given full access to the historic Orioles video library, which lived in the warehouse next to Camden Yards. I couldn't wait to get started and prepared for awesomeness.

The atmosphere in the warehouse was pretty spectacular. The general offices for the Orioles resided there and memorabilia lined the great historic hallways. I looked out every window I could to absorb the different views of Camden Yards. Even the men's room overlooked the field. You could actually stand at a urinal and take in a baseball game. Are you kidding me? I could have been struck by lightning and would have died happy right there while in midstream.

The library itself was still years away from being digitally organized, so highlights lived on random VHS and ¾-inch tapes. I found one that was simply labeled "Double Plays," and watched in awe as players like Belanger, Grich, Aparicio and Johnson turned the twin killings with ease. Navigation was difficult because lots of footage was being gathered and stored, but the labeling and retrieval process was still being created. One day, I found rookie footage of Brooks Robinson walking through the spring training locker room. He looked like he was 12 years old. The majority of the older stuff was black and white, but looked normal to me as that was how I viewed the games. We had a black-and-white television until 1970, which meant, for five years I wondered what "The FBI" looked like in living color. Baseball looks great in any color.

For weeks, I worked with a great script, original inspirational music, beautiful graphics and perfect Orioles' footage, along with highlights from their six World Series. The 40th anniversary video was so special to me and showcased relationships like Weaver and Palmer, the Robinson boys and Eddie and Cal. Unfortunately, the relationship between fans and the game became unraveled as Major League Baseball went on strike. They didn't even finish the season, meaning the World Series was cancelled. I felt like George C. Scott in "Patton," when he learned he was on probation. "The last great opportunity of a lifetime- an entire world at war, and I'm left out of it? God will not permit this to happen, I will be allowed to fulfill my destiny. His will be done!" Okay, maybe I'm a bit extreme, but I couldn't believe it. Everyone was so mad at baseball they refused to purchase the tape. Crown couldn't give them away. It was the best of times it was the worst of times.

Two years later, I joined a bus trip to New York City to watch the Orioles play at Yankee Stadium. The bus was noisy, full of bar patrons and alcohol, and the driver quickly lost control of the crowd. To calm them down, he put on a video and you guessed it, the 40th Anniversary of The Orioles. Again, I was excited, but nobody cared. After a while, I couldn't wait to get off the bus, and when we pulled into a parking lot I stood and looked out the window. The bus was slowly being surrounded by Yankee fans and they were all wearing "Baltimore Blows" T-shirts. Oh perfect, could the day get any better? Just then, a friend of mine yelled, "Look at the screen. That's this guy right here!" My name just happened to be on the screen as the editor of the video and everyone started clapping and giving me the shoulder slap signifying a good job. It wasn't such a bad day after all, maybe baseball was going to make a comeback.

The Comeback Kids

Do you remember when you were a child and Christmas or your birthday couldn't come fast enough? Anticipation to a kid had no time limit, therefore, celebrations and events seemed to take forever and a day to arrive. There were short-term celebrations like getting a snowball after dinner or going to get pumpkins prior to Halloween, but their combined anticipation only lasted a few hours or days. In 1994, I was again bitten by the anticipation bug and it lasted a whole nine months.

To the layman and midwife, nine months can be associated with the allotted time to create a new tax write-off. Preparing properly for a new housemate is not just purchasing a litter box and a 10-pound bag of kibble, room colors and border patterns must be decided along with names, nicknames and what college they will attend and all in a notary-attended family meeting. For me, it was like that times 30 over and I couldn't wait for September to arrive.

The birthdate of one of my daughters was in September, but not until seven years later. I was not looking forward to my own baby, but one delivered by filmmaker Ken Burns. On September 18, PBS aired the first episode of his documentary on baseball. I seriously could not wait and had read up on every aspect of all 18.5 hours of his epic, and even cleared my schedule of hinderances, like sleeping, for all 10 days.

My learning experience was overwhelming and I was hooked with the very first quote by Walt Whitman, "Let's go forth awhile, and get better air in our lungs. The game of ball is glorious." John Chancellor was an award-winning anchorman for NBC news for 25 years. He brought millions of Americans up to date on the latest events, tragedies, and political blunders for over a generation, however for me, his voice will be forever associated with my knowledge and love of baseball. When I was editing a television project, I became so involved I literally breathed it. There are 30 frames, or pictures, in a single second of video. Film has 24 frames per second and each one of those are very important to an editor. Removing one or adding one can make the world of difference to the viewer and the editor has the power to harness the emotions generated to tell their story.

Once, in Hollywood, I was hired to make "dirt" fixes, which were pieces of dirt or hairs on a single frame of video. I spent a week removing them or cleaning them up one frame at a time. It was better than paint drying. My eyes were trained to do that and my observational skills improved greatly. Imagine the ability to see things no one else can see, it is a blessing and a curse. When I watched a movie, I could seriously see the individual frames as they went by. Many times, I paused a DVD, turned to whoever was watching it with me and uttered, "Did you see that?"

Usually, when I was done editing a project, I was physically and mentally done as well. I had seen the product start to finish so many times, by the unveiling or first public viewing, I couldn't watch it again. That was the sole reason I was happy I was never hired to work with Ken Burns. I can't even imagine growing tired of watching his baby, ever. Everything about it was appealing, from the musical selections, to the stories shared on screen by writers and historians. So much, in fact, nothing will ever hold credence to me unless it contains a relatable story conveyed by Shelby Foote.

Where else would I have learned about Bud Hillerich, the creator of the Louisville Slugger, or Henry Chadwick, who invented the box score and the letter "K" as the symbol for a strikeout. So many aspects about the game I love were not even thought about by most who played it. The racial divide, which existed for so long in the game, was brilliantly documented by Burns and I had tears in my eyes when I saw footage of Jackie Robinson running onto the field the first time. The passionate way in which Branch Rickey believed in Robinson was palatable, and watching smiling Buck O'Neil tell Negro League stories warmed my heart every time I saw him.

When the Black Sox scandal rocked professional baseball and dismayed so many Americans, the national pastime seemed doomed. It took a Baltimore-born man, Babe Ruth, to save it. Seventy-seven years later in 1995, I sat along the first base side of Camden Yards when another Baltimore-born man tried to do the same thing. Cal Ripken Jr. was setting his mark as the new Iron Man. I attended some of those last few games and when they changed the number on the warehouse after the top half of the fifth inning, you could taste the excitement in your mouth. The way the music sounded, the way the baseball rule 4.10(c) was displayed on Diamond Vision, and the way sellout crowds cheered, were just ceremonial perfection. Whoever thought of that ceremony should have been presented with a lifetime supply of crab cakes. It was no secret, Cal Ripken Jr. saved baseball.

I watched 2,131 from home with crazy anticipation. I seriously prayed he wouldn't get injured, but if he had, he still would have dragged his bloody body to shortstop for five innings. When he homered in the fourth inning, I jumped right off the couch. An inning later, when the record became his and he slowly made his way around the stadium shaking hands with strangers, I had tears streaming down my face. What a wonderful moment that would had been to have shared with my father. Oh, to be an Oriole.

I Just Killed A Camper!

I grabbed the mail and walked down the driveway sorting through all the Black Friday ads. It was late November and one of the return addresses caught my attention. It was from the Baltimore Orioles and was addressed to "Neil Beller - 2003 Camp Participant." I opened it to find a letter from Steve Freeman. I immediately thought it was a joke, because camping was frowned upon at Camden Yards, and I didn't know a Steve Freeman. Also, I had a habit of procuring stationery from certain places and sending important letters to my friends from various agencies and corporations. Some of them received letters from law firms informing them of inherited monetary gains, some received complimentary season tickets to The Ice Capades, and some even received thank you letters for their donations to sperm banks. I just assumed the Steve Freeman letter was a payback.

The previous year, I had edited 20 episodes of "Orioles Magazine," which was the last show produced before the start of the Mid-Atlantic Sports Network or MASN. It was a local show hosted by the beautiful and effervescent, Elena Russo, and featured many Orioles doing segments on the hidden aspects of the game like stealing, bunting and how to throw a slider. These hidden aspects only referred to the 2002 Orioles, as the other major league clubs could do all that stuff with ease.

The show's producer, Steve Farrell, was also a game day cameraman, whom I bothered on a regular basis. I became familiar with the rest of the production staff as well, so much in fact, I would call them at their camera positions during the game, and tell them where we were sitting so my daughter could make an appearance between innings on the big screen. They always found us and she never disappointed. I assumed one of them had sent me a letter on official stationery, to inform me I had been barred from the park because of production staff manipulation or my extreme Italian sausage intake.

I looked through the letter in the garage to find a welcome announcement and a preliminary work-out schedule to attend Orioles' fantasy camp. It had an entire schedule layout, travel itinerary and hotel information for the Hyatt in Sarasota, Florida. Someone went to a lot of trouble to play a joke on me, but I wasn't having any part of it. I went inside with the letter and walked over to where my wife was feeding our daughter lunch. I started to fill her in on the failed practical joke and when I mentioned to her that I received a letter from some guy named Steve Freeman she gasped. Before I could continue, she started to get angry and while struggling to maintain a poker face, she let it slip she had sent the letter. Well, she really didn't send it but had it sent. For a Christmas present, she had purchased me a week at Orioles Fantasy Camp. She was mad because she was going to surprise me on Christmas morning and had no idea, they would be sending out a mailer. I was mad because I only had two months to lose 20 pounds and get in baseball shape!

For the record, I was extremely gracious she tried to surprise me and to this day it remains one of the greatest gifts I have ever received. I learned it cost an arm and a leg so it was considered a once-in-a-lifetime event and I wanted to take full advantage of it.

The leagues I played in were summer leagues and getting in shape followed the natural progression of the seasons. I had never played baseball in January before, so my body was still in "holiday" mode where it craved cookies of a chocolate consistency and many of them on an hourly basis. It was extremely cold outside, so I immediately put into place an indoor training facility, which basically included our basement utility room and a double bed-sized mattress. Every night after dinner, I propped the mattress up on our large, chest-style freezer and threw baseballs at it. I even made a square out of tape in the middle of the mattress so I had a target. I was only about 20 feet away and had no idea how far my actual throws would go, so I visualized throwing from center field to home. I even had a perfect ball-retrieval system as my two little girls rushed to pick them up off the concrete floor and place them back in my 5-gallon bucket. Human ingenuity at its finest.

I had edited a story for "Orioles Magazine" on fantasy campers and from what I remember, it was a comedy of errors. Balls dropping all over the place, out-of-shape people falling down in the baselines and all while wearing the sacred Orioles orange. Most of the participants seemed to be between 45 and 102, so my thinking process was I'd be in better shape than most. However, I was so super-excited to meet and be around former Orioles, comparing my competition level to other campers wasn't on my mind. The year was 2003, and to celebrate the 20th anniversary of the Orioles winning the 1983 World Series, almost every player on that team was going to be present. I could not wait for Christmas and New Year's Eve to come and go so I could finally board a plane for Florida and find my youth.

When the big day came, I had to be at the airport at 6:30 a.m. to check in. The majority of the campers were on the same plane and were gathered at the terminal. The first person I met was Jan Vance and we hit it off immediately, because he displayed the same excitement in his eyes. He had recently been to another fantasy camp for the Cincinnati Reds and told me he heard the Orioles camp was way superior. Well, if you saw the 1970 World Series, you would already know that.

The first Oriole I met was Dave Johnson. Not the former manager and second baseman Davey Johnson from the powerhouse teams of the '60s and '70s, but the pitcher Dave Johnson from Middle River, Maryland. He attended CCB a year after me, so when I mentioned I was good friends with Dr. Strange Glove, he smiled and we bonded. (I took a great chance as that could have gone either way.) I actually had brought a picture of the two of us taken on the field at Memorial

Stadium prior to the last game. He gladly autographed it for me. Dave was as down-to-earth as they come.

It was very early in the morning but I was wide awake. A very sleepy looking man approached and sat across from me. I glanced at him several times and knew who he was instantly. I wanted to approach him but didn't want to look like a giddy school girl, so I just sat back and waited. It only took a few minutes before another camper walked over to him and said, "You are Paul Blair!" He looked up at him and said, "You are correct, what is your name?" To this day, whenever I am jogging to or from any baseball position, I hold my glove like Paul Blair. He was the model of how to be a center fielder and I just loved watching him play. The man introduced himself and they started a conversation. Now I was angry at myself for not talking first. The one thing that stuck with me while meeting former Orioles was how gracious they were. Here we were all excited to meet them and talk about their careers and they were just as interested in what we did for a living and our families. I loved that about them. It also says a ton about the Orioles organization. It was strange, however, to see them in street clothes.

When the plane landed in Tampa, we all boarded a bus for the Orioles complex at Twin Lakes. I decided to get brave and sat right next to Paul Blair and started a conversation. I felt like I was in the presence of Orioles royalty. In talking with the man, I learned he was quite human. I also learned he had some animosity towards all of major league baseball. He told me after his career ended, he contacted all 26 major league teams looking for a coaching job. No one responded and it really hurt him. That made me sad. He still had that fire burning inside though, and looked like he could run one down in deep center. Man, I would love to see that again.

When we arrived at the complex, I couldn't even believe what waited for us. I found a locker with my name engraved on it and opened it up. Inside were two complete Orioles uniforms with my name on the back. One was the home uniform and the other was the away version, plus an Orioles jacket, and all kinds of memorabilia. I sat on the bench and tried everything on and it felt wonderful. If there were any issues, we were instructed to find the real iron man, Ernie Tyler. Seriously? Ernie Tyler had been the equipment manager for the Orioles since before I was born. He rubbed down baseballs for every home game for the past 44 years and he and his son ran the clubhouse. I had seen him 1,000 times running baseballs out to the home plate umpire and here he was helping me to pick out my official 7 ¼-inch Orioles' hat. My uniform was complete.

We were told to put on the home uniform and venture out to field No. 1 for a pregame practice. The itinerary had us warming up and drilling with each other before playing a three-to five-inning game, which would be watched by the over 50 Orioles in attendance. The idea was for them to chart us and take notes to use for a draft later that afternoon. Ten teams would be chosen in this manner, and three to four Orioles would coach each team. My God, if they handed out hot dogs randomly, I might never leave!

As I walked to the field, I saw Orioles everywhere I looked. The actual Orioles wore bright orange shirts, so they stuck out and I was eyeing them like vacationers spying for vintage stars in Hollywood. Martinez, Gentile, Bumbry, Etchebarren, Drabowsky, Buford, Grimsley, Cruz, Roenicke, Swaggerty, McGregor, Stoddard, Shelby, and on and on they went. I was smiling huge and couldn't turn it off. We took infield and outfield and practiced covering the bases before playing a five-inning game. I took balls at left field and shortstop, before putting on the gear and taking my natural position behind the dish.

My previous thoughts were correct and I quickly learned that the majority of the campers were indeed living out their fantasies. They had never competed at a high level and some of them hadn't played ball since they were in grade school. They were living out a dream that even I couldn't comprehend and that really impressed me. I was excited for them as well, but worried they didn't understand how special it was to be in the presence of such greatness. I wasn't talking about myself, but the plethora of former major league ballplayers, who were presently littering the land. Knowing the talent range, you'd think I'd take it back a few notches, but it didn't matter to me because I was going all out.

Sitting on the bleachers behind home plate were all the Orioles with clipboards and rosters. While I was catching, I was jumping all around blocking every bad pitch and firing to first at will. I mean World Series MVP Rick Dempsey was sitting back there. When a batter popped up behind the plate, I quickly ran over and dove for the ball. I completely laid out when I caught it and jammed my shoulder when I hit the ground. Instantly, I heard them all react and the name "Beller" could be heard as they jawed about drafting me. Glenn Gulliver yelled out, "Hey Beller, can you pitch?" which was followed by laughter. I was about to answer when I looked to my left and sitting in a golf cart about 10 feet away was Frank Robinson. Frank Robinson! He was smiling and returned a small hand wave when I greeted him. Holy cow, I contemplated if he saw me dive and catch that ball. I felt like that child who would wonder if their parents were proud of an accomplishment. For a brief minute, I felt silly. Seeing Frank was amazing, because there were Orioles, and then there were ORIOLES! Earl Weaver was also driving around in a golf cart and Jim Palmer was walking up the first baseline. I convinced myself I was living in a dream, either that or someone had slipped me some serious acid because I was tripping!

When we changed innings, I had the chance to bat and ripped a double. My shoulder was a little sore and as I stood at second base I heard again, "Hey Beller, can you pitch?" followed by more laughter. Just then a camper, who I learned had been participating as a catcher for the last 12 years, walked up to me and calmly said, "You are a great catcher, probably the best one I have ever seen here." Embarrassed, I thanked him and he went on, "You do know there is no stealing here, don't you? They will never play someone with your skills behind the plate." At once, all the air deflated from by balloon, I was shocked. I had been planning both mentally and physically to catch, and now I learned that was the last place I'd be. What the hell do I do now?

The next inning, they brought me in to pitch with a man on first. The coach told me to take it easy and let them hit the ball. When he departed the mound, I instinctively turn to the second baseman and said, "You've got the bag okay?" He nodded in agreement, so I turned to pitch. I threw a fastball right down the middle and as luck would have it the batter hit it right back to me. I fielded the ball, turned towards second and, while crow-hopping, fired to the player covering. He reacted in slow motion with his glove and the ball struck him solid on his forehead causing him to drop backwards like a stone. Holy hell, I just killed a camper! I ran over to him and upon seeing blood on his head, I was overcome with guilt. Here this guy was living out his fantasy and before it even started, I drilled him in his noggin. My only thought was about all the money he spent and how pissed off his wife would be.

The actual Orioles trainers and medical staff were also in attendance and he was ushered off the field quickly. I was apologizing to him endlessly, and before he left, he looked at me and asked, "Why did you throw the ball so hard, I thought you would lob it?" At that moment, I realized my trying out for the team days were not going well. As much as I dreamed and fantasized, I was never going to be a major leaguer, so maybe it was the perfect time to face reality. As I stood there feeling terrible, someone started to massage my shoulders from behind and quietly said, "Don't worry about it, you made the right play." I recognized the voice...it was Jim Palmer. When I think back on that moment, I am immediately reminded of Jim Carrey in "Dumb and Dumber," "So, you're saying I still have a chance."

P.H.O.F.

When I ventured into the locker room after the game, I was greeted by three giant gray bins on wheels filled with ice and beer. Everyone grabbed a cold one and headed to their locker to talk baseball. I took my beer into the trainer's room to find out if I really killed a camper. I learned he needed stitches, a quicker glove and he had a whopper of a headache. What a great start to the week, and what a great reason to have another beer. While in there, I had the trainers stretch out my shoulder, which was getting pretty stiff. They paid a little more attention to it than I had hoped and seemed concerned at my sudden lack of mobility. I took a couple Tylenol and went back to my locker and changed. A mesh bag and a giant safety pin with my locker number on it was hanging in my locker. I placed the dirty uniform in the bag and dropped it into another bin when I walked out the door. These guys have thought of everything.

The bus ride to the hotel was full of excitement as campers were getting to know each other and letting their inner baseball batteries discharge. Beer was allowed to leave the clubhouse, so the atmosphere resembled a bachelor party. I was drinking one and holding another on my shoulder. It seemed to be getting stiffer so I kept moving it. I was mad at the inconvenience and timing of the pain. What a waste of a mattress.

After a short and unfulfilling nap, I dressed and went downstairs to find Jay and his friend Greg Updike, who went by the nickname

"Stick." We shared a beer at the bar and headed to the welcome room. I tried to hide the pain in my shoulder the best I could, and even though it caused my eyes to water, I shook hands with every Oriole I could find. One of the friendliest veterans I found was Bill Swaggerty. He had pitched in the major leagues just prior to the "Mullet Era," and I found him to be relatable. Bill went by "Swaggs" and during our initial short conversation, he totally edified me to the extent I thought I had been the ex-major leaguer instead of him. I walked away secretly hoping I was on his team.

Before any of the festivities started, I made sure I hunted down the man I almost killed. He was easy to spot because he was sporting a head bandage just like the fife player in that famous trio. I apologized again and he was very cordial. I posed for a picture with him so he could show his wife the attempted murderer and then found a table with Jay and Greg. Greg's favorite Oriole by far was Brooks Robinson. He even wore his number and couldn't wait to meet him. He kept scanning the room for the icon, but he hadn't arrived yet. I wore the number 33, not because I loved Eddie Murray, but because it was my number. For the longest time, members of the Overlea Anxious and other teams would say motivating things like, "C'mon threes, hit the damn ball." Still warms my heart to think about it.

The teams were announced that evening and as names were being read, campers went up front to meet their new teammates. I heard my name being called and looked up to see Andy Etchebarren at the mic. I was an official member of Etch's Thumpers, which made me giggle with glee. A big-league catcher was going to be my fantasy coach, this kept getting better. Flanking him were future minor league manager Gary Kendall and pitching coach Scott McGregor. You need to understand the level of excitement associated with these coaches. Between Etch and McGregor, they played in six World Series, six! A lawyer who was interrogating little boys on the number of times they lied about washing their hands after going to the bathroom couldn't hold a candle to the number of questions I had for these guys.

I was also excited about my teammates. One of them was Steve Geppi, who I knew as owner of DC Comics, but he was also a minority owner of the Baltimore Orioles. During the week, it seemed most of the Orioles ventured into our dugout to hunt him down. He knew everybody and treated me the same as everybody else, like a ball player. They came from all walks of life like Gary Eikenberg, who sold cars, and David Kelpin, who when blowing out his birthday cake in 1972 wished to play baseball at Machu Picchu, and did. Jerry Michael was a school teacher, who later in the week pitched a perfect game, the first one ever recorded at fantasy camp. We even had a young woman named Stephanie on our team as well as the Kendzierski brothers. My other teammates were Howard Trager, Roger Ralph, and Gerry Uehlinger. They all made my week of baseball that much more fulfilling. So many heroes and fans on one bench, I couldn't wait until the games started.

After the teams were announced, I went to dinner with Jay and Stick. Jay had rented a convertible and even burned a special CD for the occasion. He called it his "Island CD" and on it were all the songs he would choose to be stuck with on a deserted island. As we drove though Sarasota, I heard older songs that were motivational and many that were instrumental in getting the listener pumped up for the game. So, when a slower folk guitar song started, I sat back in my seat and prepared to enter a lull. The song was called, "The Greatest," and sung by Kenny Rogers. It was about a little boy who was getting in some baseball before dinner by throwing up a ball and swinging at it. Each time he threw up the ball, he was telling himself he was the greatest hitter of all time, but he swung and missed three straight times. The song ends with him not letting the strikeout get him down, but realizing he was in fact the greatest pitcher. It was adorable and instantly landed on my own Island CD, as it nostalgically caused me to reflect on my baseball upbringing with my dad. Now, those memories were the greatest.

The next morning, I woke up excited to play, but my shoulder had other plans. As soon as I arrived at the park, I made a beeline to the trainer's room with hopes of finding some relief. These guys were amazing and had the ability to stretch my arms in such a way I felt I could throw a ball through a concrete wall. However, while in there I had the revelation that baseball trainers were the ones who had invented the play toy, Stretch Armstrong, and they used players as demos. I left feeling great but it only lasted about an hour. With doubleheaders scheduled every day, I was going to need a little more than stretching. Hello Tylenol!

In all seriousness, they told me in their "professional opinion" if I were their player, they would instruct the coach not to play me. I met briefly with Steve Freeman to go over my choices and the only other option was to go home. It was time to suck it up. I have played while injured half my life, so this was nothing new, just a minor inconvenience, plus there was alcohol!

After a team breakfast, we all met as a very large group to receive announcements and to see just how hilarious baseball players actually were. The rookie campers were joined by the veteran campers who were there a day early for their own tournament, so we all piled in to find a seat facing front. The Orioles coaches, in their bright orange shirts, were scattered around the room and I noticed their candor to be that of a festive nature. I was in the last row, so it was interesting to see all the strange names on the backs of Orioles jerseys. The Hall of Fame Orioles weren't assigned to a team, so they could roam throughout the camp. Everywhere I looked, I saw memories from my youth, which left me with perma-grin.

There was an announcement made about the rope ceremony. I immediately thought it had to do with hitting a line drive, which are sometimes called "frozen ropes." I was mistaken. Campers, who achieved some form of greatness in the previous day's game, were brought up front to be recognized. "Greatness" referred to things such as going two for three or striking out the side. At the time, I thought their accolades to be trivial, but all that changed after I participated in a game and witnessed the caliber of play. The recipients sat in a row facing the room, while one at a time, their coach placed a golden lasso around their shoulders. Everyone clapped and congratulated the players as their feats were mentioned. Then, they brought out the brown rope, which in my eyes compared to Frank Robinson's Kangaroo Court.

For those not in the know, Frank Robinson would hold court in the clubhouse after each win to basically bust the balls of anyone who made a mistake during the game. He wore a mop on his head, so he'd look like a judge and brought down some harsh punishments on his defendants. It really added to the camaraderie of the team and they all looked forward to it.

So, a camper's name was called and right away half the room started laughing. When he sat down in the chair facing us, they put the brown rope around his shoulders and started the process of public humiliation. It was all in good fun and fun it was! The story was very animated and quite hilarious, but usually very mundane, like someone wearing the wrong uniform shirt or forgetting how many outs there were. Leaning against the wall was a toilet seat painted red. I was told it had been invented a few years earlier when coach Jim Gentile was thrown out of a fantasy camp game. They brought him up and put the seat around his neck and presented him with the "Red Ass" award. The ceremony was a great way to start the week, and I couldn't wait to see what was going to happen at the next day's meeting.

The fantasy camp experience didn't just include Orioles meetings, Orioles uniforms and Orioles players coaching us to play Orioles games as pretend Orioles; the perks were never-ending. A top-notch photographer walked the fields taking hundreds of action photographs, which were developed overnight and put on display in team albums the next morning. He also took a special photo for your very own baseball card. When camp was over, a whole stack of them showed up at my house by mail. I used them as business cards and giveaways for a whole year. Every morning, an in-house newspaper had stories and highlights of all the previous games and let us know what was going on around camp, and the standings of each team. Fortunately, the writer had a knack for humor, and often mentioned the unmentionables like the Golden Sombrero. That was not a reference to a beautiful Cinco De Mayo celebratory hat, but to striking out four times in a single game.

The schedule was the same all week. Breakfast, baseball game, lunch, baseball game, beer. Every night there was an event at the hotel for us to get autographs and pictures with various Orioles, as well as Q-and-A sessions and, of course, beer. For no reason at all, memorabilia would randomly show up in our lockers. When the first game was over, we changed uniforms before eating lunch. When we returned to our lockers after the second game, we discovered our first uniform was cleaned and hanging neatly, as well as gifts like a signed Mike Flanagan baseball. The swag was unexpected but very much appreciated.

One day between games, they set up a light blue backdrop to act as a background for a photoshoot. Rick Dempsey sat on a stool next to a little table with an empty stool on the other side. They brought out the 1983 World Series Trophy, sat it on the table and one at a time we all sat down and had our picture taken with the trophy and the series MVP. I treasured it and it still hangs in my office. Many times, I wondered how that thing traveled. Can you imagine that baby sitting next to you on an airplane?

The first game pretty much set the tone for the whole week. I think there were seven walks and six errors and that was just the first inning. I quickly learned the caliber of play was below what I was familiar with, but it really didn't matter. These guys and gals were having the time of their lives and the thrill on their faces warmed my soul. Of course, there were a few players who were seriously good and just like every team I ever played on, they let everyone know it. The very coolest aspect was the interaction with the coaches and the Orioles. You would think they were just baseball 24/7, but I found they were more interested in who we were and what we did for a living. They asked me more questions than I asked them.

Scott McGregor and I had a serious discussion about television production because his son was interested in the field. He was very excited to learn I had worked in Hollywood, so much in fact he called me a few weeks after camp and left a message on my answering machine at work. He was the pitching coach for the Frederick Keys at the time and jokingly asked me to drive up, because they needed me to pitch for them. I kept it for 10 years and played it for every single person that ever entered my office, even the FedEx dude.

When Rick Dempsey wandered into our dugout during a game, I immediately sidled up to him. Unabashedly, I pulled out my catcher's mitt and asked him to sign it. He didn't hesitate and signed his name followed by 1983 World Series, MVP. I marveled at it after he left but then panicked because I was still going to have to use my mitt. The Orioles players knew why they were there and signed anything you handed them. One guy had them signing a taxidermic pig's head and I'm not lying. They were gracious about it and if they had been bestowed with any serious accolade, they represented it in their autograph.

I came home with pieces of memorabilia signed by players as, "20 game winner," "'70 AL MVP," "'96 HOF," and even "PHOF." The latter was written on a baseball by Moe Drabowsky, who informed me it stood for, "Polish Hall of Fame." I believed him. Moe was hilarious and the practical joker of the camp. During lunch, he would walk around and pile shaving cream on top of somebody's hat. It had no weight, so the recipient didn't know it was there and went about business as usual with a giant glob of white foam on his head. You would watch Moe in the distance performing his trick to an unsuspecting camper, and after laughing, slowly remove your own hat to check if you too had been punked.

He was never short for a story or humorous interaction. He told me one about how he would wait until someone went into a bathroom stall and get down to business, before taking the stall next door. Then he would pull out a can of lighter fluid, which every ballplayer carried, and squirt it under the neighbor's stall. They would think he was peeing at them for a brief second and react verbally, before he threw down a match. He laughed so hard as he demonstrated how guys would run out of the stall with their pants at their ankles and on fire. In his day, he was a great pitcher, but an even greater teammate. I heard that from several Orioles.

Walking through the lobby after a long day, I spied Wayne Gross relaxing by himself in an easy chair. He looked super-content and was smiling like he knew something nobody else knew. Sitting next to him was a giant black garbage bag, which looked rather suspicious. He smiled at me and said, "Want a beer?" My standard answer was, "Of course," so he reached in the bag, pulled out a cold beer and tossed it to me. Apparently, the last person out of the trainer's room was responsible for bringing all the beer back to the hotel. He dumped all the coolers, ice and all, in a garbage bag and walked out like Santa carrying his sack. Just the thought of that makes me smile.

All week long, members of the 1983 team were showing up and it was wonderful watching the reunion. The bro hugs and fat jokes were everywhere and they were giggling like schoolyard children. There was a certain bond between teammates, especially World Series-winning teammates. Some of these guys were in the minors together and over the years spent more time with each other than their own families. To them, it seemed no time had passed, to us it never would because we will always see them as they were.

One special evening, we all gathered in a giant room for a massive Q-and-A. Across the front of the room facing us were Rick Dempsey, Brooks Robinson, Boog Powell, Earl Weaver and Jim Palmer and all the way down each side of the room, at very long tables, were many members of the team from 1983. The stories that came out of the room that night left my sides hurting from laughter. I had my video camera with me and taped as much as I could, but on occasion, at the direction of others, I turned it off. We were not sworn by threat of bodily harm or forced to take a blood oath that certain stories should never leave the room, but it might have been for the best.

To see teammates, pick on Tippy Martinez or to hear Earl Weaver describe his relationship with Curt Motton was a "you had to be there" type of thing, and anything I could share wouldn't do anyone justice. Jim Palmer had the place rolling when he accused MVP Rick Dempsey of winning because he "hit a few doubles," but it was Mr. Dempsey who stole the show with his story about El Guapo. I would not even consider repeating Rick's rather colorful story, but I will reveal it had to do with Key Biscayne, three roommates, a burglar dubbed "El Guapo," and a perfect Tony Montana impersonation, which left Lenny Sakata on his knees praying out loud. Hilarious.

Payback

I hardly slept and when I got out of bed Friday morning I considered not playing. Luckily, I talked Etch into letting me start at second and I didn't get one ball hit to me. I didn't warm up either, so after the stretching and the ibuprofen, my shoulder was maintaining an even keel, but that was about to change. During lunch, Etch asked me if I could start game two. We were completely out of arms and I could see the desperation on his face. I told him I would start and maybe eke out a couple of innings, but inside I knew I had just told a complete lie.

Our pitching coach, Scott McGregor, had been called away and a new one was assigned to our team. He found out I was starting and asked me in the cutest way, "Lemme see whatchoo got." His name was Mike Cuellar and he had 185 professional wins and was asking to see what I had. Oh yea, he also won this thing called the Cy Young award. Holy shit!

How do you tell Mike Cuellar you don't have anything? Well, you don't. I walked to the warm-up area and summoned our catcher. When I threw a pitch, my interior warning system kicked in and I heard a voice inside my head say, "What the hell do you think you are doing?" I told it I had no idea, but when it learned Mike Cuellar was making me do it, it shut up. He had me throw again and again until I had thrown about 15 pitches. It was then he thought it the proper time to teach me how to throw a screwball.

Mike Cuellar was one of the four 20-game winners on the 1971 Orioles and it was because of his screwball. When I was a kid, I tried to be like Mike, but could never master his pitch and here he was in person attempting to teach me. I looked around and none of the other coaches had shown up yet, so I summoned my adrenal glands and pressed forward. He showed me how to hold the ball, how to use the seam to my advantage and how to snap my wrist when throwing. I threw about eight more pitches and knew I was completely done. I could not throw one more pitch. A few minutes later, Etch called the team in and I headed over. When he told everyone Beller would start I had to interrupt him. I informed him on what went down and that I could not throw one single pitch and I will never forget the shock on his face. I will also never forget how he turned and screamed, "CUELLAR! What did you do to my pitcher?"

Mike was kind of chuckling and then walked over to assess his damage to my shoulder, but told me he had a solution. Looking me straight in the face, he explained how this had happened to him in the past, but it was easily corrected. That was because trainers performed miracles. He told me to follow his instructions exactly, so I memorized them. In the future, if you ever need to cure a dead shoulder, here is an exact quote on all you need to do, per Mike Cuellar.

"You go to the training room and ask them for a stick. You put the stick in your mouth and you bite down real hard. They will take their thumbs and jam them into your shoulder. This will hurt very bad, so you will need to bite down on the stick. Bite down hard because it will hurt, so you need to bite down. Tears will drop from your eyes, and you might even pass out, but that don't matter, keep biting. They push the thumbs in deeper and deeper and move them all around. You see your shoulder is tight and their thumbs untighten it. They push and push and you bite and bite and scream and then soon your shoulder gives up and stops tightening. Then you can pitch again. Go, go to the trainers and get that done." Oh, my dear God.

I walked to the trainer's room and stood there. They were all cleaning up after their latest sessions when they noticed my presence. One of them asked me what was going on and I told them I needed a stick. Now, I had all their attention. When I explained how Mike Cuellar told me to bite on a stick while they jammed their thumbs in my shoulder, they laughed. The following history lesson they taught me was about Ralph Salvon. Before he became known for his tomato plants in the left field corner, he was an elite baseball trainer and helped to make some of the great Orioles even greater.

Apparently, he had ginormous thumbs and used them exactly how Cuellar demonstrated. I was relieved to learn they no longer practiced such a barbaric procedure and ventured back to break the bad news to Mike. He seemed very sad and went to the dugout to reflect on all the sticks he had bitten down on. My fantasy camp pitching days were over. Phew!

My favorite event was the game against the pros. At a predetermined time, our team ventured to a field where a number of Orioles were waiting. Etch divided us into two teams and the rest of the slots were filled with Orioles. That was what I was waiting for, finally living my dream as I took the field to play with and against major leaguers. Oh sure, they were past their prime, but I defy any of you to stand in the batter's box and face Mike Boddicker, because he could, as they say, bring it!

I played short and was flanked by Rich Dauer at second and Rick Dempsey at third. How freakin' cool was that? Elrod Hendricks was catching, Elrod! He was certainly Mr. Oriole in my opinion and his constant smile was even evident through his mask. Tito Landrum was in amazing shape and legged out an infield hit like he had never stopped playing. When he ran, it looked almost effortless and he was laughing the whole time. Juxtapose to Todd Cruz, who was in horrible shape. I had heard he lived a hard life after baseball and even sold his World Series ring, but back in the day he had a rocket arm at third.

The only new rule was when a camper was up at bat, a pro had to pitch to them and when a pro was up, the pitcher had to be a camper. Earl Weaver let it be known they were not going to take it easy on us. If we wanted the "real Orioles" experience, we had to face real pitching.

The highlight for me was when I walked on four straight pitches from

Ken Dixon. As I started to jog down the line, I was stopped and told to go back and get a pitch I could hit. When I grabbed my bat, Earl went ballistic. He started yelling at me, saying I couldn't do that and that I had to take first base. Etch said, "Oh Earl, let him hit," and then he really got bent. "That man has to take first base and he needs to do it now. We are not changing the rules of baseball to accommodate him!" Then he looked at me, pointed, and yelled, "Go!" I dropped my bat like a spanked toddler and laughed to myself as I jogged to first. My entire baseball life had been made. Earl Weaver, who was third on the all-time list for managers being ejected from major league ball games, yelled at me. That alone, was worth the price of admission. Two innings later, I one-hopped a Ken Dixon fastball off the left field fence for a double and Earl smiled as I later scored. Life was good.

When our game was over, I grabbed my video camera to film some of the guys. Jay and Greg were playing next and I thought it would be a real treat to give them some footage of their game with the pros. I had no idea I would be capturing greatness. Jay's demeanor had been calm, cool and collected all week, but Greg was always wearing a serious face while playing. He was having great fun and was laughing all the time, but was constantly making sure he didn't embarrass himself. Earlier in the week, a massive group of players and campers ventured out to a dance club and Greg didn't crack a smile the entire evening. I thought he was internally trying to solve the square root of pi, because his game face was unbreakable.

In the second inning, Greg went in to pitch. He wasn't a pitcher by trade, but we learned the hard way, arms were a premium at the end of a long week. While warming up, he was somewhat erratic and gave people cause for worry. His all-time hero was standing in the on-deck circle and watching with concerned eyes. When Brooks speaks, everyone listens and as I videotaped him, he walked towards his dugout and said, "Tippy, I think this guy is going to hit me." Tippy Martinez laughed along with the whole dugout as Brooks made his way to the plate. Greg threw a few more pitches and then Brooks stepped in.

Greg looked as serious as a heart attack and I'm certain he was freaking out on the inside. He stood on the mound proudly wearing the same number as the Hall of Famer in the batter's box. Brooks was definitely the greatest third baseman of all time and I would argue that fact with Mike Schmidt himself if the need would arise. People in Baltimore didn't just love Brooks, they named their children after him. I had seen him hit a double earlier, so I know he was still a threat at the plate. Greg took the signal from the catcher, reached back and fired a fastball. Brooks started to step into the pitch before quickly turning, only to be plucked right in the middle of his back. Oh my God, Greg drilled Hall of Famer Brooks Robinson!

The whole diamond let out a collective groan for a few seconds before laughter took over. Brooks turned to Tippy and said, "I told you so," before tossing his bat and jogging to first. Greg stood on the mound dying a little inside. Like most legendary events, which become even more epic over time, this one was still in progress.

By the time Greg was to bat, half the camp had already heard about the plunking and ventured over. A bunch of the pros were leaning against the fence feverishly watching as Greg walked to the plate. When he arrived, Mike Boddicker, who was looming on the mound quipped, "Hey, aren't you the guy who hit Brooks?" Everybody laughed, which was followed by lots of people uttering, "Oh boy, this is going to be great." Greg stepped out and walked a few steps to gain some composure before stepping back in to face the ace. Mike went through his motion and fired an 85+-mile-an-hour fastball right over Greg's head. It cleared Elrod's mitt and slammed into the backstop with great force. Don't be afraid to try and decapitate Greg, shit!

Greg didn't even see the pitch because he was sprawled out in the dirt. I remember everyone's reaction to be quite loud. Mike was just having fun, but I'm not sure Greg believed him. When he got up, and was cleaning himself off, he was considerably shaken. I remember Elrod asking him if he was okay before retrieving the ball. I walked away with two thoughts. This would be talked about for years to come, and even at fantasy camp, paybacks were a bitch.

The next day, even though we had the best record in camp, we lost the first game of the play-offs. In the afternoon, I sat on the bleachers watching David Vidi, a man who had recently overcome a personal loss, pitch and win the championship game for Jim Gentile's Diamond Jims. It was an amazing performance by an amazing player and I was certain he didn't need to bite down on a stick to pitch such a gem. One of the last outs was a line shot up the middle, which Vidi caught. I was sitting right in front of Bill Swaggerty and together we discussed baseball and how beautiful it was. All my pain had disappeared.

I think I made more memories that week than any other and that included the time I found all my dad's Playboys. Fantasy Camp was in fact a reality now and I had a uniform, my own baseball cards, signed memorabilia and an extremely sore shoulder to prove it. One more amazing perk associated with the incredible baseball experience was a reunion game at Camden Yards. Later in the summer, while the Orioles were on a road trip, we were all to gather again, but this time in downtown Baltimore to play a game at Oriole Park. It was the exact opposite of the Olympics when they announce the youth of the world will gather again because it was now the old people of the world. In any event, I was slated to play a game at Camden Yards and that was to be pure awesomeness.

Two months after the season ended, a rookie reunion was held at the Ellicott Mills Brewing Company on Main Street, in Ellicott City. The establishment just happened to be owned by my teammate brothers, the Kendzierskis. All of the first-time campers were invited with the hope of keeping their interest alive long enough to sign up again. Along with the memories and the telling of fish stories, rookie awards were handed out. The little ditty about my catching tryout was relayed, and I was presented with a special trophy. The foot-tall statue depicts a swimmer who appears to be in the middle of a swan dive. An engravement on the base says, "Neil Beller, National Diving Award." It is proudly displayed on my bedroom dresser.

It reminded me about the status of my shoulder, which was getting worse, so I decided to do what most men like myself wouldn't do, and that was go to a doctor. I hated going to the doctor and not because of getting on a scale, it was because I sat in the lobby waiting for them to call my name and then I sat in a room counting ceiling tiles until someone came in to tell me I needed to sit and wait. I hated waiting. Another reason was my uncanny ability to self-diagnose. I learned that at an early age from my father whose response to me saying, "It hurts when I do this," was "Don't do that." There you go.

When the doctor finally assessed my shoulder, he told me I needed more assessment and that included an MRI. Anybody who loves sizzling steak fajitas knows MRI is an acronym, which stands for Mexican Restaurants Incorporated, however the medical community appropriated it to mean, magnetic resonance imaging. Silly I know. The idea was to lie perfectly still in a metal tube, while 75 medical assistants banged on the outside with ball-peen hammers. Somehow, that process generated an image, which the doctor examined and determined he needed to open me up using real knives. The assessment was a 3-centimeter tear in my rotator cuff, which meant surgery and a very long and horrible physical therapy with the possibility of using female professional wrestlers and leeches.

He wanted to schedule it immediately but I opted to put it off four and a half months until after the reunion game. There was no way I was going to miss that, and if I had the surgery when he wanted me to, I might not even be able to tie my shoes by then, much less wipe my own, well you know.

The reunion game was just a spectacular way to reconnect with everyone. What made it even more special was we were set to play Swag's Stags, which of course was Bill Swaggerty's team. They opened up the stadium to any family member or guest who'd like to attend, so my family gathered as well as my sister Karen and her family. She was reliving my baseball dreams with me and was super-excited about my experience. Etch knew about my impending surgery and let me play second base again. My thought was I wouldn't need to make many throws if at all. Of course, that changed when instinct and muscle memory took over. With a runner on first, someone hit a single to right. I ran out to act as the cutoff and when I received the ball, I immediately turned and fired to third. I have made such a throw many times in my life without even thinking and usually could hit the corner of the bag at will. This time my arm had no strength whatsoever, so the ball landed about 30 feet in front of the bag, hopped and then rolled to its destination. I was mortified at my pathetic throw but the rest of the team applauded anyway because they knew my condition and we almost had an out.

It was very interesting to look at the stands from the field's perspective, as it didn't resemble the Camden Yards which I knew and loved. When I was up at the plate, my face was all over the Diamond Vision screen with all my Fantasy Camp stats. It was unbelievably cool, but distracting at the same time. Like anything else in the major leagues, I'm sure players would get used to it and I pretended I did, but inside I was thinking, "That is cool as shit!" Fortunately, when they announced me as the hitter, they called me Neil instead of Ned and for that I was extremely grateful. All in all, I had two hits and it wasn't until I received a VHS of the game a few months later, I learned the broadcasters labeled me the MVP of my team. All that because I had two hits. I'll take it. Two days after the game, I had surgery and was happy my baseball career ended at Camden Yards.

The Brown Rope

My brain continued to play games and lie to my inner soul because right smack in the middle of my therapy, I started thinking about throwing a baseball again. We all know thinking and doing are two different animals and if they weren't, we would all be incarcerated. Those who disagree with that statement need to think about the last time they were speaking face-to-face with someone and fought off the impulses to smack the living shit out of them. Thinking and doing are just an impulse away and when something enables those impulses such as alcohol or mother in-laws, bad things can happen.

I had stopped playing competitive baseball and intended to live vicariously through my daughter, Libby. I was certain she had fallen in love with baseball while still in the womb. Every single night during my wife's pregnancy, I laid my head on her stomach and quietly sang, "Take Me out to the Ball Game." During the third trimester, the baby would start moving around when I sang. I need to clarify that I was unaware I was singing to Libby. I thought I was singing to little Neil or since I was 'Little Neil," I was singing to Littler Neil. We had no idea the gender of our child until she arrived. I was not disappointed at all with a girl and anticipated teaching her the game as soon as she was able to hold a 35-inch bat.

When she was younger, we would sing "our song" together every night before she went to bed. It was our ritual right after the 50 some books she required me to read. She loved to wear her Orioles hat and

247

her Orioles raincoat and when the whiffle ball equipment came out, she tore up the yard. I had been checking out the softball website for a few weeks waiting for the sign-up information and when it finally landed, I became excited.

I woke up early Saturday morning and nudged Libby. My plan was to take her out to breakfast and then head over to the Optimist Club and sign her up for softball. It was going to be a surprise and I could almost picture her in her cute little uniform already. When my wife questioned why I was up so early I filled her in on my plan. She grabbed my shoulders and looked me in the face like she was about to inform me my puppy died. Instead, she told me the day before she had signed Libby up to play lacrosse.

Now I had seen looks of disappointments on many faces, usually on the other side of a blind date, but I can't even imagine what my wife saw. Lacrosse? I was crushed, devastated and blindsided. My wife played lacrosse in high school so I understood her motivation, but I felt betrayed by my little girl. When I went in her room to ask if she wanted to play lacrosse or softball, she excitedly interrupted me to tell me mom had signed her up to play lacrosse. She was so freaking cute I couldn't stand it, so I didn't push the issue. My thought was Libby would tire of lacrosse and I would lean her towards softball. Jump ahead 12 years and you'd see her playing defense in high school for the Liberty Lions lacrosse team. Damn.

A few years later, my arm was all back to normal and I was itching for some baseball. As luck would have it, I received an email from Jay who told me he wanted to make another fantasy camp appearance and was wondering if I was thinking about it. Thinking about it? Of course, I was thinking about it. I had autographed pictures hanging all over the place and I was wearing my cup for no apparent reason. So, a once-in-a-lifetime experience became two lifetimes and I signed up for my second fantasy camp in 2005.

One of the many perks of being a veteran was a veteran's tournament, which takes place a day before the regular camp starts. It was a way to play in two more games just to make sure you filled up on baseball and everything associated with it. It was equivalent to the cocktail party before the big dinner.

This time felt different from the start, due to the low capacity of campers at the airport. The reason for that was simply that not all the veterans lived in Baltimore. They were spread out all over the country just like those Steeler fans who crawl from the woodwork every fall with their terrible towels. It wasn't until I arrived in Tampa and got on the team bus before the reminiscing started. The January weather alone was reason enough to be excited as it was cold and snowy when I left home. The week was slated to be the best ever, because after a solid week of baseball, I would arrive home just one hour before the start of Super Bowl XXXIX. Nothing can detox a tired baseball player faster than watching grown men knock each other over, only to be interrupted by hilarious million-dollar advertisements.

Players were already warming up when I arrived, so I jogged down the left field line and laid in the outfield grass to stretch. Palm trees nearby were methodically crinkling in the wind and the sky was so blue it looked like a calm ocean. It was time to play some ball.

The second fantasy camp was a little more laid back for me only because it wasn't new. I felt very comfortable and became more friendly with the coaches. These men were great people and not just figureheads. I laughed very hard with Glenn Gulliver, Ross Grimsley, Dave Johnson, Wayne Gross, Dave Ford, Tim Nordbrook, Gary Kendall, Bill Swaggerty and Andy Etchebarren. I had great conversations with Rocky Johnson, Pat Kelly, Jack Voigt, Grant Jackson and John O'Donoghue and I reveled to discuss baseball with Don Buford, Jim Gentile, Rocky Johnson, Elrod Hendricks and Scott McGregor. Jeff Tackett had a hilarious side to him and loved to have fun and Moe Drabowsky, well, he was the definition of fun. I ended up being drafted by Etch again and for the second year was one of his Thumpers. There were also many camp favorites on my team like David Vidi, Marc Cohen, Alan Tilles, Pete Monaldi and Robin

Henderson, who was one of the biggest Orioles' fans I had ever met. Local television stations were flying reporters in just to interview us, we were that good. It was going to be a great week.

When the first day ended, 75 other campers and I ventured to the trainer's room for ice. They had a great system and used a Saran wrap contraption to wrap ice right to your body like you were being "palletized." They addressed any other ailments, which I kept acquiring, such as tight thigh muscles, lower back pain, leg cramps and bloodied knees. I saw them at the end of each day and again in the morning before breakfast. I would get my arm stretched, my groin wrapped, my back massaged and all while other players were lying on tables next to me getting similar things done. They probably would have performed an appendectomy if I had asked. I will go on record and say if trainer Dave Walker and the other training staff weren't present, I wouldn't have been able to play, much less stand upright.

On Wednesday afternoon, there wasn't a game scheduled and a bunch of us headed out to a nearby beach, which was 30 minutes away. I didn't know about the surrounding area but was so glad I learned. Jay, Greg and I ended up at Siesta Key Beach. If you have never been, stop reading and go right now. It had the whitest sand I had ever seen and resembled baby powder. The three of us walked around for about an hour in our bare feet just taking in the atmosphere. It was one of those moments mentioned in "Escape (The Pina Colada Song)," by Rupert Holmes and for the record, Jay also likes taking walks in the rain.

The week went by very fast. I had pushed myself as hard as I could and taxed my body beyond its capacity. Twelve games in six days will do that to a 43-year-old catcher. These camps had been the greatest baseball experience of my life and I really didn't fret on my body because I just loved the atmosphere. It was sunny, it was breezy, I mean it was baseball and I engulfed it.

Thursday afternoon, Etch put me in to pitch. I had pitched a few innings earlier in the week and held my own by striking out a few. I even received two golden ropes based on my display of power and precision. That's what I heard anyway, but it might have gone down as "He got on base once."

One game was different and they had my number. I struck the first guy out and then gave up a double. Then I gave up another double and another double and another double. I think I have the record for pitching consecutive doubles and before I knew what had happened, I gave up six. When Etch took me out, we were both dumbfounded.

After the game, one of the other players told me I was telegraphing my pitches, which was something I prided myself on picking up as a hitter. I never even thought about it as a pitcher, because, well, I was not a pitcher. It really goes to show you baseball was a mental sport. That evening, I called my wife to fill her in on my day and to hear about the daily antics of our two children. Since the birth of our lacrosse player, we had another girl and I was assured she was a softballer. Not that anything was assured, and I wasn't going to force her, as I had seen overbearing parents and swore, I'd never be one. It was just the look she gave me when I talked about split-fingered fastballs and Connie Mack.

After learning about the kids, I started to talk about my day. Kate was a baseball connoisseur and not only understood the game, but my contributions to it and my skill level. Knowing that, here was our exact exchange. "So, Etch put me in to pitch today."

"Did you get your tits ripped?"

Oh my God, how did she know? Upon informing her I was a new record holder for giving up doubles, she just laughed and told me to have fun. Later that evening at the Q-and-A session, I told my coaches about the phone call and they thought it hysterical. I went down there worried about my shoulder but that was the least of my concern because apparently, I had pitching batting practice down to a science.

The next morning, I thought I might be called up to the front of the room so I brought my video camera and showed Jay how to use it. Sure enough, during the rope ceremony, Etch called my name. He was holding a gold rope at the time and I thought maybe he would be kind. I thought wrong. When I sat down, out came the brown rope. Right away people started laughing and as I faced the room, I saw lots of anticipation in regards to my embarrassment.

Etch launched into a vaudeville act which brought the whole room down. He was telling the story about how doubles were happening so fast and with such force, he almost received whiplash for jerking his head from home to center. He even demonstrated how the third base coach, John O'Donoghue, was so bored, he got down on one knee and just kept his arm swinging in a circular motion, while waving runners home. Then Etch stood and said, "When he called his wife to tell her he pitched, she asked him if he got his tits ripped." A complete outburst of laughter took over the room, and he added, "Even your wife knows you can't pitch." It went from embarrassment to hilarity and I walked back to my seat high-fiving other campers whose wives knew they couldn't pitch either.

On Friday, we had a new event as they instituted an All-Star game before the game with the pros. I was honored to be voted in by my teammates and made sure I didn't pitch. The day was perfect and was one of my favorite days ever at fantasy camp. Saturday was the play-offs in the morning and the championship game in the afternoon. We didn't qualify for either and were scheduled to play an ancillary game with another unqualifying team. Saturdays were always surreal because they were the last day of an experience that we didn't want to end.

I was in the on-deck circle before my last at bat, when I noticed Brooks Robinson, had walked over and was sitting on our bench. He was the epitome of graciousness and kindness and was just a joy to have met. It was my understanding he hadn't been drilled yet that year, so he was having a great camp as well.

Everyone wanted to end their camp on something spectacular and I was no different. I was looking for a first-pitch fastball and when I saw one coming, I jumped on it. The connection was solid and had gapper written all over it. My first thought was triple, however, due to my lack of speed, I had been known to turn many triples into doubles. I took off as fast as I could and halfway down the line started to swing out so I could cut the bag hard and head for second. Out of nowhere, a sniper's bullet caught my left calf and in midstride I immediately hit the ground and stuck like a lawn dart. What was happening? What was that pain? Where was it coming from? I couldn't move and I didn't know why. I heard lots of chatter and screaming by the other team and my own teammates were yelling, "Get up! Get up! What are you doing?"

A few seconds later, after relaying the ball to four different fielders, I was tagged out while lying in the baseline. The pain I was experiencing was from a pulled calf muscle. It was like a charley horse but about 100 times worse. I just laid there looking at the sky as players walked up and leaned into my vision. There were lots of looks of concern and sympathy at my current condition and some players touched me like I was a racehorse about to be put out of my misery. All of a sudden Brooks Robinson leaned in to my view. He looked worried and showed his caring side. He was about to say something that I knew I would cherish and talk about for the rest of my life. Then, while everyone was silent, he said, "Just think son, you'll get preboarding tomorrow." He burst out laughing and turned to walk away. Holy cow, Brooks Robinson just slammed the door in my face. Soon everyone was laughing, including me. Of course, he was right.

Almost instantly, a golf cart rolled up and two of the trainers secured me and headed inside. The only things missing were the blinking red light and the siren. They iced me and wrapped me and gave me a set of crutches. Embarrassment doesn't even scratch the surface. That night at the final suit-and-tie dinner, awards were handed out. Guys were receiving best hitter and best pitcher plaques and the championship team was recognized. When Dave Walker took the stage and called my name, my teammates congratulated me with excited applause. I had just won The Trainer's Award. As I hobbled to the stage on crutches, Dave went on to describe some of the camp injuries that year before adding, "Neil Beller wins this award because he came early and he came often."

Before we left we were given a baseball signed by every Oriole in camp and if that wasn't enough, we also received an autographed group shot of ourselves with Brooks Robinson, Earl Weaver, Jim Palmer and Boog Powell. Hardly a day goes by when I am not glancing at the wall where that picture hangs. In my baseball room on the top shelf, you also will see a pyramid of various colored tape rolls topped off with a beautiful fan made of tongue-depressors and the words "2005 Trainer's Award." I displayed it proudly.

Wisely, I decided not to tell my wife about the latter, until I arrived home. I did get preboarding, but left the crutches back in Florida. My thought was to inform her about the whole trip after the kids were in bed and we were watching the Super Bowl. As I was approaching the door from the garage to walk in the house, it abruptly swung open and my wife and Libby darted by me as they headed over to the neighbor's house. They didn't say welcome home or anything, they just scooted next door. A few minutes later they came back and my wife was inconsolable. Our next-door neighbor was a school nurse and had just verified my wife's concern. Libby had head lice.

Oh, dear lord. Immediately, we stripped the house of every piece of linen, every towel and every pillow and stored them all in the sun room. We proceeded to scrub the house from top to bottom. We never even turned on the Super Bowl, or discussed fantasy camp and when I went to bed at one in the morning, I couldn't even remember going. The fantasy was over, welcome back to the real world.

Your Loft

Since 2001, professional baseball had experienced new blood as the normal teams were not winning the World Series. Teams like the Yankees, Dodgers and Braves were replaced with the Diamondbacks, the Angels, the Marlins, the Red Sox and the White Sox. It was interesting to see these other clubs win, but when you looked closely, they weren't that different.

Former Oriole Curt Schilling was on the 2001 Diamondbacks and the 2004 Red Sox. Free agency had been around for years but clubs were now buying World Series teams faster than grandmothers could crochet a toilet-paper holder. Homegrown talent was still important but money did the real talking. My Orioles were maintaining a losing record and needed some help. I came up with a plan to find them some talent and signed up for yet another "once-in-a-lifetime experience," Fantasy Camp 2007.

The way I looked at it, my arm died the first time I went, and my legs the second so maybe the third time my heart would just explode. I wasn't worried because if it did, I was sure the trainers would put it back together, they were that good. I landed on Glenn Gulliver's team and became one of his Travelers. His coach was Ross Grimsley and together they drafted a juggernaut of a team.

We had hitting, we had running and most importantly, we had pitching. Jeff Carr was one of those guys who just looked like a ball player. He could play any position and excelled on the bump. He even wore a headband to accentuate his talent, it had magic in it. Jack Kelly was another man who was born with a ball in his hand and would become emotionally erect when discussing baseball. He had tremendous integrity and we hit it off so well, I even hired his daughter when camp was over. Catcher Bryan Adkins loved catching so much he had his knees surgically removed so he could live behind the dish. Rick Angelini, John Gavin and Todd Donnelly were bulldogs and loved the game almost as much as Pete Rose. Alan Tilles had been on my team before and played a mean first base. He was also a lawyer, which meant he could represent me if Earl Weaver got mouthy with me again. We even had a father-son duo on the team known as the Lees. I couldn't even imagine how cool it would have been to go to fantasy camp with my father.

Last and certainly least was my roommate, Tim Tremblay. Tim had been coming to fantasy camp every year since 1995. He obviously was financially independent from having invented something like Velcro, hair gel or nonstick frying pans, because this venture was not cheap. Tim was one of those guys who could run for mayor and win because he knew everybody and always seemed to be around when they needed him.

One evening, a bunch of us went out to dinner. There were some great restaurants in town, so we made our way to a Chinese shop and headed in. As we entered, we were startled to hear a very loud and obnoxious alarm screaming. The owner was in the lobby waving us off, telling everyone they had to close because the alarm was stuck. She was visibly upset and had no idea how to solve the problem. Sitting customers were standing to leave and others waiting to be seated were starting to move on as well. Tim stepped up and said something techy which resembled, "I'm ascertaining a Macpherson valve malfunctioned causing the asset prevention sensor to experience a reversed polarity commencement creating argiulation. Where is your security panel?" Tim followed her around the corner towards the sound and in seconds it stopped. He came back with a smile on his face and the owner threw her arms around him joyfully because he totally saved her night.

Minutes later, we were all sitting at a table and she was dropping off bottles of champagne. We didn't pay for a thing all evening and it was due to Tim's knowledge of alarm systems. I remember thinking he must have been a manufacturer, an installer or a retired diamond burglar.

I became friends with some great people who were not on my team, but if you read the papers and listened to the stories, you knew who they were. Plus, everyone had their name plastered on their backs for instant identification. Cal Alt was truly living his fantasy as he was a pharmacist by trade and never even played baseball as a kid. I was inspired by his learning ability. Dick Thompson caught just about every game and I was jealous of his knees, which he obviously stole from a teenager. John Giles, whose nickname was "Bam-Bam" hurt the ball when he hit it. I heard it scream.

Steve Murfin or "Murf" was always smiling and when his wife hired a belly dancer to entertain us for his birthday, I understood why he smiled. Bob Moore shared my profession as a cameraman and his love for the game. I ran into him in Cooperstown once, when he was shooting for Gerry Sandusky, of WBAL-TV. I had an amazing conversation with Robb Riddle, which was so intense, I can't recall its theme, meaning or contents. Joe Pavlock was a former policeman, who I'm sure was casing the joint looking for seedy people to start a jacket on. Due to his investigations, he has been the point person for all the campers to keep in touch with each other and I appreciated his detective work. Jon Darby was a great player and looked the part. He worked for a secret government organization, which had something to do with finding people who were needing to renew their car's warranty. Fred Creutzer was familiar because I went to middle school with his brother. He also looked like a fashion model. I believe he was in finance because he could calculate batting averages at will, as well as the caloric intake minus the number of carbs burned that were associated with all the alcohol we were drinking. Everybody needed him around.

The third time must have been the charm, because I started banging doubles and pitching better than I had in years. Between Jeff, Jack and myself, golden ropes were abounding and other teammates were stepping up to make sure we were playoff-bound. The camp seemed more laid-back to me and I made it a point to really appreciate all the people who were putting it on. Mike Flanagan, who was the Executive Vice President of Baseball Operations at the time, came down and held a Q-and-A talk about the future of the Orioles. He was the first Cy Young Award winner to hold such a position and he was very down-to-earth. After the session, I asked him if they needed a catcher and without pausing, he let me know they were always looking for talent. In hindsight, he could have laughed in my face, but he was too professional to do that. Later, when I told Gulliver and Grimsley the story, they laughed in my face and with great gusto. You'd have thought I would have known the dream was over. I didn't.

Just when everything was running smoothly, my inner child had a meltdown and held his breath until I tweaked a groin muscle. I really hate that little guy. Up until that point, my icing was just a daily ritual for my arm, now it was completely necessary to get wrapped and ice for my groin every day. For the record, ice and groin don't go together very well, at least not without uncontrolled singing. By singing, I was referring to one high-pitched note being held for a very long time.

The unknown reporter of the daily updates had some fun and labeled me as, Neil "One-Wheel" Beller. I was still hitting doubles but was doing my best "Festus" impersonation as I limped in to second. Our team was doing exceptionally well, but I kept waiting for the wheels to come off, because I was a realist. It really never happened and the only strange thing that took place was when Alan Tilles tried to stop his throw and hit himself in the foot with the ball. Other than that, things went peachy.

At the banquet on Saturday night, our table was full of laughter. Stories and impersonations were flying all over the place. Coaches, Glenn Gulliver and Ross Grimsley were right there in the middle of it, yucking it up with the rest of us. They were seriously down-to-earth guys and I could imagine sitting with them in a dugout for 162 games must have been epic and exhausting. The highlight of my evening was when I won the "Hitter's Award" along with Dom Staiti. When they announced the winners, my table jumped up with excitement and congratulated me with sincere enthusiasm. I was super-appreciative all the way down to my iced groin. Dom, another player whose journey took him through Parkville, was a solid person as well.

I found baseball friendships aren't limited to the diamond. Every year, The Country Club of Maryland in Towson, held a golf tournament and Tim Tremblay was always good for about 10-12 foursomes. He would wrangle up some Orioles, which made the event a great draw. One year, I had the wonderful opportunity to play golf with Ken Singleton, who can crush a ball. Interestingly, he didn't bend down and remove three imaginary pebbles before his swing. Another year, I played with Dave Johnson, whose entire golf bag was full of woods. I'm not kidding either, he had an 8 wood and a 9 wood and so on. He was super-competitive and once called the pro shop in the middle of play to get a ruling on the mulligans we had purchased. I had always wanted to play a round with he and Dr. Strange Glove and have added that to my bucket list.

It was hilarious to hear these pros yelling at each other on the golf course. Ken Singleton was yelling at Al Bumbry during his backswing and he was two foursomes away. I can still hear him calling him "B" as it echoed through the trees. However, playing with Glenn Gulliver and Bill Swaggerty was my all-time favorite. It was the first time I saw someone fall out of a golf cart because they were laughing so hard. When Glenn hit a bad tee shot, Bill told him he had trouble with his loft. Glenn said, "My loft? What do you mean?" Bill replied, "Lack of Fucking Talent!" I laughed for 10 straight minutes.

At the time, I was a regular on WBAL's "The Shari Elliker Show" and I repeated that story on the air. It was for a segment called "Ask Natalie," and received a great response. You can hear it at www.smellslikefoot.com

The E.S.K.

When I was growing up, I was totally spoiled because the Orioles were always winning. During the first 10 years of my life, the Orioles were in the World Series four times. In the 50 years since, they had only managed it twice. However, it didn't matter if they won or lost, they will always be my team. Some people experience that one dream where they forgot to drop a college class or study for a final causing them to wake up in a panic. My bad recurring dream was based on the Colts sneaking out of Baltimore in the middle of the night and fearing it might happen with the Orioles. I usually wake up sweating about it.

I like other major league teams as well and even follow some of them closely, but when it comes to the home team, I am a gamer. Thus, any and all milestones need to be celebrated. In July 2003, one of those milestones was the Hall of Fame induction of Eddie Murray.

Who else would I choose to celebrate with other than the Wilkins brothers and Tom Howard? I was only a few weeks post-shoulder surgery and really couldn't drive, so together with Tom and Caroline Howard, and Bill and LuAnn Wilkins, we rented a Winnebago and headed north. Kevin had moved to California for work and was slated to fly to Albany, rent a car and drive down to meet us. That way, we would have an automobile to cruise around Cooperstown, rather than bringing the colossal camper on wheels.

Tom was the driver of the Winnebago, and based on the control and maneuver skills witnessed, I was confident he could parallel park a train. He and Caroline picked up Bill and LuAnn and headed to Carroll County to gather Kate and myself. We decided to hit a grocery store for snacks but our shopping cart ended up at a liquor store instead. The drive to Cooperstown was wild, and although it was 342 miles away, we only had to stop for gas 12 times.

We were late getting in our reservations, so we booked rooms at a motel 15 miles north, parked the house and drove in to Cooperstown. During previous visits, the place seemed quaint, but induction week had all the living Hall of Fame members showing up, so the place was mobbed with baseball fans from all walks of life. The other inductee in 2003 was Gary Carter, making the majority of the visitors Orioles, Expos and Mets fans. I had followed Carter's career as well, as he was a catcher and won the World Series while with the New York Mets. I loved his spunk.

There were events going on all over the town and current members were out and about signing autographs. When I say "out and about" I meant they were under a financial obligation to sit outside various hardware stores and other establishments, for strictly scheduled periods of time, charging anywhere from $20-$100 to sign their name. The majority of them didn't experience the huge contracts younger players had and those sessions were a major part of their income, so I couldn't blame them. I blamed their agents, though. Outside a laundromat, I scored a Rollie Fingers autograph.

After cruising the town for a while, we thought we saw the actual ghost of Babe Ruth walk around a corner and into a bar. My first thought was that if it were Babe's full-body apparition, he would haunt a hot dog stand or a brothel, but a bar works, so we followed him in. It turned out to be a man who looked remarkably like Babe Ruth. He basically walked around Cooperstown in a vintage Yankee uniform and took pictures with excited tourists. Bill struck up a conversation with him and they hit it off pretty well.

Most Orioles fans could regale at least three to five stories about negative interactions with a Yankees fan. In Baltimore, whenever the

Orioles are besting the Yankees, their fans immediately pull-out statistics about how great they are in an overarching manner. Once, in the ninth inning on the losing end of a game, a visiting Yankees fan turned to me and yelled, "27!" to which I said, "Excuse me?" "We've won 27 World Series dude." I had no idea what that had to do with the fact they were currently getting their asses kicked but it made him feel better. They had also been playing 55 years before the Orioles even existed, but he wouldn't have understood math at that point in the conversation.

Bill kept the Babe, and a few of his groupies, busy with enthralling conversation and hilarious Yankee jabs. They were having so much fun, they didn't notice the influx of Orioles fans who had entered the bar. After a while, Bill deemed the bar an "Orioles only" establishment and kept vigil at the front door questioning everyone's loyalty before they could enter. It was pretty funny to see him standing there in his Orioles hat deciding who could come and go. The Babe and company bought Bill several beers hoping to sway his loyalty, but that would never happen. Finally, the owner stepped in and asked Bill to stop as it was bad for business. Bouncer Bill and the Babe. Sounds like a great title for a '70's movie.

As we made our way around town, most of the fans were cordial, however, one obnoxious Expos' fan got under our skin. We were standing on the street for an hour and a half waiting for the parade of current Hall of Fame members to show up for their annual banquet. That happened on a Friday night and the following day they participated in the Hall of Fame golf tournament. They were chauffeured around in open-air vehicles, and one by one were dropped off in front of the hall, so screaming fans could appreciate them. One guy was complaining out loud because he couldn't see "The Kid."

When he first entered the league, Gary Carter had a very youthful appearance and was nicknamed "The Kid." The man directly behind us must had been the one to name him that, because he let it be known for 90 straight and unrelenting minutes, "The Kid was coming. The Kid was on his way, soon you'll see the Kid, the Kid was the best catcher of all time, the Kid was near, get ready to cheer for the Kid."

Now, I had been around Bill, Tommy and Kevin many, many times and knew their threshold for tolerating irritating people. Just having Bill in the general area was acknowledgement not to be irritating, I mean ask the Babe. His build alone exuded fear. I was sporting a sling and couldn't partake in anything physical, although my verbal cannon was loaded and waiting to go off. Upon every kid reference, I shot sideways looks at Bill waiting for him to explode, but it was his wife, LuAnn, who finally turned and said, "Will you please shut the hell up about "The Kid!" At that moment, the LOL emoji was invented.

We had been in town all day and were ready to remove ourselves from the festivities at hand, so we found a nice Italian restaurant and settled down to dinner. Kevin was excited about all he saw and we talked baseball nearly the whole time. The actual induction ceremony was an outdoor event at Clark's Sports Center two days later, and along with Murray and Carter, Hal McCoy and Bob Uecker were going to be presented with awards. The excitement had libations flowing at dinner, which was just the warm-up to a long evening.

Kate had one glass of wine and decided not to partake in any more alcohol, which turned out to be the smartest move all night. We cruised the town some more, stopping at various pubs, before piling in Kevin's rental to head back to our glamorous rooms at The Village Motel. We sure hoped they left the light on for us. As Kate was driving along non-lit windy roads and endless acres of cornfields, her non-buzz status was applauded and she received the nickname "Straight Kate."

Out of nowhere, Tom yelled, "Pull over!" For a second, I thought he was going to hurl, and I was sitting next to him, so I leaned the other way. Kate was confused because we were flanked by cornfields and there was no place to pull over, so she kept driving. Minutes later, he requested it again, and that time with more urgency. We all started laughing when he let it be known his emergency involved his southern exposure. Kate quickly pulled off in a cloud of dust and Tom shot out of the car and disappeared into the cornfield like Shoeless Joe Jackson.

Tom had experienced an urgent situation known as brown-capping.

He literally had no more room in all 15 feet of his intestines, so his bowel duct had reached maximum capacity. We sat in the car, as Tom experienced his own field of dreams. Caroline didn't bat an eye, which made me think she had been down this road, I mean Hershey highway, before.

After a few minutes, Tom trotted back to the car, much happier and a few pounds lighter and requested a beer. Straight Kate drove us right to the nearest beer joint. During the short ride, we were all questioning Tom on his instant need for a cornfield and the desire for a new product to help out with such a condition. What we came up with could have rivaled the excitement associated with the launch of Diet Coke. Lucky for us, the tablecloths of the high-end saloon we visited were made of white paper and came equipped with a small box of crayons for inventing such a product.

Right then and there, Tom and I wrote out all the items required to combat any situation in which a cornfield would be urgently needed, even when there was no cornfield available. What if you were driving through a desert, a mountain or along the beach? What if you were in the city, the county or on a gravel road being shared by a chain gang? What if you were still wearing your Sunday best after a church social, which involved all-you-could-eat beef burritos? We thought of everything. Carabiners, magazines, disposable wipes, extra socks and road flares were only a few of the components in what we labeled the E.S.K. or Emergency Shit Kit. Soon, every automobile and truck on the planet would be equipped with one, but Tom will sell you one from the trunk of his car.

The next morning, we made our way to town for breakfast and to visit the actual Hall of Fame. Kevin and I walked around checking every display and commenting on just about everything and everyone. The cackling hens in "The Music Man" had nothing on us. He also made it be known there was no one in the hall with the nickname "Cut Home."

We stopped in a shop to look around and Tom struck up a

conversation with a local. He was questioning him for some time before shaking his hand and walking back over to us. Apparently, he made some kind of deal and soon we were doing something I had never done on my prior trips to Cooperstown; we rented a boat and headed out on Otsego Lake.

The day was beautiful and the lake was calm and although I only had use of one arm, I was totally relaxed. Everybody had a good time and the only standing rule was that if we were to come across another vessel that was called "The Kid," we were required to sink it immediately.

Tom could pretty much drive anything and even though we were not technically "driving," he took us all over the lake with extreme precision. The day was uneventful because no one was forced to use the makeshift E.S.K. we had manufactured in the car. Our baseball break was very nice but we were excited about the next day, which was the induction ceremony.

An outdoor stage was constructed at Clark's Sports Center and a VIP section for families, friends and dignitaries was right in front. The rest of us crowded together in a large field resembling Woodstock, minus the rain, lack of food and antiwar songs. It still felt like a rock concert with large screens on either side of the stage and there were Orioles fans everywhere. When our man hit the stage, chants of "Eddie, Ed-die, Ed-die" went on until he acknowledged the crowd. His speech was very humbling and he even became choked up at times. I was very proud to be there and experience such a pastoral event. I wondered about the previous members of the great brotherhood and if they knew what they were starting.

Bob Uecker owned the whole event and stood out as the best speaker. His speech rivaled the funniest things I had ever heard and that included the very first Steve Martin concert I attended at Merriweather Post Pavilion. Uecker was truly hilarious and I was belly laughing the entire time. I couldn't even imagine sitting on the bench with him but I would have given a year of Kevin's life to have done it. I'm sure he wouldn't have minded. It was a nice weekend and we all agreed we would gather again in four years when Cal Ripken Jr. was inducted, and we did.

We tried something new in 2007 and rented a house just south of town. Tom and Caroline couldn't make that trip due to family obligations, so we gladly ate and drank their portions so they felt wanted. They were missed. Bill ran the grill, which meant steaks were abundant and LuAnn ran into a local cornfield, but thankfully she just purchased corn. I always had fun with these people, so in retrospect I'm glad I knocked over all those beer cans years earlier. I forgot to mention, LuAnn makes a mean snickerdoodle and when visiting once, I ate at least two and a half dozen in one sitting and she will verify that.

We knew it was going to be crowded, but we had no idea it would be the largest crowd in the history of the Hall of Fame. Eighty-two thousand fans showed up to see Tony Gwynn and Cal Ripken Jr. enter the hall and to celebrate Kate's birthday. Steve Freeman secured us five passes for the VIP section so we were sitting pretty close to the action. Johnny Bench sang the national anthem, which was quite impressive. I tried to get him to sing "Happy Birthday," but failed. I loved to learn Tony Gwynn retired a few days after Cal, so they could go into the hall together. Kevin and I walked around with my video camera and a handheld microphone and pretended we were a news crew. We interviewed random people about their experience and assured them it would be seen and heard nationwide. The love they felt for both players was off the charts, as it should have been.

Before we left Cooperstown, we had a serious conversation about who the next Oriole inducted to the hall would be. We came up with no one. I seriously think I won't see another one in my lifetime, and that is just sad.

Coach Neil

When Natalie was of age, I immediately signed her up to play softball and never looked back. I was prepared to sleep out at the Optimist Club the night before registration, just like people had done in the past for Rolling Stones or Sponge Bob Live tickets. She was born late in the year and was always one of the youngest kids in her class. That seemed okay in school but on a softball field with varying degrees of talent and growth, the age of little girls could be deceptive. I remember my wife coming home from dropping her off at the middle school dance and saying, "Some of those girls look like they were in college!"

Natalie liked softball and I was glad. While soft tossing to her one day before practice, the head coach, Robert Milstead, asked me if I'd like to help out. Moments later, I had my own hat and was hitting grounders to these little women. I couldn't get over how tiny they were and how big the equipment looked on them. Every child was required to purchase their own helmet, a lesson we learned during the great head lice Super Bowl experiment of 2005. Gloves needed to be big enough to catch a softball, but small enough to fit on their hands. Their uniforms were literally falling off, so they would tie their shirt in a big knot in the back, therefore, it no longer resembled the nightshirts worn in Charles Dickens' "A Christmas Carol."

Robert's daughter was named Madelyn and was quite the player, plus she was adorable. I learned she was the last of many sisters, who he also coached, and they all were very talented. I ended up assistant coaching for four years and head coaching for three and I immediately learned how wrong Tom Hanks had been, because there was crying in baseball and lots of it. I am not referring to watering eyes and a few sniffles, I mean blubbering beyond control and for great lengths of time. The pressure on these little girls must have been enormous and internally they placed each at bat as a life-or-death struggle. I explained to them that when professionals failed seven out of every 10 times, they would still be considered some of the best players around. Their little brains hadn't learned the laws of algebraic equations yet, so they didn't buy any of that and continued to cry.

However, whenever it would happen, all of the other girls would come over and console each other. They would put their arms around one another and try to make everyone feel better. It really warmed my heart how much they cared for each other. I loved how they became teammates, well, until the singing started.

I enjoyed coaching first base just so I could say, "Run through the bag!" 74 times a game. We practiced this drill all the time, but for some reason, they all liked to coast into the bag and stop once they reached it. One game, I was clapping at the batter when I channeled my UMBC coach, John Jancuska, and said, "Let's hear some chatter!" Like a finely tuned glee club, all the girls stood on the bench and started singing.

"Open up the barnyard, kick out the hay, 'cause we are the girls of the USA. Turn on the radio and what do you hear, Elvis Presley singing a cheer. We're gonna …F...I.. .GHT, we're gonna fight, fight, fight for victory!" Now where in the hell could they have learned that? Did they get together and practice? Did someone hand out sheet music? I was quite impressed. Then they started singing it again, and again and again. Oh my God who handed out the sheet music? I wouldn't put it past the other team.

I wrote that in jest, but I do have firsthand accounts of sabotage by other coaches. The first year I coached, the head coach informed me he would be late and asked me to start the game. I created a lineup and warmed everyone up through infield drills. Keep in mind, these girls were so young most of them could not conquer the simple task of playing catch. Actually, the majority of the time, playing catch consisted of one girl throwing the ball and the other girl running somewhere to pick it up, which meant they were all running all over the place. The whole time that was going on, one little girl was lacing and attempting to put on her cleats.

We turned the field over to the other team and were waiting for the umpire to show so we could start the game, when one of my girls came over to me and said, "Coach Neil, I forgot my glove." I realized she was the one working her cleats or I would have noticed sooner. I had an extra glove in my car, so I asked them to wait on the bench and I'd be right back. I sprinted to my car, while constantly looking over my shoulder to make sure none of them wandered off. Many times, parents would drop their kids off and then come back right before the game started, so at that time I was the only adult present. I ran up, got the glove, ran back and was gone only a matter of minutes.

When I returned, every one of my girls were covered in chocolate. Their faces were a mess, and chocolate was all over their mouths and hands. "What went on here?" I was in complete shock and then one of the girls pointed, "She gave them to us." She was pointing at the coach of the other team. I walked around the backstop to inquire and discovered, as soon as I left, the other coach walked over to my bench and gave every one of my players a chocolate cupcake. She told me she had brought them for her team, but thought they would melt during the game. She considered it a very nice gesture to give them to the other team instead and thought I should thank her. So now, I have 12 little girls sitting on my bench in a chocolate coma. Their energy was gone. One of them laid in the grass under a nearby tree to take a nap. I didn't sign up for that.

Coaching little league softball wasn't as easy as you might have thought. We needed to arrive early to rake and line the field. We needed to lug equipment to every game. We needed to make daily lineups and a rotating manifest of girls who were sitting out, and which innings that would take place. We needed to constantly reach out to each and every team member to make sure they would show up to the scheduled practices and games. We also needed to keep calling the "weather line" to confirm games were going to happen. During softball season, if it were to rain, it would happen at 5:58 and by 5:59, I would receive calls to see if the game had been cancelled. Keep in mind, for a 6:00 start, I started setting up the field at 4:30.

It took a lot of coordination and for that, every coach needed a team mom. It was ideal to pick a team mom who was plugged in, had some free time, and enjoyed being around other people's children. Sometime that alone could be a game changer. My mom of choice was Laurie Facius, who happened to be the mother of my daughter's BFF, Samantha. We immediately scheduled a meeting at the local drinking establishment and the only thing we decided at that meeting was to have more meetings.

Team moms have to set up the snack schedule, coordinate the distribution of uniforms, make sure team birthdays are celebrated, chart all the family vacations, distribute team pictures and attend weekly meetings at the local drinking establishment. Laurie was perfect for the role. She also kept a mean book and charted all the action on the field. I can still hear her calling out the batting order every inning.

Samantha was a pure athlete and I'm certain will be for the rest of her life. One of my favorite drills was to divide the team in two, place one half at home and the other half at second base. One player would take off from each base at the same time, and needed to circle the bases as fast as they could. When they touched their initial base, the next runner would take off. Samantha would always run the last leg and usually caught the runner from the other team. I could tell she really enjoyed running and felt that was the only reason she actually hit the ball.

I enjoyed teaching little girls how to play softball and I started at the very beginning. The times I yelled, "Ready positions!" from the bench were infinite. I would have thought most of them had a little knowledge of the game, but every year I had at least one new player who had never played before. For them, it was how to step when throwing the ball and how to catch. It really began with the basics. Teaching them about positions, bunting, backing up and how to maneuver under a pop-up was way down the road, because some of them were perpetually putting their helmet on backwards. For the record, it was very hard to see the ball that way.

When they were very little, they were required to sit on the bench in their batting order or they would never know when to get up to strike out and cry. Several years later, they would yell out the name of the player who was on deck and who was in the hole. I always loved the expression, "in the hole," which referred to the player who was slated to hit after the player who was "on deck" who was following the player who was "in the box." Baseball and softball had the best vernacular.

The league we were in didn't have a drafting system I was a fan of. When I was a kid, every player went into a big hat and was drafted one at a time. When done correctly, each team would be different every year and usually with a different coach. This league had a system where each girl could name one girl who they wanted on their team. By naming each other two friends were guaranteed to be on the same team. My understanding was that rule was instituted when parents complained and threatened that their little girl wouldn't play unless they could play on the same team with their little friend. Some coaches figured out the flaw in the system and instructed their players to act accordingly.

What happened was some girls wouldn't name each other but another girl and that girl would name another and pretty soon they had the same team they had the year before, and it was guaranteed. A few years of this created a dynasty and an unfair advantage in the league. The same teams won the championship every year.

We played teams who were stacked and putting on double steals and attempting hidden ball tricks, while I was teaching my team not to eat chocolate cupcakes on the bench. The bottom line was the system was flawed, parents became angry and the league suffered because kids started going elsewhere. With kids leaving, the divisions had to become larger, so the fifth- and sixth-grade division grew from fifth to eighth grade. The disparity in age coincided with talent and an eighth-grade pitcher could be bringing it to a fifth grader. Yikes! Soon the singing Elvis cheer was replaced with, "Cookies, cookies, cookies and cream, what's the matter with the other team, nothing, nothing, nothing at all, they just (clap, clap) can't play ball." Ahh, little girls and their cheers.

Other things came into play, which I had not accounted for. Jewelry of any kind was not allowed during games, which included earrings. These girls were at the age where they were starting to get their ears pierced, which was considered a rite of passage, and I wasn't going to stand in the way of future body piercings. From my own daughter, I learned when she received the initial piercing, the studs shouldn't be removed for at least six to eight weeks. That wasn't for fashion reasons, but to train the hole just punched through her skin with a medieval device to remain open. To combat the human body's desire to heal itself, we had to place Band-aids over the jewelry on their earlobes. For the record, I had never seen that on a softball field before or anywhere else for that matter and I went to college!

I had a ton of fun though and had special players on each team. One of my first favorites was Lili. She practiced like a champ, always throwing and catching and running during drills, but when the game started, she would freeze at the plate and I mean solid. Lili would walk to the plate, hold her bat in the air and never move it. Never. She wouldn't even swing and stuck out with amazing frequency. I remember explaining to her that in order to obtain a hit, the heavy aluminum thing she was holding in her hands needed to connect with the ball in such a way, it would move in the opposite direction of which it came. She just looked right through me as if to say try and make me. I accepted her terms.

As a parent, I learned that discipline stemmed from motivation, so if I found out what motivated them, discipline could be controlled. For

Lili, it was the United States commerce system. On my way to coach first, I stopped by the on-deck circle and whispered in her ear that if she swung the bat, I would give her a dollar. She didn't even need to make contact, all she had to do was swing the bat. The first pitch sailed over her head and when the next pitch arrived, she swung her bat. She didn't hit the ball, but tried. The whole bench cheered and I was flabbergasted and called time out. Right then and there, I walked to home plate and handed her a dollar bill. She took it proudly, smiled and stuffed it in her pocket. Motivation. Two weeks later, she was ripping doubles. I seriously loved coaching these girls.

Working with the kids was the easiest aspect of coaching, the most taxing part was dealing with the parents. Most of them were very pleasant and very appreciative of my time and knowledge, but there were always a few who knew better than the coach. I tried to have one little girl step a little closer to the plate and was told, "My mom told me to stand here." I calmly said, "Well, she's your mother, but I am your coach and I'd like you to move up to here." Before the next game, I was visited by her mother who told me in no uncertain terms, that she knew what she was doing and I should never send a message to her, through her daughter again. Okaaaay.

Another time, a brand-new player named Sarah landed on my team and was just learning how to throw and catch. Before her first game, her mother walked up and asked me where her daughter would be playing. I told her due to her skill level she would be starting in right field.

"Well, that's not going to work. She needs to play third base."

"Third base?"

"Yes, third base." She played right field.

There were strict league rules that no girl could sit for two innings in a row, so girls were changing positions constantly. With 14 girls on the team, four of them had to sit every inning, and it all had to be configured prior to the game using flow charts, slide rules and phone apps. They would always bat in their initial order whenever it came up, but they might not have been playing in the field at the time.

A few innings later, a player was injured and needed to be replaced, so I walked up to Sarah, who was sitting on the bench, and told her to go in at second base. She looked up at me with a huge shock on her face and shook her head no. When I inquired as to why, another girl spoke up and told me that she had just shoved five doughnut holes in her mouth. What the hell? She physically couldn't talk or even chew due to the Munchkin overload. After the game, I had a meeting and told all the parents, pastries of any kind were forbidden on the bench during the game. I'm certain some girls just played for the snacks. Third base coach, Steve Fry, volunteered to "look after" all the snacks until after the game. I wish I had thought of that. Things had certainly changed since I was a kid. We never experienced sweets on the field, unless you considered an orange wedge a "sweet."

I chuckled as I thought that everything I had ever learned and loved about this great game had come down to pastries and Band-aids. A key observation happened when I visited young Jake Facius during one of his recreational baseball games. I was there to recruit his father, Dennis Facius, as a coach, because he wanted to have his own meetings at local drinking establishments. Jake was one of the funniest kids I had ever met and earned the moniker, Bob Phun, however, what I saw had me questioning my own participation in youth sports and that was years ago.

Jake's team was full of 10–12-year-olds, but they dressed and acted like pros. Some of them were wearing eye black, had sunglasses perched on their hats, wearing matching wrist bands and batting gloves and had bat bags with their names on them. That didn't shock me because many times I tried to act like a major leaguer, but it was usually delegated to their swing or pitching style. I mean, how many times did someone you were playing with imitate Joe Morgan's twitch or Luis Tiant's look to the sky before each pitch? With the way sports and advertisers have placed huge impacts on representing players and having them push their products, I was not surprised at the outcome. What affected me the most was they all had their own huge package of sunflower seeds. Their mouths were full and instead of watching the game, learning and cheering on their teammates, they seemed to be more concerned about chewing and spitting and were constantly reaching to their back pockets for more. A saw a runner score and when he approached the bench, no one said a word or even noticed. To me they seemed to only care about how they looked and acted and not how they played. I hoped I was wrong, because I only witnessed one inning of their whole season, but that was my walkaway observation. It was the new way and the precursor to establishing a copious number of views to their TikTok videos. Sadly, a few months later, I found myself handing out participation trophies to my girls. Ugh, I hated the new way.

Eyelashes

Natalie had grown up and reached her last year of youth sports eligibility, so I knew it would also be my last year of coaching. She had no desire to try out for high school as her singing and saxophone skills had her involved heavily in the music program, which didn't translate well to second base. I heard her in the shower, she was good. No, not the saxophone, the singing. Anyway, two years earlier, the league had changed their posture on slow-pitch and decided to transition over to fast-pitch. It seemed local high schools only had fast-pitch teams and were struggling to obtain players who were up to par and didn't consume pastries during the game. Winter camps needed to be held to teach girls how to windmill the ball and how to hit the erratic windmill pitches, which were sure to be headed all over the place, including straight up in the air. Some of the girls picked it up immediately, like Megan Fry, who used that form to put her laundry away, but I had to admit, even I struggled. The game was faster and for safety reasons, face masks were required for all the fielders. This was another cost for parents and I can't tell you how many times I had to call "time out" to secure a player's mask properly.

Pitching machines were used at the beginning of the season, until pitchers could take the mound without walking 39 straight batters. To curb that, a limit of five runs an inning was established. At least once a game, a pitcher would walk eight straight batters, and end that half of the inning only to switch sides, and have the other team do the same thing. We lost one game 24 -8 and only gave up three hits. The scores of games skyrocketed, but slowly the girls caught on.

When I grew up, all of our teams were sponsored, but the league didn't have such a luxury so the girls had to come up with their own team's name. I coached the Banshees, the Queen Bees and the Twister Sharks. They sound impressive, don't they? Weird nicknames seemed to be the rage and I handed them out at will. One particular girl stands out in my mind because she was slightly vertically challenged, but had a very strong throwing arm. Her name was Samantha, but we already had a Samantha, so I called her Sam. That actually happened a lot, as I had two Katelyns and two Graces as well. Sam had been on my team for a few years and steadily improved and insisted I called her, "Eyelashes." She had no reason why, but insisted, so I called her anything but Eyelashes.

One strange game, she was playing third and the ball was ripped right to her. She wasn't in "ready position" but standing straight up with her glove out in front of her like she was about to catch a falling bird. Without missing a beat, she stopped the ball with her right foot, picked it up with her right hand and fired to first, all the while without moving her glove. I couldn't believe my eyes and was reaching for a verbal retort when my new assistant coach, Dennis, yelled out, "What the hell are you doing?"

I glanced at her mother, Stephanie, who telepathically head nodded me permission to reprimand her daughter. I called time out and sprinted to third before she even turned around. I launched into an explanation for the object on her left hand. "Hey, that thing right there, it's called a glove. It was specifically designed to aid the wearer when attempting to apprehend a sphere which was hit or thrown in their direction at a velocity that could be damaging to the bare hand. That thing down there is called a foot. Gloves do not fit on feet. Why didn't you catch the ball with your glove?" She held out her glove and it was filled with sunflower seeds. I finally caved, "Eyelashes, why is your glove filled with sunflower seeds?" She looked at me with the most-sincere face,

"Coach Neil, I don't have any pockets." What could I say to that? She was right, she had no pockets. I slammed the bottom of her glove sending all the seeds airborne and replied, "Now you don't need a pocket, use your glove." Her mother applauded my disciplinary actions and suggested I throw in some extra running after the game as well. Loved her.

Things like that happened all the time. My all-time favorite took place with one of the Graces. Earlier in the year, her mother, Amy, reached out to me via email to inform me that Grace had Type 1 diabetes. Occasionally, her blood sugar would drop, so she wore an insulin pump and just wanted to make me aware in case she needed to come out of the game for a while. Amy was a very caring mom and proved it more than once. After one game for no reason at all, she purchased snowballs for the whole team. It was a nice treat on a very hot day. However, it was on a very cold day she impressed me the most.

Practices were at a premium my last year because the weather was being super-uncooperative. I'd go as far to say she was being a real bitch, like a "Mommy Dearest" kind of weather bitch. We only had a few weeks left before games started and I called a practice for an upcoming Saturday morning. Without my permission, a polar vortex visited like an unwanted cousin and brought with it the ability to key a car just by walking past it.

The morning was extremely frigid and very windy and as I was carrying equipment to the field, I started second-guessing my decision. The field we were assigned was below a small hill, which I thought would shelter us from the wind. Unfortunately, it had the opposite effect and added to the discomfort by creating an aerodynamic wind tunnel so severe, NASA would had been jealous. I am guessing the wind chill was about 30 below zero and I'm crapping you negative.

Parents refused to leave their heated cars and for good reason. Looking back, it was pretty hilarious to see these girls showing up for softball practice wearing parkas, scarves and knit hats. Hitting the ball became a procedure accompanied by pain and more than once I heard a girl scream after catching a ball. I was surprised at the number of girls who showed up, but even more amazed when Amy walked to the field with a large jug of hot chocolate and insulated cups. It took some forethought to be that prepared and I appreciated it almost as much as the little ladies she warmed up. I took of picture of all of them in a huddle and later at a game when it was 85 degrees, I had them all sign it. It's hanging on my wall.

At that same game an interesting thing happened. We were playing a good team, which usually owned us, but that time we were right in it. We had scored a run and only needed two more to tie it up. Grace had reached on an error and then a Samantha walk moved Grace to second base. I was always communicating with the runners on base, making sure everyone was on the same page. You know, those normal things you hear coaches yell, "Line drive you freeze!" "Take off on a ground ball!" "Crack of the bat you are gone!" "Stop looking for clovers and pay attention!" Well, the latter only happened a couple of times. All at once, the batter ripped a line drive and contrary to what I was yelling, everybody took off. Coach Dennis and I immediately started screaming, "Everybody freeze!" Fortunately, the calamity confused the other team. The pitcher caught the line drive and turned to look at every base, not knowing where to throw the ball. When she finally made a decision, it aided us, as she threw the ball to third. Grace had sprinted off second towards third and was now heading back. Samantha took off from first for second, but now both girls were heading for the same base. When they realized it, they both stopped and started going in the other direction. I yelled, "No, go back," and they both stopped again, so I had to redirect, "Grace, go to second, Samantha, go to first!" Meanwhile, the third baseman threw the ball to first and Samantha got back just in time. Phew! I never smoked a day in my life, but was craving a cigarette. I chuckled to myself and when I turned to look at the parents, they were all laughing.

The next batter was Eyelashes. (Yeah, I know.) She was no longer storing sunflower seeds but had a mouthful of bubble gum. I was really hoping she could scratch out an infield hit, which would leave bases loaded for our next batter, who had doubled in both her previous at bats. I yelled to Grace, "Two outs, you are moving at the crack of the bat!" She acknowledged with a short wave.

Seconds later, Eyelashes, who obviously had caffeine in her gum, smacked the ball into the outfield. "Go to War Miss Agnes," I didn't see that coming! "Go! Go! Go!" I started rotating my arm like a madman. Samantha took off from first base so fast she was almost pushing Grace in front of her. I knew Grace and Samantha would score, so I was concentrating on Eyelashes. She rounded first and was smoking towards second when I heard a soft voice below me, "Coach Neil?" I looked down and Grace was standing on third base. Over her shoulder I could see Samantha barreling towards third. "Go, Grace, go! What are you doing?" "I can't Coach Neil, my blood sugar is low, I have to stay here." I immediately assessed the situation. Samantha was almost to third and Eyelashes was nearing second. The left fielder was about to pick up the ball and Grace was married to third.

At that moment, I had been involved with some form of baseball for over 50 years. I had seen bats thrown on purpose, human parts extruding from safety devices, major leaguers firing fastballs at grown men, I even saw a foul bad ricochet off a man's head and carom all the way to center field, but I had never seen the will of a little girl, diminished by diabetes.

"OK, Grace, just take a breather." With the intensity of a traffic cop directing tanker trucks on the 895-tunnel thruway, I threw my arms in the air and yelled, "Stop! Go back! Grace has low blood sugar!" Samantha was only a few feet away and screeched to a halt before turning back towards second. Eyelashes was only a few feet behind Samantha and she stopped as well.

I had three girls running bases and they were all about 10 feet away from each other. The left fielder picked up the ball and threw it towards the infield. Samantha turned to Eyelashes and in single file both of them ran back towards second. The third baseman ran out to get the rolling ball and then ran back towards third. Eyelashes touched second and headed back to first as Samantha landed on the bag. Coaches on the other team had no idea what was transpiring and probably couldn't believe their eyes. They started yelling "First base, first base!" so the third baseman threw the ball to first. By the time Eyelashes reached first base going the wrong way, she had already run more than the equivalent of an inside-the-park home run. It was the only time I had seen the same runner called safe at first base twice on the same play. That had to be something for the baseball and medical journals.

Third Degree

I caught a rumor an all-star team was being created from fantasy campers to compete with other fantasy campers from other major league teams. It came to fruition when I received a call from one of the players asking me to come. We flew to Clearwater, Florida and won the inaugural tournament against teams from the Yankees, Cardinals and some others. To me, it seemed we had much more talent, but then again, we were the Orioles.

Standouts like Marc Cohen, Jeff Carr and Jack Kelly nailed down the pitching and we cruised every game.

The next year, our team flew to Arizona for another tournament. The talent pool for this tournament was much better and the competition reflected it. I played second base still and my partner up the middle was Tim Favazza. Tim loved baseball through and through and like me had daughters he hoped would play. It turned out he was an amazing coach and thanks to his tutelage, all of his daughters went on to become tremendous players. His coaching took them much farther than mine and they are still involved. He was definitely one of those coaches you want to have on your side, as he not only made you better, but he made you want to be better and there was a difference.

Matt Williams happened to be there as a guest coach for another team. He was only five years removed from playing for the Diamondbacks and stepped in the box during batting practice. He launched about eight balls over the left field fence in the simplest of fashion. I remember thinking, "And he doesn't even play anymore!" The men who play professionally are literally in a class by themselves.

I was struggling with the heat from the moment I departed the plane. Growing up in Baltimore, I had experienced humidity just below 54,000 percent. If you have straight hair during the summer, you are either abnormal or sporting a Mr. Ray's hairweave. It was instantaneous and a part of Baltimore just like Berger's Cookies or Old Bay Seasoning. Arizona heat was road runner hot. It was the type of heat that hits you when you open the oven and received a blast which made you recoil. It made you think of skulls half buried in the sands of Death Valley when you felt it.

It knocked me on my ass and I couldn't get out from under it. I started drinking Gatorade, which left me bloated, so I was hot and swelling at the same time. Baseball players not only played on the hottest days of the year, but they covered every inch of their body with layers of clothing. Shirts, 50/50s, shorts, sliding pants, pants, sanitaries, stirrups, hats and batting gloves cover everything except the wrists, forearms and the back of your neck. It made for an interesting tan. Following an afternoon game, I trudged to my rental car to sit in some air conditioning as I drove back to the hotel. When I opened the car door, the heat coming out was at least 250 degrees and knocked me right over. I could have roasted a turkey in my midsized Toyota Corolla. I left the door open for a minute before climbing in and when I reached for the seat belt, I flinched so hard I banged my elbow on the steering wheel. As the belt was coming over, the metal clasp hit my forearm and gave me a third-degree burn. Oh my God did it hurt. It was balls hot!

We had played a few games and I was less than 100 percent all around. To make matters worse, I hadn't managed a single hit. I was popping up and flying out, but no line drives and nothing solid. Marc Cohen invited a few of us to the movies, which was a very welcomed air-conditioned break. We saw "Tropic Thunder" with Jack Black and Robert Downey Jr. and laughed at the absurdity of it. Afterwards, I spoke about how disgusted I was with my play and they shook it off telling me to just have fun.

The next day, in my first at bat, I ripped a triple down the left field line. When I arrived at third, Marc was coaching. To welcome me, he simply said, "Where the hell have you been?" I guess he knew I was playing below par too, but didn't rub it in my face. I appreciated that.

Later that summer, Jack asked me to try out for an over-40 league, called Ponce De Leon. Every game was on a Sunday and only about 30 minutes from my house. I had dabbled in another league a year before fantasy camp, with my old friend, Chris Manouse.

I hadn't played in years and found it wasn't like riding a bike. They already had a catcher on his team and I was an afterthought, so I didn't play much. One game they put me in at third base and it seriously was the first time I had played another position in over 30 years. When you spend that long viewing the world from a squat, third base is another planet. Behind the plate, you are in charge of what was coming. It was quite the opposite at the hot corner as you have no idea what was coming. It turns out, snagging a line shot, which turns into a one-hopper was scary as hell and nowhere as easy as Brooks made it look.

It was an interesting league and I was surprised to see how the seven degrees of separation worked in baseball, because one game I looked over and there was Dan Fielder sitting on the bench. "Has it been 20 years?"

"Yeah,"

"Huh,"

"Yeah,"

"Huh,"

"One score!" Think about it. He was called in as a ringer and they used him periodically. Inquiring on the last few decades, I learned he had been the baseball coach at Western Maryland College. I was certain everybody he coached was drilling the ball between first and second. He seemed concerned that I had stopped playing and was an advocate for getting me back behind the plate, but it didn't happen.

The Ponce league was more comfortable because of fantasy camp. I had played other positions, and no longer caught, which made for a smoother transition. At the initial try-out practice, I was running down balls in the outfield like I had been doing it my whole life. They put me in at short and I loved it. It felt great to participate in something I only had seen. Cut offs, backing up throws and turning double plays were things I had never done, but knew through osmosis how to achieve. I felt more comfortable at the plate as well. I guess when you have nothing to gain from playing, you relax a little more. I finally figured everything out.

Jon Darby was on my team and I was still quizzing him on what he did for the government, because he would disappear for weeks at a time. I'm pretty sure he didn't yank Saddam Hussein out of a spider hole, but he might have taught him how to hit a curveball.

I was still on WBAL radio with Shari Elliker. It was a comedy talk show and just about any topic was allowed. The only thing she knew about sports was it rhymed with Bermuda shorts and she occasionally wore them. I quickly learned what was funny to me, wasn't funny to everyone. When practicing comedy, it was important to know that and turn on a dime when necessary.

I was regaling a story which had taken place earlier in the day and I was still reeling from it. I was playing third base and Jack Kelly was on the mound. We were ahead by a run and in the last inning the other team managed to get a runner on second. There were two outs and the batter hit a hot grounder my way and I picked it up flawlessly. I was in the middle of my crow-hop to first base, when the runner heading to third caught my sight. He was only a few feet from me and my attention turned to him. Now I had been a witness to such a play from behind the dish and it was a no-brainer to ignore the runner and throw to first. It was drilled into us as kids and again in high school and college to the point it wasn't even discussed anymore. However, for some reason I turned to tag him and immediately Jack Kelly screamed, "NO!"

I was having an out-of-body experience and as the runner jumped

285

past me avoiding the tag, my only other play was to throw to first. I recoiled and fired, but was too late, everybody was safe. I immediately wanted to throw up. What hurt the most was, I knew that wasn't the play, but I went for it anyway. What internal major malfunction makes that happen? Thankfully, Jack struck out the last batter and we won the game. It didn't matter though because in everybody's eyes, I made a mental error and that was the very worst kind of error to make. It would have been better if I sailed the ball over the first baseman's head. As I was laughing at myself while telling the story, I glanced at Shari who was wearing her, "What in the hell are you talking about" face. My guess was, she was waiting to hear that my pants had fallen off or something. In baseball, as well as life, you have to laugh at yourself and I did.

Haunted

So, I had been frozen in midair for several chapters now, and it was time to come back to earth. My wife and kids were sitting about 40 feet away from me in the third base bleachers and I could already feel the look of disgust being aimed at me. The ball just touched the very edge of my outstretched glove and continued on into left field. I hit the ground with a giant thud, as all the air left my lungs in an instant. The sound resembled the mating call of a Sasquatch looking for some late-night deep-forest action. The pain in my side only temporarily shielded the pain which emanated from my ribs for the next few weeks. I shot a look at my family as I was getting up and only two of them had the "Oh, Daddy are you okay?" face. The other look was the "You're an idiot and an old one at that," face. I had seen it many times before.

After the inning, Jerry Kovack made sure to smack me on the side with his glove while saying, "Nice try." He scored a direct hit and generated a tear to drop from my right eye. It was finally obvious to me, my days of being a professional ball player were coming to an end, however, it was impossible to remove the burn for it. I played in a few more leagues and flew to participate in a few more tournaments, but just to do it.

According to "Bull Durham," baseball is easy, "You throw the ball, catch the ball and hit the ball," and I had been doing it most of my life. Nothing was guaranteed, even your skill level. While working on a pilot for a woman's fast-pitch television show, I ended up in a batting cage with a local deejay from 105.7 The Fan, who claimed he could hit any pitcher. Two outstanding female players from Arizona were present and making him look extremely foolish. He didn't hit one pitch and almost celebrated when he finally fouled one off. The pitcher was Taryne Mowatt, who pitched on the 2006 and 2007 World Championship teams for the University of Arizona. Also, she held her glove like Paul Blair. She was amazing and blazing and I was super-happy I didn't face her while playing medium-pitch in California.

Baseball still touched my life on many wonderful days. One memorable Father's Day, Natalie took me in the basement and we laid on giant throw pillows as we watched, "Field of Dreams." She knew of my connection to it and wanted to become a small part of it. She forever was.

In my television career, I came across many commercials dealing with the baseball motif where they said things like, "We are located a long fly ball from Camden Yards," or "Buying from us is a home run!" I have never been a fan of those, but would like to hear "Our cars shift better than Chris Davis." That would sell, as there is truth in advertising.

In 2012, I was cutting the grass on a hot, cloudless June day. I had just returned from coaching softball and had high hopes for a wonderful season. As I was carrying a bag of grass to the woods, my foot slipped out from underneath me and I tweaked my knee. I stood there on one foot about to pass out from the pain, before slowly lowering myself to the ground. I couldn't move. I remember thinking if I were on "Naked and Afraid" and a lion roamed by, he would eat me without a fight. I was all alone, with the exception of my cell phone, which I used to call 9-1-1. I couldn't believe I was calling an ambulance for myself, but that was the case. My diagnosis was a full quad tear in my left knee. Falling in love with the tools of ignorance came back to haunt me, as love does.

My playing days were over, as well as my ability to wipe my own ass. When he was 11 years old, my father broke both his arms in a horse

-riding accident. When I asked him how he went to the bathroom he replied, "You find out who your friends are." There was a lot of truth in that statement. All summer long, I hobbled on crutches to the back yard and listened to the Orioles on the radio. It always brought me back to my youth and the love of the game.

Every now and again, a moment happens which excites a generation. Who can possibly forget the bases-clearing double Delmon Young hit in the 2014 playoff game against the Tigers? When J.J. Hardy scored from first base behind a cheering Steve Pearce with Nelson Cruz falling over backwards, I yelled as loud as I ever had in my life. In my mind, I see that play over and over again and it reminds me baseball is a wonderful game.

Two of my all-time favorite baseball moments involved my daughters. On June 30, 2015, Libby auditioned and was selected to sing the national anthem before a Frederick Keys baseball game. Two years later, on July 1, 2017 Natalie accomplished the same feat. I was so proud of both of them. To watch them stand behind home plate, facing center field while singing their patriotic hearts out, warmed my soul to no end. There were many future Orioles on both of those teams, as well as close friends and family members in the stands. They were both truly magical evenings, and proved to me any baseball field, regardless of its purpose, was a field of dreams.

Whenever I watch a baseball game on television, a part of me plays the "what if?" game. I run useless scenarios in my head about the career I never had and all the accolades I never experienced. It only lasts a minute before I realize it was not meant to be, and I snap back to the present. I remind myself that somewhere, a former professional player is sitting in his living room doing the same thing. He is rubbing his once -powerful arm, which is now useless at his side, wishing he could throw the ball once again.

Baseball is haunting, but I love it so. As a dreamer, a player and a coach, I desire to pass on that haunt, which is why, I pray for grandchildren.

Made in the USA
Middletown, DE
16 January 2022

58183739R00172